The Legal Foundations of Free Markets

The Legal Foundations of Free Markets

EDITED BY STEPHEN F. COPP

WITH CONTRIBUTIONS FROM

NORMAN BARRY

DAVID CAMPBELL

STEPHEN F. COPP

RICHARD A. EPSTEIN

SAMUEL GREGG

PETER T. LEESON

JULIAN MORRIS

ANTHONY OGUS

CENTO VELJANOVSKI

The Institute of Economic Affairs

First published in Great Britain in 2008 by
The Institute of Economic Affairs
2 Lord North Street
Westminster
London SW1P 3LB
in association with Profile Books Ltd

The mission of the Institute of Economic Affairs is to improve public understanding of the fundamental institutions of a free society, by analysing and expounding the role of markets in solving economic and social problems.

A CIP catalogue record for this book is available from the British Library.

ISBN 978 0 255 36591 8

Typeset in Stone by MacGuru Ltd
info@macguru.org.uk

Printed and bound in Great Britain by Hobbs the Printers

CONTENTS

ABOUT THE AUTHORS

Norman Barry

Norman Barry is Professor of Social and Political Theory at the University of Buckingham. His research interests include analytical political philosophy, welfare theory and business ethics. His books include *Hayek's Social and Economic Philosophy*; *On Classical Liberalism and Libertarianism*; *The New Right*; and *Welfare and Business Ethics*. He has been a Visiting Scholar at the Social Philosophy and Policy Center, Bowling Green State University, Ohio, and the Liberty Fund, Indianapolis. He is a member of the Academic Advisory Councils of the Institute of Economic Affairs and the David Hume Institute (Edinburgh).

David Campbell

David Campbell is a professor in Durham Law School at Durham University. He was educated at Cardiff University (BSc, 1980), the University of Michigan (LLM, 1985) and the University of Edinburgh (PhD, 1985). He is a Fellow of the Chartered Institute of Arbitrators. Since 1985, he has taught at a number of British universities and in Australia, Hong Kong, New Zealand, Spain and the United States. Professor Campbell has written on a wide range of legal and social scientific issues. He is currently working on a book refining Fuller's model of contractual interests and another on Coase's critique of intervention.

Stephen F. Copp

Stephen Copp gained his LLB (Hons) from Exeter University in 1982. He holds the dual qualifications of solicitor and barrister, having been called to the bar in 1985 and admitted as a solicitor in 1989; in 1994 he was made an Honorary Fellow of the Institute of Indirect Taxation. In 2004 he completed his PhD on 'The early development of company law in England and Wales: values and efficiency'. He is currently an academic, based at Bournemouth University, and does not practise. Dr Copp speaks and publishes widely on company law and corporate governance.

Richard Epstein

Richard A. Epstein is the James Parker Hall Distinguished Service Professor of Law at the University of Chicago, where he has taught since 1972. He is also the Peter and Kirstin Senior Fellow at the Hoover Institution (since 2000), a visiting professor of law at New York University Law School (since 2007), and a director of the John M. Olin Program in Law and Economics. He has also served as editor of the *Journal of Legal Studies* (1981–91), and editor of the *Journal of Law and Economics* (1991–2001). Professor Epstein is the author of numerous books and articles on a wide range of legal and interdisciplinary subjects.

Samuel Gregg

Samuel Gregg has an MA in political philosophy from the University of Melbourne, and a D.Phil in moral philosophy from the University of Oxford, where he worked under the supervision of Professor John Finnis. He is the author of several books, including his prize-winning *The Commercial Society* (2007), and a regular writer of newspaper opinion pieces. He is Director of Research at the Acton Institute, an Adjunct Professor at the Pontifical Lateran University, a Fellow of the Royal Historical Society and a member of the Royal Economic Society.

Peter T. Leeson

Peter T. Leeson is BB&T Professor for the Study of Capitalism at George Mason University. Previously he was a Visiting Fellow at Harvard University and the F. A. Hayek Fellow at the London School of Economics. He has been an Adjunct Scholar of the Mackinac Center for Public Policy since 1997, and has served as an Associate Editor of the *Review of Austrian Economics* since 2005. In 2007 he received the Fund for the Study of Spontaneous Orders Prize for his research on anarchy and the Olive W. Garvey Prize for his paper, 'Escaping poverty: foreign aid, private property, and economic development'.

Julian Morris

Julian Morris is Executive Director of International Policy Network, a London-based think tank that works on global policy issues relating to health, environment, trade and development. He is also a Visiting Professor at the University of Buckingham. Professor Morris holds degrees in law and economics and has published widely on matters relating to the environment, health, technology and development. Prior to founding International Policy Network in 2001, he was director of the Environment and Technology Programme at the Institute of Economic Affairs.

Anthony Ogus

Anthony Ogus is Professor of Law at the University of Manchester and Research Professor at the University of Maastricht. He has held visiting posts at a number of European and North American universities. Since the late 1970s Professor Ogus has specialised in the economic analysis of law, having been one of the first European legal scholars to work in this field. He is currently a member and vice-chairman of the Social Security Advisory Committee, and for this work he was awarded a CBE in 2002. In July 2007, he was elected a Fellow of the British Academy.

Cento Veljanovski

Dr Cento Veljanovski is Managing Partner of Case Associates, an IEA Fellow in Law and Economics, and an Associate Research Fellow at the Institute of Advanced Legal Studies, University of London. He was previously Research and Editorial Director at the Institute of Economic Affairs (1989–91), Lecturer in Law and Economics, University College, London (1984–87), Research Fellow, Centre for Socio-Legal Studies, Oxford (1974–84), and has held academic positions at UK, North American and Australian universities. Dr Veljanovski was the first economist appointed to a lectureship in a law department at a British university. He has written many books and articles on industrial economics, economic reform, and law and economics.

FOREWORD

Free markets do not exist within a vacuum, but need a legal framework that protects property, enforces contracts and allows free exchange to flourish. This statement would tend to be accepted by most economists and, increasingly, forms the basis of meaningful discussions of development economics. This type of statement also leaves many of the most important questions unanswered, however. What should this legal framework look like? What are its limits? What systems should we use for determining it? And, perhaps most importantly, who should determine it? After all, if freely transacting parties within a market are capable of designing contracts and even designing very detailed systems of private regulation, such as those that used to be found within stock exchanges before government regulation took over, then why cannot freely transacting parties design systems of law that are widely applicable?

In particular, those involved with development economics and issues of bad governance within poor countries would like urgent and simple answers to these questions. But there are no simple answers, and our understanding of many of these problems is cloudy. One especially important question stands out. Do legal frameworks evolve naturally within societies or can they be designed, at least in outline, and imposed from above? If it is possible to impose effective legal frameworks within which free exchange can take place, then perhaps we can solve problems of underdevelopment fairly rapidly: at least where there is an absence of war and conflict. Provisionally, however, it seems as if the evidence points to the conclusion that many aspects of effective legal frameworks have to be allowed to evolve within communities – a process that can take time.

In this excellent collection, put together by Stephen Copp, and containing chapters by many of the leading law and economics scholars in the world, many of the authors deal with subjects related to the questions posed above. In one of the early chapters, Peter Leeson asks quite simply whether free markets need government. The relative merits of common law versus codified law systems; the relationship between government law and natural law; whether concepts such as limited liability need to be defined by government law; and whether environmental protection requires state regulation or can be attained through private legal actions are then addressed in an engaging and straightforward style by the authors.

Even upon settling these issues, there remain many questions on which free-market economists legitimately disagree. The other authors in this book deal with some of these questions. How should we deal with monopolies and cartels? If courts have a responsibility to enforce obligations agreed in contracts, how should they do this in practice? What is the relationship between law, regulation and economics? Should human rights and economic freedoms be protected in a special way, such as through treaties and constitutions? And has an obsession with human rights undermined economic freedom?

The importance of the subject area of law and economics is being increasingly recognised – though it still does not have the prominence it deserves in the UK. This collection is an important contribution to the debate in this field. It is important both for economists who wish to understand more about the origins and purpose of law and regulation, but also for lawyers who need to understand more about the economic foundations of sound legal systems.

The views expressed in this monograph are, as in all IEA publications, those of the authors and not those of the Institute (which has no corporate view), its managing trustees, Academic Advisory Council members or senior staff.

PHILIP BOOTH

Editorial and Programme Director, Institute of Economic Affairs

Professor of Insurance and Risk Management, Sir John Cass Business School, City University

July 2008

TABLES AND FIGURES

The Legal Foundations of Free Markets

1 THE LEGAL FOUNDATIONS OF FREE MARKETS

Stephen F. Copp[1]

Introduction

The achievement and maintenance of economic prosperity are among the central concerns of economics. It is clear that law, broadly defined, plays a very important role in this. For example, the Heritage Foundation/Wall Street Journal/IEA *2007 Index of Economic Freedom* (2007: 3) found in a survey of 157 countries that the world's freest countries have over five times the average income of the fifth quintile of countries. Their definition (ibid.: 5) of ten key economic freedoms is dominated by measures dependent on law, such as the ability to start and close an enterprise easily, labour freedom reflected in wage, hour and other restrictions, strong property rights, and freedom from corruption. What is immediately apparent from this is that some laws are regarded as contributing to economic prosperity, whereas others are damaging to it.

The matters with which the law is, or should be, concerned are much more controversial and diffuse than the achievement and maintenance of economic prosperity. Typically, most academic lawyers would instead respond that law is concerned with questions of rights, justice or fairness, though it must be suspected that many would have difficulty defining such concepts with any precision. Properly, such questions are the subject matter of the discipline of jurisprudence – the science of law – but economic analysis typically receives little prominence within this and, where it does, offers little positive guidance on how the law might contribute to economic prosperity. Such indifference seems dangerous

1 I am grateful for the comments made by the anonymous referees on this chapter.

in countries whose present prosperity may well have been built on legal foundations conducive to this.

The essence of a free market is that it is one where parties can compete freely through voluntary exchange on terms settled by agreement, on their own or with others, free from interference with their person or their property. Because free markets are based on the economists' model of perfect competition that can lead to a Pareto-optimal (i.e. first best) outcome, they offer a real hope of increased economic prosperity. The behaviour consistent with free markets is not an accident but the product of laws, based on strong moral foundations.

The legal foundations of free markets in England and Wales (and which indeed form the basis of the laws of many other countries through the former influence of the British Empire) are commonly associated with the mid- to late nineteenth century, with strong laissez-faire influences in both the courts and Parliament, though their roots can be demonstrated to be much older. As Stephen Smith (2006: 9–10) has expressed it:

> The English law of contract has roots going back to the Middle Ages, but most of the general principles that underpin the modern law were developed in the eighteenth and nineteenth centuries ... To the judges of this period, theories of natural law meant that individuals had inalienable rights to own property, and therefore to make their own arrangements to deal with that property, and hence to make contracts for themselves. The philosophy of *laissez-faire*, for its part, was understood to mean that the state, and thus the law, should interfere with people as little as possible ... In general, the law was not concerned with the fairness or justice of the outcome ... The judges were not even greatly concerned with the possibility that a contract might not be in the public interest (say because it restricted competition).

It was not only in the fields of property law and contract law that such thinking can be seen: it was true in the area of company law, too. Not all was sweetness and light in the Victorian era, though, and some forms of government intervention can be traced to that era too (see, for example, ibid.: 11). There is now a risk that these foundations are under threat. The old legal maxim used to be that 'hard cases make bad law'. The current approach appears the opposite of this, with the courts, Parliament and European legislators all too often reflecting the priorities of the chattering classes, enshrining in law fashionable concerns. Norman Barry in Chapter 6 warns how an 'an all-embracing concept of freedom', a unity of liberty from which economic liberty flows, is being abandoned in favour of recognition of particular liberties only, without recognition of the intimate connection between them.

The contributors to this book were asked to push back the boundaries of current thinking on the legal foundations of free markets. They were selected on the basis that the book should reflect some of the diversity of views that exist on the role of law and regulation. The major questions that the book covers are:

- Do free markets need rules?
- How can the rule-making process be made more consistent with free markets?
- What particular types of law contribute to free markets?

Do free markets need rules?

The title *Legal Foundations of Free Markets* might at first seem to be an oxymoron – a 'figure of speech with pointed conjunction of seemingly contradictory expressions' (*Concise Oxford Dictionary*). As Anthony Ogus comments wryly at the beginning of Chapter 5, on the topic of regulation, it might seem perverse to write a chapter on a concept that is the very opposite of free markets. The question as to whether free markets are consistent with laws, and consequently governments, is a difficult one. We will start simply with whether free markets need rules, leaving open, for now, how those rules might be made and enforced.

The economic justification for free markets owes much to the microeconomic model of resource allocation by voluntary exchange in competitive markets. The purpose of this model in its simplest form is to demonstrate at an abstract level how the most efficient (i.e. first best) – Pareto-optimal – allocation of resources can be achieved (Maughan and Copp, 1999: 112–13; 2000: 15–16), differing therefore from a free market, which may be imperfect. Like many simplified models it performs a valuable role in enabling us to explain and predict the consequences of change. Generally, it is expressed in simple terms, emphasising property rights, and making assumptions such as rationality, voluntariness, specialisation, competition, information, mobility and the absence of transactions costs (Maughan and Copp, 1999: 113). It excludes, however, many important and pervasive features of the real world, in particular institutions such as government (Maughan and Copp, 2000: 16). This simple model, therefore, says little superficially about rules but much about how people are assumed to behave, in terms of what motivates them and the choices they make. Curiously, it assumes the existence of property rights because of the importance these have in providing people with incentives, while omitting other rights the absence of which can produce equally important disincentives, such as the right to personal security.

The economic model, in turn, developed as a series of independent models, designed to explain diverse moral and economic phenomena in societies where laws, institutions and practices were based on biblical and classical values and developed from inductive and deductive observations of early market economies (Maughan and Copp, 2003: 249, 256). The patterns of behaviour reflected in the model, therefore, were shaped by the existence of rules conducive to it and which might have been very different in the absence of these rules. Samuel Gregg in Chapter 3 traces the contribution of natural law reasoning to free market ideas and practices, in particular the development of property rights and contract and their influence on behaviour, as well as the tradition of liberty under law. Natural law, for Gregg, is concerned with discerning the moral good or evil of the choices people make and reflects the Judaeo-Christian understanding that man was created by God and that certain moral truths are as a result permanently inscribed into human nature, whether people believe in God or not.

Freedom of choice and human rationality do not necessarily result in behaviour consistent with free markets (or for that matter the perfect markets of the model). There is much scope for behaviour that can undermine such markets, including theft, fraud, duress, collusion on prices, and so on. From an economic perspective, such behaviour diverges from the assumptions of property rights, voluntary exchange and competition. Rules, especially legal rules, can be highly effective ways of discouraging undesirable behaviour, for example by increasing its price through criminal sanctions (Becker, 1976: ch. 4). How law can do so is discussed in more detail towards the end of this chapter. The use of rules is not, however, limited to discouraging undesirable behaviour; they can also be valuable in providing incentives for desirable behaviour (Veljanovski, 2006: 61). Property rights appeal to self-interest and incentivise people both to look after property and use it benevolently (Gregg, this volume: ch. 3). The conditions under which people have to take decisions also diverge from the model. Instead of being based on perfect information, decisions are taken under conditions of uncertainty, and people can be irrationally risk averse; rules can reduce the level of uncertainty by addressing the effects of error resulting from decision-making under uncertainty (Campbell, this volume: ch. 7). Given that the economic rationale behind many rules can be to render behaviour more consistent with the Pareto-efficient model, then such rules are not inconsistent with free markets, even if a free market need not be a perfect market.

This of course paints a very rosy picture of what rules might achieve. In real life, however, rules have equal potential to achieve the exact opposite of these desirable functions. There are many illustrations in this book of this. Badly drafted rules, for example, instead of reducing uncertainty, can increase it, a problem which Epstein laments in Chapter 9 over the brief drafting of Article 82 of the Treaty establishing the European Community[2] in relation to competition law, discussed below in relation to the rule of law.

2 Nice consolidated version.

Rules may not be the only means, or the best means, of facilitating market behaviour. Problems of risk can often be addressed through market means, most importantly through insurance. There are many ways of resolving issues of uncertainty. For example, North (1990: 138) identifies the role that informal constraints, such as cultural values, might play, an issue highlighted by Fukuyama (1995: 30) in his distinction between low-trust and high-trust societies. What we believe matters.

How can the rule-making process be made more consistent with free markets?

So far, we have been careful to discuss the relevance of rules to markets regardless of whether those rules have the status of 'law' or not, to avoid prejudging how rules can be made or enforced. The significance of giving rules the status of law is that legal rules are derived from an institutional source socially recognised as having the power to create law (in England Parliament, the courts, the European Community and the European Convention of Human Rights) (Holland and Webb, 2006: 3–4). The distinguishing feature of a law, of course, is that it comes with all the supporting coercive power of the state, including the power to punish.[3] It can therefore be very effective at achieving behavioural change.

'Do markets need government?' is the provocative question posed by Peter Leeson in Chapter 2. He sets out to challenge the belief of most economists that markets need government to enforce the rules of market exchange, arguing instead that markets may be better at producing their own institutions of enforcement than is widely acknowledged. Leeson illustrates this from commercial law and criminal law. International

3 As Becker puts it (1976: 49), 'Mankind has invented a variety of ingenious punishments to inflict on convicted offenders: death, torture, branding, fines, imprisonment, banishment, restrictions on movement and occupation, and loss of citizenship are just the more common ones ... The cost of different punishments to an offender can be made comparable by converting them into their monetary equivalent or worth ...'

commercial associations can be seen to work because they provide for information sharing and multilateral punishments, such as boycott or embargo, as well as reputation acting as a bond to behave well. Perhaps more surprisingly, evidence is shown for the spontaneous evolution of self-enforcing criminal law in the effectively stateless English/Scottish borders between the thirteenth and sixteenth centuries. The latter discouraged crime by the creation of mutually recognised juries, the use of hostages and the deadly feud (protracted slaughter of another's family). Leeson's argument indicates that there may be few types of behaviour that pose special problems for which government can be said to be the only solution.

Whether law should be the preferred route, and if so what type of law, is likely to depend on the respective costs and benefits, with different types of law giving rise to a hierarchy of cost, with constitutional rules tending to be the most expensive rules to change and the rules in individual contracts the cheapest (North, 1990: 47). There are, however, unique problems that the use of law, as opposed to other approaches, can cause. For example, law can increase uncertainty and risk, for example by resulting in transactions being held ineffective (Black, 2004: 52–4), and can undermine incentives, for example by replicating steps that market participants would otherwise take themselves (Cheffins, 1997: ch. 4).

The authors of this book provide a number of illustrations of government failures in law-making and discuss ways in which the process may be improved. These include alternative means of rule-making (market-generated regulation and greater use of judicial law-making), as well as mechanisms that can provide safeguards against inappropriate law-making (greater jurisdictional competition, strict adherence to the rule of law, restoration of economic rights, and constructive engagement between economists and regulators).

Government failure and the law

The most important source of law, at least in terms of volume and intrusiveness, is government, despite the increasingly well-known problems it can cause. As Coase (1964: 195) put it: 'It is no accident that in the literature ... we find a category "market failure" but no category "government failure". Until we realize that we are choosing between social arrangements which are all more or less failures, we are not likely to make much headway.'

The problems of government regulation can be seen to be deep-rooted, with Norman Barry in Chapter 6 criticising the workings of representative democracy, with parties needing to secure majorities by offering favours to significant interest groups, resulting in redistribution and over-regulation, to the detriment of the community as a whole. Julian Morris, for example, in Chapter 10, argues that the impact of lobby groups that favour legislation is one reason why statutory regulation has become dominant in environmental law, together with the dilution of the common law of nuisance over the last 150 years and the high costs of legal action. Nonetheless, these criticisms need to be set against the advances made in the design of regulation emphasised by Ogus in Chapter 5.

Market-generated rules

Markets are perfectly capable of generating their own rules without government. As Leeson points out in Chapter 2, in common-law countries, state judges were initially seen as discovering pre-existing legal principles that governed commercial transactions as well as others rather than creating them *ex nihilo*. The ability of markets to produce and enforce their own rules in the shadow of government-provided rules is well known. For many years the London Stock Exchange provided an excellent example of this; the impact of it being brought within a statutory framework in the 1980s was to leave it a much less powerful organisation suffering an identity crisis (Cheffins, 1997: 368–9). Market-generated regulation can bring benefits of flexibility, expertise and lower costs (ibid.: ch. 8).[4] It is tempting to use Leeson's argument as support for market-generated regulation and the extension of state enforcement powers to markets. Where there is government, however, market-generated regulation must be suspect. While the costs of regulating may be reduced, the existence of rules will still impose costs on non-consenting third parties[5] (Copp and Maughan, 2001: 241). The existence of government provides an opportunity for vested interests in such regulation, such as professional bodies, to lobby for statutory support for barriers to entry, which conflicts with the need for competition.

Greater use of judicial law-making

While an effective legal system is widely regarded as desirable in economic terms to ensure that constitutional and other legal rules are adhered to (see, for example, North, 1990: 59–60, 101), many economists go farther, expressing a strong preference for the common law as a rule-making system itself. Holcombe (1983: 140) expresses it nicely as 'The Invisible Hand in the System of Precedent'. There are many reasons for this. The courts are associated with the development of core areas of property law and contract law, seen as consistent with markets. Judges are perceived as independent from government and therefore less susceptible to short-term political pressures from panics or lobby groups. But perhaps above all the courts are seen as a form of spontaneous order rather than a form of planning. Easterbrook and Fischel (1989: 1445) put it this way:

> Court systems have a comparative advantage in supplying answers
> to questions that do not occur in time to be resolved ex ante.
> Common law systems need not answer questions unless they occur.

4 Though this will depend on the extent to which governments allow private associations to administer punishments among freely contracting parties.

5 For example, in the case of a self-regulating stock exchange, the costs of lack of access to credit – though only if a monopoly is established.

> This is an economising device; it avoids working through problems that do not arise. The accumulation of cases dealing with unusual problems then supplies a level of detail that is costly to duplicate through private bargaining.

Posner (2003: 250) explicitly links the common law to free markets: '... the common law establishes property rights, regulates their exchange, and protects them against unreasonable interference – all to the end of facilitating the operation of the free market, and where the free market is unworkable of simulating its results'.

The common law is compared favourably with civil law in Chapter 4 by Cento Veljanovski, who points to empirical studies that show greater economic growth in common-law countries than in civil-law countries, though he concludes that the nature of legal processes and their effects remain poorly understood. While the common law might facilitate economic growth better than civil-law systems in some areas and some jurisdictions, considerable variations in common-law systems have to be recognised too. Morris, in Chapter 10, demonstrates how private regulation based on the common law could well discharge in a more efficient manner many of the functions of environmental law that are more usually associated with statutory regulation.

Yet common-law systems are not immune from problems. Governments can control in legislation the extent of judicial discretion through the level of precision employed in statutory drafting or other means; judges may be subject to incentives to respond to what politicians want (Cheffins, 1997: 350–51). Posner (1995: 117–23), in the strikingly entitled book chapter 'What do judges maximise?', suggests a desire to maximise popularity, prestige, avoiding reversal, reputation, deference and the satisfaction derived from power. But it is not hard to think of recent cases where judges have shown little deference to politicians or popular opinion.

There has to be a worry that, despite the superiority of the common law as a system, judicial values may be changing and taking us into uncharted territory. Veljanovski in Chapter 4 and Copp in Chapter 8 show how the common law and the statutory development of company law respectively in nineteenth-century England were influenced by the laissez-faire views of a glittering list of political philosophers and economists. Epstein (1996: 235) has commented on how nineteenth-century judges often delivered judgements that better reflected sound economic principles than their counterparts today. Campbell in Chapter 7 is very critical of recent judicial developments in the law of contract, which seek to improve on practical economic wisdom with abstract legal reasoning as to 'justice'. Is the golden age (if there truly was one) of the judiciary over?

Ensure greater jurisdictional competition

In a global economy jurisdictional competition can provide a powerful check on governments that might otherwise be disposed to over-regulate. In theory, jurisdictional competition can lead to a Pareto-optimal outcome, based on fairly rigorous assumptions, such as a perfectly elastic supply of jurisdictions (Trachtman, 2000: 338). The existence of jurisdictional competition is often not recognised because to a lawyer competition tends to imply rivalry, whereas to an economist it simply relates to how resources are allocated when prices are not distorted by monopoly (Posner, 2003: 294). While jurisdictional competition in a corporate-law context has often been derogatively characterised as a 'race to the bottom',[6] with states such as Delaware being regarded as the more successful (see, for example, Romano, 1987: 720–25), it is a vital mechanism to provide choice and to ensure that rules – whether statutory or common-law – are proportionate. Without it, a centralised decision-maker would be subject to considerable pressures from special

6 The origins of this term have been traced by Mayson, French and Ryan (Mayson et al., 2007: 23) to a judgement of Judge Brandeis in the US case of *Louis K. Liggett Co* v. *Lee* (1933), 288 US 517, where he referred to 'the traffic in charters' (at 557) and to a 'race' between states 'not of diligence but of laxity' (at 559).

interest groups, would have insufficient information or incentives to reflect local needs and would be less likely to experiment because the impact of errors would be greater (Charny, 1991: 440–41).

Stephen Copp, in Chapter 8, observes how even limited jurisdictional competition may have been significant in Parliament's decision in 1855 to allow general limited liability. The availability of limited liability in France and the USA was attracting businesses to incorporate there and investment funds were flowing out of England to countries such as South America. It had made the USA one of the most powerful nations in the world, especially in naval power.

It is important, therefore, that the benefits of jurisdictional competition be recognised and encouraged. The reality is much different. International initiatives aimed at global standards across a range of fields, which may well be motivated by old-fashioned protectionism, may replace competition with stifling uniformity.

Strict adherence to the rule of law

Amid considerable diversity in political and legal systems, the concept, or perhaps the ideal, of the 'rule of law' has been growing in importance as a characteristic thought to be associated with economic prosperity. Dicey's influential formulation of the rule of law in 1885 identified three distinct aspects (1885: ch. IV, especially 110–21):

- the absolute supremacy or predominance of regular law as opposed to the influence of arbitrary power ... a man may with us be punished for a breach of law, but he can be punished for nothing else ...;
- equality before the law, or the equal subjection of all classes to the ordinary law of the land administered by the Ordinary Law Courts ... it excludes the idea of any exemption of officials or others from the duty of obedience to the law ...;
- a formula for expressing the fact that with us the law of the

> constitution, the rules which in foreign countries naturally form part of a constitutional code, are not the source, but the consequence of the rights of individuals, as defined and enforced by the Courts.

Infringements to the rule of law are significant in economic terms because they result in an increase in risk and uncertainty and are likely to lead to behavioural change adverse to free markets, as parties try to respond. Since the actions emanate from the state, however, it may be costly or impossible to circumvent these by market mechanisms, even where they are sufficiently predictable. Paradoxically, this may provide a justification for quite complex institutions and laws, if they at least provide greater certainty.

Richard Epstein, in Chapter 9, challenges the compliance of EC Competition Law with the rule of law, specifically criticising Article 82, which broadly covers the abuse of a dominant position. As Epstein argues, its language 'should make classic liberals blanch'. In his view, the rule of law requires 'a clear and knowable line' to be drawn between conduct that is legal or illegal, such as the well-known prohibition 'thou shalt not kill'. Such a prohibition is sufficient for the purpose of notice and guidance, even if it does not set out all the details; gaps can be filled in by ordinary statutory construction. In contrast, Article 82 gives no clear indication of the everyday practices it proscribes and the delegation of administrative authority to a centralised agency may lead to its systematic expansion.

Restoration of economic rights

Categorisation of an aspiration or expectation as a human right has become enormously important. Such rights are increasingly given special status in both domestic and international law. They have the potential both to advance economic freedom – and to stunt it.

The case for economic rights is presented by Norman Barry in

Chapter 6. He argues that there has been little discussion of economic rights, such as the right to property, contract and the procedural requirements that make up a market society, and criticises how the debate over rights has placed civil rights, such as non-discrimination, to the fore. As he puts it, 'Where would the right to free expression be without the right to own a printing press and publishing company?' Barry is encouraged by US judicial approaches, where there is a constitution historically and philosophically designed to protect private property and free enterprise. In contrast, he is sharply critical of the absence of a written constitution or the formal protection of economic rights in Britain, going so far as to argue that Britain, notwithstanding the role of the European Convention on Human Rights, provides the least formal protection for economic rights of any advanced country.

Economic rights, however, need not be limited to matters such as property rights and contract. There is a strong case for economic firms to be recognised as a matter of right as being legally distinct from those who comprise them. Copp, in Chapter 8, identifies how, in contrast, prior to 1855, a company with limited liability could be formed only through some exercise of discretion – for example, by Board of Trade approval or a private Act of Parliament. The problems this gave rise to included delay, cost, inconsistencies of treatment and opportunities for obstruction by vested interests. Recognition of the statutory right to establish a limited liability company by mere registration, first enacted in 1855, as an important human right might be a major step forward in resisting encroachments upon it.

Constructive engagement between economists and regulators

Economics shows numerous ways in which the process and method of law-making can be improved, suggesting that one route forward is for more constructive engagement between economists and regulators.

Anthony Ogus, in Chapter 5, believes that we will always have regulation and that economics can have a positive as well as a negative role in its design. He argues that over the last 25 years the nature of economic and social regulation has been transformed, in part through the contribution of mainstream economic theorists. Social regulation, for example, has shifted from command-and-control measures to co-regulation, whereby industries are left to come up with rules to meet objectives set by regulators. Ogus identifies two ways in which economics may play a more constructive role. The first is in the exploration of the cost-effectiveness of different regulatory instruments, once regulatory objectives are taken as a given, where regulatory impact assessment has had the highest profile. Second, behavioural economics can assist in predicting irrationality, where unwise individual choices provide the justification for genuine paternalist regulation.

Striking illustrations of how economics has transformed environmental regulatory strategy are provided by Julian Morris in Chapter 10. The usual policy option for environmental regulation has been command-and-control regulation, the origins of which can be traced back as far as Edward I's attempt to ban the burning of sea coal in London in 1306. Examples of such regulation can be seen in the use of technological standards, flow limits and stock limits. Morris argues that alternative methods of regulation, specifically tradable emissions permits and emission charges, can achieve environmental gains more efficiently, though these are usually used to supplement rather than replace existing command-and-control regulation. Morris also identifies how the use of individual transferable quotas, which closely resemble property rights and dramatically alter incentives, to manage scarce ocean stocks, such as fish and lobster, has raised levels of efficiency.

What particular types of law contribute to free markets?

The minimum legal foundations conducive to free markets are those that ensure personal security, the protection of property rights, voluntary contracting and free competition, and the ability to associate. These owe much to the microeconomic model of resource allocation discussed above. This book points to a number of ways in which the law can establish an appropriate structure of incentives and disincentives to this end.

Law as incentive

Law can be used to provide various incentives to shape behaviour in a way consistent with free markets. Property rights are especially important because they provide incentives to use property efficiently: without such property rights there would, for example, be no incentive to incur costs in developing land (Posner, 2003: 32). The simple economic model assumes that a set of universal, exclusive and transferable property rights is in existence before exchanges take place (Maughan, 1995). Accordingly, the role of law here encourages wealth-maximising behaviour by identifying which rights are to be recognised as property rights and facilitating their transfer. In doing so, it may also significantly reduce problems of uncertainty.

A much wider range of laws is needed, however, to establish property rights effectively than is implied by the term: not only will land law be needed but laws to establish other forms of property, such as personal property, and intangible property rights, such as debts, share capital and intellectual property. The transfer of such property rights may entail contract law (since few exchanges are simultaneous), conveyancing law (since this has been arbitrarily separated in the UK from property law), family and trust law (since the individuals assumed in the simple economic model will exist in families and other relationships in real life) and probate law (since people die).

Law can also be seen as providing incentives for contractual exchange. Most sophisticated exchange does not take place simultaneously but involves an exchange of promises that are fulfilled later. The passage of time creates uncertainties and risks that create obstacles to cooperation (Cooter and Ulen, 1999: 184). The law of contract in theory enables parties to make credible commitments by foreclosing alternative actions with a high liability cost (ibid.: 187). That would imply that the role of the law of contract is essentially concerned with disincentives, i.e. raising the price of breach. In contrast, should its role instead be seen as incentivising possibly risk-averse parties to enter into contracts, by reassuring them that their risk in entering into contractual relations is limited?

Campbell, in Chapter 7, criticises recent developments in contract law. He sees the essential component of commercial relationships as the economic exchange rather than the legal contract; the main reason for such a contract being security against non-performance. The present law codified previous commercial practice and does not seek to prevent breach by ordering compulsory performance but rather to impose compensatory damages for breach. Campbell argues that mistakes in the contracting process should be seen as inevitable because of bounded rationality and that the mechanism for handling this problem is central to the efficiency of the market economy. Accordingly, he suggests that the major function of the law of contract is to allow breach, but on the right occasions and on the right terms.

If the role of law in recognising property and contract rights is seen as providing incentives for investment and wealth-maximising cooperation, then the doctrine of limited liability in company law becomes much clearer, as does its importance for a free market.

'Limited liability and freedom' is the, perhaps surprising, title of Stephen Copp's chapter. Copp traces the origins of a general statutory right to limited liability in 1855 in England and Wales through the arguments of the Victorian legislators themselves. Limited liability was seen as an integral characteristic of forming a company, following logically from the substantive differences between a large partnership and a company. Unlimited liability was impracticable to enforce, resulted in a disproportionately high risk for investors compared with creditors, and a sub-optimal level of investment, but a disproportionately low risk for creditors and an above-optimal level of credit being misallocated to unmeritorious business activities. Limited liability would remove disincentives to enterprise, working-class investment and diversification. In short, the unshackled ability to pursue economic activity with others was an important freedom.

Law as disincentive

Violence, detention and other forms of personal harm affecting the personal security of parties to economic exchange are generally inconsistent with free markets because of their compulsory, non-consensual nature; similarly, theft, forced sale, restrictions on use, damage, or trespass involving property. Fraud, misrepresentation, duress and prohibitions affecting contractual exchange are also inconsistent with free markets. They are not normally wealth-maximising activities because the loss to the party affected invariably outweighs the utility to the party responsible, and because they involve utility for one party only whereas market exchanges involve utility for both. There are also spillover effects to such behaviour, because it imposes costs on non-parties, who will invest in non-wealth-maximising precautions as a consequence. Personal security and property rights are closely linked: for example, Posner describes the function of the law of torts as 'concerned with protecting property rights, including the right to bodily integrity' (Posner, 2003: 31) and a list of torts, such as assault, with their criminal law counterparts, as involving a 'coerced transfer of wealth' (ibid.: 205).

Law can be used to increase the price of, and therefore discourage, such non-wealth-maximising behaviour, thereby signalling parties towards wealth-maximising behaviour instead. The sorts of threats faced by natural persons will vary and may originate from outside the state (such as insurgency), from the state itself, state organisations (such as the army or police) or from other persons and organisations (such as trade unions). To protect against such a wide range of threats, a wide range of laws and the ability to enforce them may both be needed. At the broadest level, there may need to be an effective system of international law, a constitution to guarantee the rule of law; perhaps some carefully crafted human rights law; at the least, there will need to be an effective criminal law to deter deliberate injury and a law of torts to ensure that injurers internalise the cost of accidents (Cooter and Ulen, 1999: chs 11, 8).

Norman Barry, in Chapter 6, claims that property rights, in particular, as a form of economic right, have been poorly protected in legal systems throughout the world, with neither common-law nor civil-law countries being effective in preventing invasions of property by the state. He argues that the main threat to property rights comes through excessive regulation, for example zoning laws that prevent a person using property profitably, but with little compensation in most legal systems for those adversely affected by government action. Barry sees some encouragement in the USA, with its written constitution, in judicial approaches as to whether compensation should be paid where there is, in effect, a partial taking of property through regulation. In contrast, he is sharply critical of the protection of economic rights in Britain, dismissing the role of the European Convention on Human Rights, the First Protocol of which guarantees the 'peaceful enjoyment of possessions', because of its qualification that the use of property may be controlled in the general interest, on the ground that the whole point of an individual right is that it is held against the general interest.

A much more complex picture is painted as to whether or when the law should provide disincentives for behaviour that conflicts with the ideal of a perfectly competitive market. In the, not always helpful, neoclassical model, a perfectly competitive market is assumed to be one where there are a large number of buyers and sellers, a homogeneous product, perfect information and no barriers to entry or exit (Jones and Sufrin, 2008: 7). So if, for example, it is assumed that people in real life try to be efficient and allocate resources as suggested by the simple economic model, then the approach to monopoly would focus not on the behaviour of the monopolist but on the constraint that produced the monopoly in the first place: monopoly may simply be a response to huge economies of scale (Maughan and Copp, 2000: 19). Conversely, monopoly may be inefficient where there are barriers to entry, where regulation may be justified (ibid.: 19). Others see competition law, in contrast, as a means of achieving non-efficiency goals, such as the supposed benefits of curbing perceived corporate power or promoting small enterprises.[7]

Richard Epstein, in Chapter 9, argues that any regulation of unilateral practices should identify those that deviate from a competitive market in ways that generate systematic social loss. Yet instead, broad uncertainty is embedded in the EC's Article 82[8], without any information as to the paradigmatic cases to which it applies. For example, there is no real definition of the term 'unfair' that is used, despite it possessing multiple connotations. He concludes that Article 82 is much more intrusive and mischievous than the US case law under s.2 of the Sherman Act. The impression created is that the EC is much more corporatist and less individualistic in its mindset than US courts. The effect of such decision-making is likely to hurt the cause of innovation and competition.

The law and market failure

Since a free market is a real-world market, and not an abstract concept of a market, it may well be imperfect, for example, in terms of the parties' bounded rationality, asymmetric information, transaction costs and negative externalities. Market failure, a rather elastic concept justified by reference to such factors, provides the theoretical justification for a great many apparently independent fields of law that in reality represent qualifications of those described above. For example, employment law largely represents extensions to contract law, impinging substantially on freedom of contract. Should a market continue to be regarded as free if there is state intervention to address such problems?

The difficulties of regulating for market failure are discussed by Julian Morris in relation to environmental policy, in Chapter 10. He observes how conventional economic theory suggests that, in the absence of regulatory intervention, individuals and firms will generate negative

7 For a summary of such arguments, see, for example, Jones and Sufrin (2008: 16–18).

8 See n.2 above.

externalities which impose an uncompensated cost on third parties, the policy solution for which is to require the internalisation of this cost. Such internalisation does not, however, require such third parties to be fully compensated or for the harm to be eliminated, but simply that it be reduced to the socially optimal level – that is, where marginal social benefit equates to marginal social cost. Identifying this optimal level is, however, challenging. As Morris points out, it rankles with notions of equity: how can it be optimal that some people are harmed? On whose say-so? Morris suggests that the solution to this problem lies in the type of regulation adopted – the common law would enhance the ability of individuals to achieve their own environmental objectives.

Conclusions

The law, together with the institutions associated with it, plays a central role in economic prosperity, which concerns all of us. The legal foundations of free market economies, which have delivered enormous improvements to the quality of life of countless people, evolved over centuries. Their justification does not lie simply in utilitarian concepts of economic efficiency but also in moral concepts of natural law and a broader concept of freedom. Great care needs to be taken when changes are made to areas of law that can be foundational in shaping market behaviour, to ensure that they are not undermined. Similar care needs to be taken in developing other areas of law, such as competition law and environmental law, where significant inroads may be made, often justified by reference to alleged market failure. This book suggests various practical solutions to these problems, including ensuring greater jurisdictional competition, greater adherence to the doctrine of the rule of law, the restoration of economic rights, greater use of judicial law-making, and more constructive engagement between economists and regulators.

References

Becker, G. S. (1976), *The Economic Approach to Human Behaviour*, Chicago, IL: University of Chicago Press.

Black, J. (2004), 'Law and regulation: the case of finance', in C. Parker, C. Scott, N. Lacey and J. Braithwaite (eds), *Regulating Law*, Oxford: Oxford University Press, ch. 2.

Charny, D. (1991), 'Competition among jurisdictions in formulating corporate law rules: an American perspective on the "race to the bottom" in the European Communities', *Harvard International Law Journal*, 32(2): 423–56.

Cheffins, B. R. (1997), *Company Law, Theory, Structure and Operation*, Oxford: Clarendon Press.

Coase, R. H. (1964), 'The regulated industries: discussion', *American Economic Review*, 54(3), Papers and Proceedings of the Seventy-sixth Annual Meeting of the American Economic Association, pp. 194–7.

Cooter, R. and T. Ulen (1999), *Law and Economics*, Reading, MA: Addison-Wesley.

Copp, S. F. and C. W. Maughan (2001), 'Innovative high growth companies: the case against special rules', *Company Lawyer*, 22(8): 234–43.

Dicey, A. V. (1885), *Introduction to the Study of the Law of the Constitution*, reprinted in R. E. Michener (ed.) (1982), Indianapolis: Liberty Fund.

Easterbrook, F. H. and D. R. Fischel (1989), 'The corporate contract', *Columbia Law Review*, 89: 1416–48.

Epstein, R. (1996), 'Do judges need to know any economics?', *New Zealand Law Journal*, pp. 235–40.

Fukuyama, F. (1995), *Trust, the Social Virtues and the Creation of Prosperity*, London: Penguin.

Heritage Foundation/Wall Street Journal/IEA (2007), *2007 Index of Economic Freedom*, www.heritage.org/index/research/features/index/chapters/htm/index2007_execsum.cfm.

Holcombe, R. G. (1983), *Public Finance and the Political Process*, Southern Illinois University Press.

Holland, J. and J. Webb (2006), *Learning Legal Rules*, Oxford: Oxford University Press.
Jones, A. and B. Sufrin (2008), *EC Competition Law*, Oxford: Oxford University Press.
Maughan, C. W. (1995), 'The economics of property rights', *New Zealand Law Quarterly*, 1: 78–91.
Maughan, C. W. and S. F. Copp (1999), 'The Law Commission and economic methodology: values, efficiency and directors' duties', *Company Lawyer*, 20: 109–16.
Maughan, C. W. and S. F. Copp (2000), 'Company law reform and economic methodology revisited', *Company Lawyer*, 21: 14–22.
Maughan, C. W. and S. F. Copp (2003), 'Economic efficiency, the role of the law, and the Old Testament', *Journal of Interdisciplinary Economics*, 14: 249–98.
Mayson, S. W., D. French and C. L. Ryan (2007), *Mayson, French and Ryan on Company Law*, Oxford: Oxford University Press.
North, D. (1990), *Institutions, Institutional Change and Economic Performance*, Cambridge: Cambridge University Press.
Posner, R. A. (1995), *Overcoming Law*, Cambridge, MA: Harvard University Press.
Posner, R. A. (2003), *Economic Analysis of Law*, New York: Aspen Publishers.
Romano, R. (1987), 'The state competition debate in corporate law', *Cardozo Law Review*, 8: 709–57.
Smith, S. (2006), *Atiyah's Introduction to the Law of Contract*, Oxford: Oxford University Press.
Trachtman, J. P. (2000), 'Regulatory competition and regulatory jurisdiction', *Journal of International Economic Law*, 3(2): 331–48.
Veljanovski, C. (2006), *The Economics of Law*, London: Institute of Economic Affairs.

2 DO MARKETS NEED GOVERNMENT?

Peter T. Leeson

Introduction

Do markets need government? Virtually every economist believes they do. Even the most libertarian thinkers argue that markets require government to establish the rules of market exchange and to enforce these rules. As Milton Friedman put it, 'government is essential both as a forum for determining the "rules of the game" and as an umpire to interpret and enforce the rules decided upon' (Friedman, 1962: 15). Markets, however, may be better at producing institutions of enforcement of their own than we think. Could economists have underestimated the power and beauty of markets in this regard? This question is of more than mere hypothetical interest. At least 10 per cent of the world's governments are classified as 'weak or failed' (Foreign Policy, 2006). In these countries, the state is so corrupt, fragile or otherwise dysfunctional as to create anarchic (as in the case of Somalia) or 'near anarchic' conditions. Citizens cannot rely upon the civil magistrate to uphold contracts or protect individual property rights. Furthermore, international market activity, which now comprises close to a quarter of world GDP (World Bank, 2005), has no overarching supranational authority to interpret or enforce commercial agreements. In these markets as well, government cannot be relied upon to create or enforce the rules of the game required for exchange relationships to thrive.

Nevertheless, markets, in both 'weak and failed states' and internationally, flourish. The long-standing existence of vibrant markets under conditions of real or quasi-statelessness suggests that private 'rules of the game' must be possible without government. This chapter examines these rules, how they emerge, and how they are enforced. It investigates whether there might be something like 'laws of lawlessness'. I consider two major areas of law: commercial or contract law and criminal law. The first part of this chapter examines how contract law might be provided privately and supplies evidence for this possibility. The second part examines how criminal law might be provided privately. Unlike contract law, the question of criminal law under anarchy has received almost no treatment. In addition to exploring this issue theoretically, I also consider evidence for the spontaneous evolution of criminal law without government.

Does the social dilemma imply the need for government?

The traditional argument for government is rooted in the work of Thomas Hobbes (1651 [1955]), which famously described life under anarchy as 'solitary, poor, nasty, brutish and short'. Hobbes's description has been subsequently formalised by game theorists in the form of the prisoner's dilemma, the classic game of conflict. Without an agency of formal enforcement, individuals in this environment have nothing preventing them from stealing, defrauding, and generally failing to recognise the ownership claims of others. Since each individual stands to gain more by plundering his fellow man than interacting with him peacefully, society ends up in a 'war of all against all' in which everyone does worse than if they had interacted peaceably with one another. This situation is depicted in Figure 1.

Individuals may follow one of two basic strategies when dealing with others: cooperate or defect. Cooperation refers to any individual behaviour consistent with the ends of the other members of society, such as trade, respecting the property claims of others, and so on. Defection refers to the opposite form of behaviour. Here, an individual acts in a way that benefits him at the expense of others. Fraud, theft and physical violence are examples of this. When both individuals cooperate, they both receive α. If one cooperates and the other does not, the cooperative

Figure 1 **The social dilemma**

	Cooperate	Defect
Cooperate	α / α	θ / γ
Defect	γ / θ	β / β

individual of whom advantage is taken receives θ, while the defector receives γ. If neither individual cooperates, they both earn less than they could by cooperating and each receives only β. In this game, $\gamma > \alpha > \beta > \theta$, where $2\alpha > (\gamma + \theta) > 2\beta$, which is to say that mutual cooperation is socially efficient.

The unique equilibrium of the one-shot version of this game is for both individuals to defect. Strictly speaking, the logic of the game suggests that in the state of nature individuals will never cooperate and will always attack one another. This situation – the game's pure strategy Nash equilibrium – is clearly Pareto dominated by that in which both agents behave peacefully towards one another. According to this reasoning, to prevent the degeneration of social interaction and facilitate cooperation, one form of which is market exchange, society requires a formal authority of rule creation and enforcement – a government. Without such an authority, the members of society are stuck in the mutual defection equilibrium; there is no trade and only war. On these grounds, it is easy to understand why everyone from Thomas Hobbes to Milton Friedman sees government as indispensable for the market to operate.

Both casual observation and recent research, however, suggest that the strict game-theoretic outcome of this situation is too strong. Where formal enforcement is absent, agents do not immediately and always try to kill one another. The presence of international anarchy, for instance, has not resulted in all countries adopting a first strike policy, leading to perpetual war that ends in world annihilation. In fact, most countries, most of the time, are in a state of peace, not conflict. Similarly, among primitive people, anarchy has not led to endless fighting and zero trade (Leeson and Stringham, 2005). On the contrary, in primitive stateless societies, as well as internationally, substantial trade and peaceful cohabitation overwhelmingly prevail (Leeson, 2006). The traditional rendering of anarchy in Figure 1 incorrectly predicts the outcome of statelessness because it fails to account for institutions of governance besides government. Although it is true that in the absence of any rules whatsoever society may break down, as I discuss below, it is evidently not true that in the absence of government society lacks rules.

This should really not be that surprising given the assumptions about individuals that the game in Figure 1 makes, namely that they are rationally self-interested. This, after all, is what leads agents to defect in this game in the first place. Individuals are able to calculate their prospective pay-offs and on the basis of this calculation see that no matter what others may do, they do the best by defecting in their interactions with others. Rational self-interest is, however, a double-edged sword. While it enables individuals to make the calculation that encourages them to defect in the absence of state enforcement, it also encourages them to develop private solutions to the social dilemma that would otherwise stand in the way of their ability to capture the gains from exchange. While irrational or selfless actors might sit by and let the absence of government prevent them from profiting, rationally self-interested actors would not. Thus, rational self-interest is both the cause of and the solution to the problem that Hobbes identified. Of course, recognition of this possibility is far from demonstrating that private solutions will, in fact, develop. For this we need to establish how individuals might go about establishing and enforcing private rules – laws – that support social cooperation and exchange under anarchy, and determine whether, in fact, any such rules have emerged without government. I turn to this task below.

Self-enforcing commercial law

The development of commercial law, particularly as it relates to contractual agreements, is not particularly difficult to imagine without government. At the most basic level, this requires rules against fraud and contractual violations. As Berman (1983), for instance, points out, what is now state-enshrined commercial law in common-law countries is really just the outgrowth of rules governing exchange that existed in customary law long before government became involved. Hayek (1960, 1973) and others have similarly emphasised that most commercial laws 'created' under the purview of government in fact existed before state courts. Indeed, at least in common-law countries, state judges were initially seen as 'discovering' pre-existing legal principles that governed commercial, as well as other, interactions rather than as creating these rules *ex nihilo*. Thus, virtually no one denies that broad rules outlining legitimate and illegitimate conduct can and did in fact emerge to govern commerce without government.

Probably for these reasons, the determination of commercial rules has not been seen as the primary or most important objection to the operation of markets under anarchy. Instead, the enforcement of these rules without government has received the focus of most attention that deals with stateless commercial order. Commercial rules, such as those against fraud and contractual default, might emerge without government. But how, in the absence of state enforcement, shall these rules be enforced?

A burgeoning literature demonstrates the effectiveness of private institutions of self-enforcing exchange where government is absent (see, for instance, Ellickson, 1991; Greif, 1993). In most of these cases, multilateral punishment in conjunction with the shadow of the future is used as a substitute for state enforcement of commercial agreements. For instance, imagine a version of the game played in Figure 1 where cooperation refers to fulfilling one's obligations under a contract with the other player and defecting refers to reneging on this agreement or in some other way breaking its terms. There are many examples of this. Credit agreements are one such example. In the absence of any institutional mechanisms of governance, debtors have no incentive to repay their creditors. Once they have received credit, their pay-off is maximised by defaulting on repayment – a form of theft. Fraud is another example of this. In the absence of any mechanism of contractual enforcement, sellers who agree to provide buyers some good of, say, quality X have an incentive to take payment from buyers only to provide them with a good that upon later inspection by buyers is of some lower quality, Y. Realising that this is the debtor's or seller's dominant strategy, creditors will not offer credit and buyers will not contract with sellers, leading the market to shrink and gains from exchange to go unexploited.

If the interaction between a buyer and seller or a creditor and debtor is repeated, however, this problem is quite easily overcome. In this case, provided the debtor or seller wants to enjoy the benefits of contracting with the other party again, he cannot cheat his exchange partner. If he does, his partner will refuse to deal with him again, causing him to lose the discounted value of the stream of future exchanges that honest conduct would have permitted. So long as this loss of future business to the dishonest agent is worth more than the one-shot pay-off from cheating, he maximises his pay-off by behaving honestly. Thus, his trading partner's credible threat to terminate future dealing if he cheats credibly commits him to cooperation, making the contract self-enforcing without government or any other form of external coercion. The self-enforcing exchange institution described here is based on what economists call bilateral punishment. Bilateral punishment, however, is not an ironclad mechanism for enforcing commercial contracts. If, for instance, individuals have relatively high discount rates, such that the discounted value of the future stream of revenue enabled by continued cooperative exchange is worth less to potential defectors than the one-shot pay-off from cheating, then cheating will occur and the market will consequently shrink in response to this prospect.

What is needed in this case is the ability to impose a greater loss on those who have a potential to renege on the contract such that, even when they are more impatient, it still pays them to fulfil their end of commercial agreements. A coordinated form of bilateral punishment, called multilateral punishment, achieves this. Under this strategy, if an agent violates his contract, a whole group of individuals refuses to deal with him again whether any individual group member specifically was the violated party or not. A common manifestation of this mechanism is boycott or embargo. As I discuss below, this mechanism of self-enforcing contracts is used by traders in the international arena where they enjoy very limited, and in some cases non-existent, contract protection from government. The way it works is straightforward. Suppose that an individual defaults on his contract with another individual. In response, the cheated agent communicates this information through his relevant network of other international traders. International commercial associations and arbitration venues, such as the International Chamber of Commerce and the Stockholm Chamber of Commerce, which I discuss below, facilitate this communication.

A number of international traders may be members of commercial associations – such as industry associations – which permit them to socialise, meet with one another, and so on. At such venues they share information about the conduct of other members of the international trading community. In sharing information about the identity of the trader who cheated him, the cheated individual coordinates the responses of his network of other traders, who, not wanting to be cheated themselves, refrain from commercial interactions with the cheater. This has the effect of cutting off the cheater not only from future dealings with the individual he cheated, but also from this individual's entire trading network. It imposes a much stiffer penalty on contractual default than the bilateral version of this punishment, which involves only forgoing future dealings with one individual. In this way, multilateral punishment is much more effective at creating contractual compliance than bilateral punishment. Since all traders know that cheating is treated with this harsh form of punishment, they maximise their pay-off through cooperation instead of defection. And, since everyone knows that this is everyone else's pay-off-maximising strategy, they can participate in the market free of fear of default, which would keep them from engaging in the market.

Multilateral punishment is effectively a way of creating reputations for individual traders which have value to those who are honest. Honest individuals have good reputations and are able to cash in on this through contractual relationships with many others who are willing to contract with them because of their good reputation. Cheating would be very costly for individuals with good reputations because doing so would destroy the value of their histories of good conduct and with it the value of their reputations and thus ability to trade with others in the future. Reputation creation therefore acts as a kind of bond that commits traders to behave honestly. If they do not, they sacrifice the value of their bond.[1] This is significant because it means that traders are likely to fulfil their contractual obligations with others even when they do not expect ever to deal with that particular exchange partner again (Leeson, 2003). In other words, even in the one-shot version of the game in Figure 1, cooperation under multilateral punishment is possible. The reason for this is reputation. Although an individual may never contract specifically with you again, he still wishes to avoid cheating you. If he does not avoid cheating you, you will communicate this to the rest of your trading network, which consists of some individuals he does anticipate wanting to deal with in the future. This creates a negative reputation for him that prevents him from contracting with these other individuals. So, cooperation does not require that he interact with you

1 On the alleged breakdown of multilateral punishment under conditions of large numbers and social heterogeneity, see Leeson (2006, 2008a).

for an infinite number of rounds. Provided reputations can be established, he will cooperate with you even if he intends to interact with you only once.

Private mechanisms like reputation are highly important for enforcing contracts even where government is present and functional. The reason for this is straightforward. Even where government exists and is highly functional, state contractual enforcement is costly and imperfect.[2] For many contractual agreements, it is not profitable to seek state enforcement even if a party has certainty he will win the dispute. The value he would receive is lower than the cost of pursuing state enforcement. Given this situation, one might expect that no contracts below this critical threshold would ever be established because, without recourse to state enforcement, defection would be endemic. But this is evidently not the case. Where state enforcement is prohibitively costly and thus cannot provide practical protection, reputation coupled with bilateral or multilateral punishment, discussed above, secures contractual fulfilment.

Evidence from the international arena

Perhaps the best evidence of the effectiveness of self-enforcing commercial law is from international trade. International commercial contracts are largely governed by an institution called the *lex mercatoria,* or law merchant. The *lex mercatoria* grew out of the need of international traders in the late tenth century to realise the benefits of exchange in the absence of state enforcement (see, for instance, Benson, 1989; Leeson, 2006, 2007a, 2007b). Traders were separated by their own domestic laws, which dealt differently with commercial contracts. Additionally, countries' laws did not have rules that governed international commercial contracts: their laws extended only to domestic contractual agreements. This was problematic in several ways. First, it meant that there

2 Furthermore, as Leeson (2007d) points out, in many cases it is inefficient to have any government at all.

was no universal law to govern international commercial agreements or to resolve international commercial disputes. For instance, which party's domestic law would apply to the agreement in the event a dispute arose? Second, there was no common enforcement body for contracts. For example, in which party's country would the state court decide a dispute? Most domestic courts would not decide conflicts involving international parties. Perhaps even more importantly, even if this could be overcome, how would a state court go about enforcing its decision? If the loser's assets resided in his home country, which was not the country in which the dispute was decided, how could his assets be seized if he did not comply with the state court's judgement?

To overcome these problems, international trading parties needed a common set of rules governing exchange and a mechanism for enforcing compliance with these rules. Out of these obstacles evolved a spontaneous system of customary law, the *lex mercatoria*, which over time established rules that governed international commercial agreements. At first, international disputes were adjudicated in private, informal 'merchant courts' – dispute-resolving bodies that rendered judgements on the basis of the rules of the *lex mercatoria*. Merchant courts consisted of international merchants who were familiar with the rules of the law merchant and so could apply them to the cases that came before them. Since they were private, the decisions they arrived at were not formally binding. Instead, reputation, in conjunction with the bilateral and multilateral punishment discussed above, created compliance with merchant court decisions. Rejecting a merchant court's decision brought no formal sanctions but could result in boycott or ostracism from the community, which created a strong incentive for international traders to comply with the rules of the *lex mercatoria*.

This system operated effectively and governed the preponderance of international commercial agreements between the eleventh and sixteenth centuries throughout Europe (Benson, 1989). Today, international commercial agreements are largely governed by the modern *lex mercatoria*, which operates similarly. In the place of merchant courts are international arbitration associations. Some of the largest of these include the International Chamber of Commerce (ICC), the Stockholm Chamber of Commerce, the London Court of International Arbitration, and the International Center for Dispute Resolution, though hundreds more exist globally. These associations are located throughout the world and privately decide disputes arising from most international commercial contracts. Upwards of 90 per cent of modern international commercial agreements contain arbitration clauses, stipulating that disputes, if they arise, will be decided by a private arbitration association (Volckart and Mangels, 1999). Parties may stipulate *ex ante* which association they will use, what law will apply to their dispute (including the evolved customary rules of the *lex mercatoria*), and so on.

Until 1958, private international arbitral decisions were not enforceable in state courts. Thus, to create compliance, international traders relied on reputation and multilateral punishment, described above. Since then, several international treaties, the most notable of which is called the New York Convention, make state enforcement of international arbitral decisions possible in theory. Recent work suggests, however, that this convention (and the others that came after it) has not contributed dramatically to the size and growth of modern international trade (Leeson, 2008b). Thus, the argument that the shadow of the state is responsible for the incredible magnitude of international trade since 1958 is mistaken. On the contrary, it appears that private arbitration and enforcement mechanisms along the lines discussed above deserve the overwhelming credit for booming international trade. This finding is corroborated by reports from the world's largest international arbitration association, the ICC, which estimates that 90 per cent of its decisions are complied with voluntarily by parties to international trade (Craig et al., 2000).

Self-enforcing criminal law

Unlike the topic of self-enforcing commercial law, the issue of self-enforcing criminal law has received scant attention. Anderson and Hill (2004), Friedman (1979), Posner (1995), Benson (1990) and Leeson (2007c, 2007f, forthcoming) have discussed this topic. Relatively little work, however, deals with the question of preventing and punishing violence without government. This is significant because, at least on its surface, the problem of violence poses a considerably more serious threat to the ability of markets to flourish without government than 'peaceful theft', such as fraud or contractual default, discussed above. The reason for this is twofold. First, although the market may be quite thin if private institutional arrangements cannot enforce commercial rules under anarchy, society itself will not be destroyed if they cannot. Individuals will be relatively poor, but violence will not ensue. Things are different, however, if private institutional arrangements cannot prevent violence. Not only will the market be thin and thus society poor, but more importantly the potential for widespread slaughter that involves the death of many individuals may result.

For these reasons, even those who are ready to defend the possibility of self-enforcing commercial agreements are not ready to jettison government when it comes to matters that typically fall under the purview of criminal law. According to this view society requires government to prevent physically stronger individuals from using their superior strength to violently plunder physically weaker individuals. Even Adam Smith held this position. As he put it,

> It is only under the shelter of the civil magistrate that the owner of ... property ... can sleep a single night in security. He is at all times surrounded by unknown enemies, whom, though he never provoked, he can never appease, and from whose injustice he can be protected only by the powerful arm of the civil magistrate continually held up to chastise it. (Smith 1965 [1776]: 670)

Despite the greater problem that 'violent theft' poses for social order compared with 'peaceful theft', such as fraud or contractual default, there is no reason to think that private institutional solutions to this problem are any less likely to emerge to facilitate trade in the absence of government than they are to emerge to solve problems of 'peaceful theft'. In fact, the greater threat that 'violent theft' poses suggests that private mechanisms for dealing with violence are more likely to emerge, as the cost to individuals if they do not are much larger.

Trading with bandits

The first example of self-enforcing exchange in the presence of violent threats I would like to consider is one I have discussed elsewhere, which examines a historical episode in pre-colonial Africa (Leeson, 2007c). This case is not so much one of the emergence of criminal law under anarchy, but instead one that demonstrates the emergence of private institutional arrangements used to facilitate market activity by overcoming the threat of violence in the first place. Thus, although it does not deal directly with criminal law, it does take up the central issue this chapter is concerned with – the ability of markets to function without government, with a particular emphasis on the obstacle that the threat of violence poses for this ability.

In late-nineteenth-century Angola there was a flourishing export trade consisting of beeswax, ivory and wild rubber, for which there was a large foreign (European) demand. These goods were produced by indigenous Africans in the remote interior of west-central Africa. There were two sides to this export-related trade. On one side were middlemen and the European agents who employed them to obtain ivory and the rest from interior producers. On the other side of this trade network were the producers themselves. Middlemen were highly mobile, often armed, and travelled in large caravans. Producers, in contrast, were stationary, often unarmed, and lived in small villages. Middlemen, then, typically constituted the substantially stronger force in the interactions between members of these two groups. Indeed, when they could, caravans of middlemen violently plundered interior producers – stealing instead of trading for the goods they desired. Peaceful trade rather than violent theft, however, characterised the preponderance of these interactions.

In fact, the export trade based on producer–middlemen exchange flourished during this time.

This occurred despite the absence of government in this society. Many of the interior communities of producers were stateless. Even the African 'kingdoms' that had more formal rulers were hardly formal from a modern Western perspective. The Europeans (mostly Portuguese) had outposts closer to the coast, but these outposts had no official authority over indigenous communities in the interior. Most importantly, since there was no overarching formal authority to oversee the interactions of individuals from different indigenous or European communities, there existed large ungoverned interstices for the interactions between members of these different groups. Social interaction was essentially anarchic.

In the face of the threat of violent theft that middlemen's strength superiority presented, producers developed a practice that through expanding use over time was institutionalised without central command to facilitate cooperation with middlemen. Producers had a strong incentive to find a solution to this obstacle to exchange since, by themselves, largely stationary and cut off from global markets, they could earn very little. Interactions with middlemen presented an opportunity for greater profits, but also made them vulnerable to violent plunder. The practice producers employed for this purpose was credit. Normally we think of credit agreements as the cause of potential opportunism. The separation of payment and provision makes the creditor vulnerable to debtor default. In the context of producer–middleman relations, however, it had quite the opposite effect. The way that credit supported cooperation without command is straightforward. In time *t*, producers would produce effectively nothing. They would leave wax, rubber, and ivory unharvested. When caravans of middlemen looking for goods to steal travelled to outlying interior producers and came upon a village, they would find little to forcibly take. This was problematic from the middlemen's perspective, as travelling to the interior could be quite costly.

Producers would then offer middlemen the goods they were seeking on credit. Middlemen would pay up front, and producers would harvest the goods after the middlemen departed. Middlemen would later return in time $t + 1$ to collect what they were owed. By indebting themselves to stronger middlemen, producers created an incentive for middlemen to avoid physically abusing them and to ensure that other middlemen did not use violence against them. The reason for this is simple: in order to repay what they owed, producers needed to be alive and in good health. The financial health of the middlemen who provided producers goods on credit became linked to the physical health of producers who were their debtors. When middlemen returned to collect on the agreement, all that was on hand to plunder was what they were owed. If they wanted more they could either contract a new round of the credit exchange or leave, knowing that the next time they returned there would again be nothing to take back to their employers for export. Middlemen frequently chose to renew their credit relationship. In this way, credit emerged as a spontaneous institutional arrangement that prevented violence and enabled both sides to realise the gains from trade, despite the absence of government and the superior strength of some members of society. Notably, these credit arrangements did not create the problem of *ex post* opportunism on the part of producers, which normally attends credit agreements. Given the superior strength of their creditors, producers knew that, if they failed to deliver, middlemen could easily punish them through their greater strength. Thus, this spontaneous order solved multiple commitment problems that emerge under the social dilemma at once and in each case substituted cooperation for conflict.

Although the credit mechanism did not create anything like an encompassing system of criminal law in late pre-colonial Africa, it did overcome the threat of violence by transforming the incentives of middlemen from banditry to trade. This historical episode is therefore instructive regarding the ability of markets to overcome the obstacle of violence. It also suggests that government is not, at least in some cases, required for individuals to capture the gains from exchange, even where some agents are stronger than others and thus tempted to use force instead of trade to obtain what they want. In short, even in the face of the potential for violence, the absence of government need not prevent markets from functioning.

Spontaneous order in criminal law

Although the case considered above demonstrated how market actors devise solutions to the problem of violence that threatens to prevent the market from operating, it did not demonstrate the private emergence of criminal law. Here, I will briefly take up this issue. An interesting historical episode on the Anglo-Scottish border between the thirteenth and sixteenth centuries sheds light on the spontaneous evolution of self-enforcing criminal law (Leeson, forthcoming). This territory was divided up into six regions called 'marches', three on the English side and three on the Scottish side, known as the English and Scottish East, Middle and West Marches respectively. Although each march was officially governed by a 'warden' appointed by its respective crown, between the thirteenth and sixteenth centuries the Anglo-Scottish borderlands constituted a significant arena of anarchy. There are several reasons for this.

First, march wardens rarely applied or enforced their countries' official domestic law, which, in any case, was incomplete and poorly defined. Second, and more importantly, since until the early seventeenth century England and Scotland were completely sovereign, there were no common, formal laws – criminal or otherwise – that extended across the border. This was a significant problem, since the border people hardly recognised their 'official' countries but instead defined themselves as members of clans that stretched across national boundaries. Thus, inhabitants on both sides of the Anglo-Scottish border interacted frequently, so much so that the borderland formed a third, almost separate, region between England and Scotland, rather than being a part of both (Fraser, 1995). Since neither England nor Scotland's domestic laws extended to the opposite realm, this third region, as it were, was anarchic in the sense that there was no ultimate supranational authority to create or enforce laws that dealt with 'cross-border crime' – criminal acts perpetrated by citizens on one side of the border against those on the other. This was problematic in a number of ways. Perhaps foremost among these problems, however, was the potential for violent chaos ruling the borderlands. The Anglo-Scottish border during this period was home to the infamous 'border reiver' – that sizeable class of cross-border criminal memorialised in the poetry of Sir Walter Scott, who professionally raided and plundered as a way of life. Without a supranational sovereign to regulate the cross-border reiving system, it threatened to plunge the borders into bloody mayhem.

In the face of this threat, the borders developed a unique international 'legal system' grounded in ancient cross-border custom, called the '*leges marchiarum*', or laws of the marches.[3] The *leges marchiarum* are somewhat reminiscent of the *lex mercatoria* described above. They accomplished for borderers in the context of international criminal law what the *lex mercatoria* accomplished for international traders in the context of international commercial law. The *leges marchiarum* were primarily concerned with rules regarding violence. They dealt with violent cross-border crimes, including murder, violent theft, maiming, etc., and stipulated punishments for these crimes. Punishments evolved over time along with the system of border rules; in most cases, however,

3 It is important to note that international border law was ultimately codified as a series of treaties between the English and Scottish kingdoms. In this sense, governments did play a role in its operation. Two caveats should, however, be recognised. First, these treaties were based on older border custom that emerged without government involvement. Second, the *leges marchiarum*'s status as a partial product of interstate cooperation does not render them unimportant for understanding the emergence of criminal law under anarchy. Like all international agreements, the *leges marchiarum* ultimately could be formed and upheld only through voluntary, interstate cooperation. No supranational sovereign existed then, just as one does not exist today, to enforce governments' promises to one another to comply with the terms of the international treaties they signed. In short, international anarchy is inescapable. Thus, the problem of cooperation, here for the purposes of dealing with cross-border criminality, is merely 'pushed up a level', to securing cooperation between states instead of individuals. Some private, informal enforcement mechanism is still required to support cooperative agreements.

they involved fines and/or delivery of aggressors to victims to ransom or otherwise dispense with as the victims saw fit.

To enforce these rules the borders developed a court-like institution known as the 'day of truce', which met monthly to settle cross-border disputes and address violations of border law according to the *leges marchiarum*. Wardens coordinated days of truce but functioned primarily in an informal fashion under border custom rather than as official agents of the state. Wardens announced approaching days of truce in the market towns in their marches on either side of the border. Border citizens then informed those on the opposite side of the border with whom they had grievance (or these individuals' wardens) of their intent to file a 'bill of complaint' at the impending day of truce. This functioned as a summons for the accused to attend the day of truce and have his case heard. At the day of truce, each side created 'juries' – the English side selecting six Scotsmen for the task and the Scottish side selecting six Englishmen. Each side's jury then heard the bills of complaint filed by the other side (the English jury heard the Scottish complaints and vice versa), and decided whether border law had been violated and what border custom dictated was the appropriate punishment. There were a number of interesting details in this well-refined institutional arrangement, which space does not permit me to delve into here. Suffice it to say that, over time, the system evolved rules regarding a wide array of criminal contingencies.

The day of truce functioned somewhat analogously to the medieval merchant courts under the *lex mercatoria*, although the day of truce dealt primarily with criminal violations, such as violent theft, murder, etc. As with merchant courts, since the day of truce institution did not fall under the purview of a supranational sovereign, its decisions could not for the most part be formally enforced. In the absence of formal mechanisms for enforcing these decisions, informal mechanisms emerged alongside the *leges marchiarum* and day of truce process to ensure compliance with day of truce decisions. Several mechanisms were used for this purpose. Space limitations again prevent me from elaborating upon all of them.

Two in particular, however, deserve further attention: bonding and the deadly feud. Bonding involved the use of human hostages – typically a family member of the accused/guilty or, failing this, one of his fellow clansmen. If, for instance, an accused borderer did not show at the day of truce to which he was summoned, one of his family members or fellow clansmen would be delivered by the accused's warden or the aggrieved to compel his participation. Only showing at the day of truce would lead to the release of the bond. Similarly, if an accused was found guilty by the jury at the day of truce and refused to comply with the jury's decision, a family member or fellow clansmen would be sent to the aggrieved as an assurance until the guilty paid the aggrieved his fine, etc.

The deadly feud was also used to enforce the *leges marchiarum* and day of truce decisions.[4] This is somewhat peculiar in that, as its name suggests, the deadly feud was a violent institution involving the protracted slaughter of another's family. The idea behind this practice, enshrined in border custom, was as follows. Murdering a man, for example, in violation of border law, could result in violent retribution by the murdered man's clan. Usually, in response to this, the clan of the original aggressor would respond in kind, and a deadly back and forth would ensue between the two clans. Obviously, if launched, a deadly feud could result in many deaths on both sides. Given a mutual, credible expectation of this response to unlawfully aggressing against the member of another clan, the cost of doing so was extremely high. This expectation created by the deadly feud institution provided a powerful incentive to behave within the bounds of border law in the first place. In addition to feuds, borderers also used duelling to accomplish similar ends. A borderer who failed to uphold his promise under the terms of border law or comply with a day of truce decision, for instance, could be challenged by the wronged party to a duty-bound duel. Of course, these enforcement mechanisms were far from perfect. Protracted feuds, for instance, did sometimes break out. Precisely because of this possibility,

4 On the stateless Nuer people's use of feuding to create social order in Africa, see Bates (1983) and Leeson (2007d).

however, borderers had an incentive to avoid violating border law, lest they be dragged into a long and bloody battle. It is interesting to note that even these rather crude mechanisms for enforcing prohibitions on violent behaviour proceeded according to well-established border rules. In some cases, for instance, a highly detailed contract elaborating the nature of a duel, the rules according to which it would proceed (such as the weapons that could be used), etc., was drawn up and provided striking structure to this violent enforcement mechanism.

The *leges marchiarum* and their mechanisms of enforcement worked remarkably well at regulating violence along the border when one considers that the society in which they emerged was effectively one of violent thugs. Of course, the system was far from perfect. But this is an unreasonable standard to hold it to in the light of the time period, the unruly individuals it encompassed, and the equal imperfection of government institutions for dealing with criminal activities that existed elsewhere in England and Scotland during this era. Whatever one can say about this episode, it does show that rather intricate informal rules and institutions of enforcement can emerge under anarchy to prevent and punish criminal behaviour.

Concluding remarks

My discussion leads to three conclusions. First, the market is more capable of producing institutions for its own enforcement than conventional wisdom permits. Where government is absent, society does not launch itself into a violent and dishonest frenzy that leads to the end of trade and the death of many of its members. Instead, private institutional arrangements emerge as the result of individuals' efforts to find alternative mechanisms of securing peace and honesty so that they can realise the tremendous benefits of exchange.

Second, commercial rules, specifically those relating to contracts, can and do emerge where government is absent. Perhaps more importantly, private mechanisms for their enforcement emerge alongside them.

Evidence from stateless societies not considered here, such as that from Somalia,[5] and from the international arena, which I considered only briefly, supports this claim. Significantly, this latter arena is a massive one and involves thousands of traders from many different backgrounds and countries who are able to coordinate on such a level that their resulting market activities constitute nearly 25 per cent of global economic activity.

Finally, contrary to prevailing wisdom, criminal behaviour poses no special problem for markets under anarchy. Like rules for dealing with 'peaceful theft', such as those that emerge endogenously to govern commercial contracts, rules for dealing with 'violent theft' also emerge endogenously without central direction to regulate the violent disposition of some members of society. Importantly, private institutions for their enforcement, including mechanisms for adjudicating claims of criminal behaviour, and mechanisms for enforcing the decisions of such adjudications, evolve along with rules regarding criminal conduct to enhance the safety individuals require for markets to function.

References

Anderson, T. L and P. J. Hill (2004), *The Not So Wild, Wild West: Property Rights on the Frontier*, Stanford, CA: Stanford University Press.

Bates, R. H. (1983), *Essays on the Political Economy of Rural Africa*, Cambridge: Cambridge University Press.

Benson, B. L. (1989), 'The spontaneous evolution of commercial law', *Southern Economic Journal*, 55(3).

Benson, B. L. (1990), *The Enterprise of Law: Justice without the State*, San Francisco, CA: Pacific Research Institute.

Berman, H. J. (1983), *Law and Revolution: The Formation of the Western Legal Tradition*, Cambridge, MA: Harvard University Press.

5 On the private emergence and enforcement of law in Somalia and its impact on Somali development, see Leeson (2007e).

Craig, W. L., W. Park and I. Paulsson (2000), *International Chamber of Commerce Arbitration*, New York: Oceana Publications.

Ellickson, R. C. (1991), *Order without Law: How Neighbors Settle Disputes*, Cambridge, MA: Harvard University Press.

Foreign Policy (2006), *The Failed States Index*, www.foreignpolicy.com.

Fraser, G. M. (1995), *The Steel Bonnets: The Story of the Anglo-Scottish Border Reivers*, London: HarperCollins.

Friedman, D. D. (1979), 'Private creation and enforcement of law: a historical case', *Journal of Legal Studies*, 8.

Friedman, M. (1962), *Capitalism and Freedom*, Chicago, IL: University of Chicago Press.

Greif, A. (1993), 'Contract enforceability and economic institutions in early trade: the Maghribi traders' coalition', *American Economic Review*, 83(3).

Hayek, F. A. (1960), *The Constitution of Liberty*, Chicago, IL: University of Chicago Press.

Hayek, F. A. (1973), *Law Legislation and Liberty*, vols 1–3, Chicago, IL: University of Chicago Press.

Hobbes, T. (1651 [1955]), *Leviathan*, Oxford: Blackwell.

Leeson, P. T. (2003), 'Contracts without government', *Journal of Private Enterprise*, 18(2).

Leeson, P. T. (forthcoming), 'The Laws of Lawlessness', *Journal of Legal Studies*.

Leeson, P. T. (2008a), 'Social distance and self-enforcing exchange', *Journal of Legal Studies*, 37(1).

Leeson, P. T. (2008b), 'How Important is State Enforcement for Trade?', *American Law and Economics Review*, 10(1).

Leeson, P. T. (2006), 'Cooperation and conflict: evidence on self-enforcing arrangements and heterogeneous groups', *American Journal of Economics and Sociology*, 65(4).

Leeson, P. T. (2007a), 'Does globalization require global government?', *Indian Journal of Economics and Business*, Special Issue.

Leeson, P. T. (2007b), 'One more time with feeling: the law merchant, arbitration, and international trade', *Indian Journal of Economics and Business*, Special Issue.
Leeson, P. T. (2007c), 'Trading with bandits', *Journal of Law and Economics*, 50(2).
Leeson, P. T. (2007d), 'Efficient anarchy', *Public Choice*, 130(1–2).
Leeson, P. T. (2007e), 'Better off stateless: Somalia before and after government collapse', *Journal of Comparative Economics*, 35(4).
Leeson, P. T. (2007f), 'An-*arrgh*-chy: the law and economics of pirate organization', *Journal of Political Economy*, 115(6).
Leeson, P. T. and E. Stringham (2005), 'Is government inevitable?', *Independent Review*, 9(4).
Posner, R. A. (1995), *Overcoming Law*, Cambridge, MA: Harvard University Press.
Smith, A. (1965 [1776]), *An Inquiry into the Nature and Causes of the Wealth of Nations*, New York: Modern Library.
Volckart, O. and A. Mangels (1999), 'Are the roots of the modern Lex Mercatoria really medieval?', *Southern Economic Journal*, 65(3).
World Bank (2005), *World Development Indicators*, Washington, DC: World Bank.

3 NATURAL LAW, SCHOLASTICISM AND FREE MARKETS

Samuel Gregg

Introduction

Serious study of the history of ideas invariably indicates that it is rare for any one set of institutions or practices to have been originally conceptualised or predominantly developed by one particular tradition of thought. In *Law and Revolution* (1983), Harold Berman articulates a convincing case to demonstrate that what he calls the Western legal tradition owed much not only to the 'papal revolution' ignited in the course of Pope Gregory VII's clash with Emperor Henry IV, but also to an evolving synthesis of royal, imperial, feudal, urban, mercantile and Roman law.

A similar explanation underlies the formation of key ideas and institutions that contributed to the growth of free market economies. As Odd Langholm remarks at the beginning of his *Legacy of Scholasticism in Economic Thought*, 'historians of economic doctrine now recognise that modern theory is the product of continuous growth over a much longer period of time than was previously assumed' (1998: vii). Even a relatively cursory survey of the literature that explores the emergence of market-oriented concepts and practices underlines the difficulty of rooting these phenomena solely in a single tradition of thought. Free market ideas neither began nor ended with the publication of Adam Smith's *Wealth of Nations*.

The purpose of this chapter is to identify and highlight prominent contributions of the natural-law tradition of moral, political and legal reasoning to the shaping of free market ideas and practices. Given that this tradition of thought stretches back to Aristotle and beyond, it does not seek to explore or summarise the particular contributions of all relevant natural-law thinkers. Rather, the emphasis is upon underlining some of the more important contributions by thinkers – specifically Aristotle, Thomas Aquinas and the sixteenth- and seventeenth-century Scholastic thinkers associated with Spain's University of Salamanca – working within the natural-law tradition.[1]

What is natural law?

Before embarking on this task, some clarification is required as to the meaning of 'natural law'. In itself this is a vast subject. Throughout history, it has involved debates ranging from the meanings of the words 'natural' and 'law' to the tradition's understanding of the precise character of free will. We confine ourselves here to delineating the most uncontroversial features of the tradition more relevant to our immediate purposes.

Perhaps the most common understanding of 'natural law' prevalent at the beginning of the 21st century is the idea that there are certain choices and actions that, no matter what endorsement by the positive law legislated by governments, ought never to be taken. A good example of the logic of natural law may be found in the 1946 Nuremberg war crimes trials. In defending those leaders of the National Socialist regime on trial, the lawyers for the accused maintained that the defendants' actions – such as confiscations of Jewish property, the euthanasia programme, medical experiments in the concentration camps, etc. – were legal insofar as they had not contradicted and, in many instances, had been legitimised by laws promulgated by the Nazi state.

The prosecution responded by maintaining that such actions were

1 By the natural-law tradition, we do not mean the natural-rights tradition associated with the thought of John Locke and some post-Enlightenment thinkers. Broadly speaking, the natural-rights tradition flows from the tradition of natural law, but is more immediately concerned with the protection and upholding of human autonomy than with natural law's emphasis on human flourishing.

not only rendered illegal by international law, but were called into question by strong Anglo-Saxon and European jurisprudential traditions that emphasised that there are indeed universal laws which no positive law – no matter how firmly sanctioned by the state – can annul. In his closing prosecutorial address, Justice Robert Jackson contended that the International Military Tribunal sought to:

> ... [rise] above the provincial and transient and [sought] guidance not only from international law but also from the basic principles of jurisprudence which are assumptions of civilization and which long have found embodiment in the codes of all nations (1947: 29).

During the trial, the phrase 'natural law' was used sparingly by the prosecutors. They preferred to use terms such as 'the laws of peoples which the peoples of the world upheld', 'the enlightened conscience of mankind' or 'higher justice' (Shawcross, 1947: 106). There is little question, however, that they were appealing to a notion that there are certain principles or goods that the state may not violate, and which indeed can nullify the validity of certain laws.

Up to a point, this accurately reflects much of the content of natural law, which is far more explicit when it comes to identifying what we may not do rather than what we should do. The question arises, however, of how we know what we ought never to do. This in turn directs us to perhaps the more substantial content of the idea of natural law, which is the notion of *practical reason*. By 'practical reason', natural-law scholars do not have in mind a type of pragmatism. For its most famous exponent, the natural law 'is nothing other than the light of understanding infused in us by God, whereby we understand what must be done and what must be avoided. God gave this light and this law to man at creation' (Aquinas, 1954: 245).

Interestingly, Thomas Aquinas's definition of natural law does not presuppose that people must believe in God to know the moral truths revealed by our practical reason. These truths, the natural-law tradition holds, are inscribed into our very reason itself, and thus are a permanent feature of human nature (hence the phrase 'natural'), regardless of whether people believe in God. Natural-law theory thus holds that man is free to discover and, if he chooses, obey these moral truths. At the same time, natural-law theory contests the notion that reason itself creates the truth about moral good and evil. This is why natural law is often described as 'right reason'. Its 'practicality' arises from the fact that the moral goods revealed by natural law can only be realised – or contravened – through human *choice* and *action*. According to Aquinas, 'Good is the first thing that falls under the apprehension of the practical reason, which is directed to action: since every agent acts for an end under the aspect of good. Consequently the first principle in the practical reason is one founded on the notion of good' (Aquinas, 1975: I-II, 94, a.2).

Sceptics point to the fact of some disagreement in almost all societies about what is morally right and wrong as grounds to doubt that human reason can reveal definitive moral truths or that moral truth even exists beyond the conventions of evolving custom and social habits. Here is not the place to debate the merits or otherwise of philosophical scepticism's case against natural law. It is enough to note that natural law theorists have produced their own objections to philosophical scepticism, such as what John Finnis and others call scepticism's self-refuting nature (1998: 60), and have noted that the fact of difference does not prove the 'unknowability' of anything beyond the power of natural science. Some people make errors in their reasoning; others are blinded by cultural and emotional prejudices.

But perhaps more importantly, natural-law theory acknowledges a diversity of views about what we may rightly choose to do, as opposed to refrain from doing. In other words, while natural-law theory posits the taking of innocent human life or adultery as acts that may never be committed, it also insists that there is significant room for legitimate prudential judgement concerning the reasonable and good options that people can choose, especially in the realm of economics. Some of these judgements may be incompatible with each other, even though they are derived from the same principles. From a natural-law standpoint, for example, there is no absolutely right answer to the question of what percentage of his income or time a rich person should give to the poor. Natural-law thinkers acknowledge that answering such a question depends upon empirical and prudential judgements reasonably in dispute among people equally well informed by practical reason.

It is, however, precisely because natural law theorists are concerned with discerning the moral good or evil of the free choices of people living in society that they have made significant contributions to the formation of political, legal and economic thought. In this regard, the approach of natural-law theory is decidedly anti-utilitarian and anti-consequentialist in its reasoning. Utilitarianism and consequentialism are characterised, from a natural-law standpoint, by arbitrariness and a futile attempt to measure the incommensurable (Finnis et al., 1990). Certainly, natural law does not suggest that the utility and consequences of human acts are irrelevant when it comes to discerning the moral worth of human choices. As we will see, the issue of utility features prominently in natural-law reflections upon economics. Nevertheless, natural-law theory insists that the morality or otherwise of a freely chosen act lies in the act's conformity to the moral law discernible through human reason. And it is precisely through its study of the mechanics of free choice that natural-law theorists have made their most significant contributions to the formation of market concepts, practices and institutions.

From Aristotle to Aquinas

If people desire to understand the nature of economic life, they need to reflect upon those engaged in it: human persons. A starting point of classical natural-law reflection is that, unlike animals, human beings can understand and therefore shape the world around them through their choices and action. This suggests that it is through the study of human intentionality and human acts that people can understand social realities, including economic activity. As the legal philosopher John Finnis notes:

> … human actions, and the societies constituted by human action, cannot be adequately understood as if they were merely (1) natural occurrences, (2) contents of thoughts, or (3) products of techniques of mastering natural materials … True, there are elements in human life and behaviour … such as the workings of one's digestion, or one's instinct and emotions, which can and should be understood as objects (subject-matter) of natural science … But human actions and societies cannot be adequately described, explained, justified, or criticised unless they are understood as also, and centrally, the carrying out of free choices. (Finnis, 1998: 22)

This attention to the dynamics of human action is manifested in the thought of the first thinker normally identified with the natural-law tradition. A leading commentator on Aristotelian economics, Ricardo Crespo, comments:

> For Aristotle, practical rationality is reason applied to *prâxis*. *Prâxis* is human action; while practical reason has to do with the capacity of guiding action toward an adequate end. Thus, practical rationality is motivated by ends, and seeks after corresponding means to achieve its objectives. (Crespo, 1998: 202)

Like most of the citizen class of his time, Aristotle had a low opinion of those engaged in commerce (Aristotle, 1988: 1.3.1257b1–1258a18). Yet it has been argued that the very idea of political economy originated with Aristotle (Newman, 1951: 138), not least because of Aristotle's critique of the virtually communist property arrangements advocated by Plato. In this, Aristotle articulated some of the most lasting arguments in favour of one of the free market's most essential foundations: private property. He observed that people tend to take better care of what is theirs than of what is common to everyone, since individuals tend to shirk a responsibility that is nobody's in particular. Second, Aristotle stressed that if everyone were responsible for everything, the result would be confusion. Finally, Aristotle insisted that dividing things up generally produces a more peaceful state of affairs, while sharing common things often results in tension.

These are primarily observations on how people typically choose and act when property is privately or communally owned. For Aristotle, however, private property was not superior to communal property arrangements simply because the former appeals to each person's self-interest and the incentives that lead to higher economic productivity. Aristotle also maintained that private property's superiority was derived from the fact that it created opportunities for people to choose freely to use their private wealth in benevolent ways. In other words, legally enforceable private property arrangements were far more conducive to an individual's free choice of virtuous acts than communal property.

Aristotle touches on other questions relevant to the formation of free markets, but these are generally scattered throughout his writings. The most significant natural-law contributions to free market ideas and institutions had to wait until the emergence of the Scholastic movement in Europe towards the beginning of the ninth century, which persisted until the seventeenth century.

As one author notes, Scholasticism was an intellectual movement that:

> ... was essentially a rational investigation of every relevant problem in liberal arts, philosophy, theology, medicine, and law, examined from opposing points of view, in order to reach an intelligent, scientific solution that would be consistent with accepted authorities, known facts, human reason, and the Christian faith. (Weisheipl, 1967: 212)

Though the names associated with Scholasticism are many, the figure of Thomas Aquinas looms prominently, not least because it is virtually impossible to discuss natural-law theory without some reference to his voluminous works.

Though Aquinas did not address economic questions in a systematic way, his work did contribute in a variety of ways to the moral legitimisation and legal protection of economic liberty. For one thing, he rejected Aristotle's view of commerce as a somewhat disreputable activity. There were, Aquinas said, many good reasons for people to engage in commercial activity, ranging from the obvious public benefits that flow from material prosperity to the ways in which commerce generally helps to alleviate the condition of the poor. Aquinas also stressed that profit-making – provided it was done in morally acceptable ways – was quite legitimate (1975: II-II, q.77).

In terms of specific institutions indispensable for market economies, Aquinas affirmed Aristotle's treatment of property (ibid.: II-II, q.66). He also, however, devoted much attention to the institution of contract. While many Roman legal theorists had examined and analysed contract (Gordley, 1991), Aquinas's particular contribution was to deepen the moral significance of contract and expand our appreciation of why unreasonable violation of contracts is immoral. Noting that making a contract involves two or more people participating in a legally recognised social practice, Aquinas underscored the moral element of promise-making in the formation of reasonable contracts. Insofar as valid contracts involve promises that demand personal commitments to other people as well as a person's free choice of the moral good of truthfulness, Aquinas stressed that making contracts with no intention of adhering to their terms is a form of lying (1975: II-II, q.40, q.110).

Aquinas also emphasised that the promise-making implicit to contract-making and implementation is much more an act of intelligence than will (ibid., II-II, q.88). Commenting on this passage, Finnis observes that for Aquinas the promise-making of contracts:

> ... projects an order, a set of relationships between a person or persons and some other act or other 'thing', and settling things in order is always fundamentally an act of practical understanding and more or less creative reason ... it is also an assertion of one's present intention to undertake and acknowledge the *obligation* to do so, and the corresponding right of the promise, such that the benefits or service of the promisor's performance can be counted, as from *now*, among the promisee's *sua* (belongings, goods) or *iura* (rights). (Finnis, 1998: 198)

From this standpoint, we see that Aquinas's emphasis on the act of intelligence involved in making contracts strengthens their binding force. It also reflects a far stronger view of the binding character of contracts than is often expressed in many contemporary legal treatments of contract (Atiyah, 1995).

There were two further areas in which Aquinas contributed to the development of market economic thought. The first arises in the context of his attention to the question of which commercial exchanges are fair and which are unjust. Reflecting upon what constitutes a just sale, Aquinas insisted that the buyer and seller involved in any one exchange are acting justly if the amount paid by the buyer and received by the seller is neither more nor less than the actual worth or value of the good or service being exchanged. This, according to Aquinas, is underpinned by the principle that any transaction must be equitable in the sense of providing mutual benefit (1975: II-II, q.77, a.4).

But how, some might ask, are we to measure the value of a given good or service? For Aquinas, such a measure is to be found in human need (1992: v.9, nn.4–5). Elsewhere Aquinas specified that people need something when they cannot accomplish ends without it (1929: d.29). Drawing upon a variety of his writings to summarise Aquinas's conclusions on this matter, Finnis writes:

> … the value at stake in justice is use-value: in the order of nature a mouse, having senses and locomotion, is of greater worth [*dignitas*] than a pearl, but in terms of utility – what people need for their use – a pearl has a higher value [*pretium*]. But utility is relative to circumstances: in a situation of necessity [*necessitates*] a loaf of bread … will be reasonably more valued [*praeeligeretur*], and fetch a higher price, than the most precious pearl. The normal manifestation of need [*indigentia*] is preference [*praeeligere*]: so 'need' amounts in these contexts to 'demand'. The conventional institution of money [*numisma*] enables us to measure demand, i.e., the demand of the buyer who has money and of the seller who needs [*indigent*] money and has what meets the buyer's demand [*indigentia*]. The normal measure of something's value, therefore, will be the price it would currently fetch 'in the market' [*secundum*

> *communem forum*], i.e., in deals between willing sellers and buyers in the same locality and time-frame, each party being aware of the thing's merits and defects. (Finnis, 1998: 202)

Like his treatment of contract, Aquinas's reasoning about the justice of free exchanges in the market is considerably more complex – and perhaps more rigorous – than many more modern explanations, such as that articulated by Thomas Hobbes in his *Leviathan* (1996: xv.14). The point, however, is that Aquinas's analysis of this matter was far more detailed and internally consistent than that of most previous writers on the subject, thereby helping to establish the moral and therefore rational legitimacy of the practice of free exchange in the West's economic practices and legal and cultural memory.

A similar observation may be made of Aquinas's treatment of the subject of usury. The history of the usury debates is complex and particularly subject to caricature. For our purposes, it suffices to note that while neither Judaism nor Christianity objected to people making honest profits, a question hovered over the matter of whether an honest profit could be earned by selling money: that is, charging a price for money or what we call 'interest'. The early fathers of the Christian Church condemned the charging of interest on a money loan. It was unjust, they maintained, when the borrower was a poor person seeking ways to survive, while the lender was a wealthy person who had resources to help the poor man if he chose to do so. Usury was thus defined as a *loan for subsistence*, as opposed to a *loan of capital* (Charles, 1998: 95). This distinction is crucial, as it does not appear that there were any serious objections to people lending others capital (Chadwick, 1988: 15).

The problem was that the distinction between money loans and capital loans was not well understood, not least because, as one historian comments, 'at the time, the wise and fruitful use of deposits for the creation of credit and, hence, of new real wealth, was not fully understood' (Giuseppi, 1966: 5). With the emergence of new commercial wealth in twelfth-century western Europe, there was a corresponding increase in the demand for money. This was not driven simply by increased consumption and the heightened processes of exchange. It was also based on the need for money as a measure and *store* of value. Once money began to serve this purpose, more people began to realise that money could be used to create new and more wealth through investment. In other words, money could be *capital*. This raised the question of whether it was right to lend money to someone in order that they might use it for a business venture and charge interest on the loan.

Such concerns arose, in part, from a static view of the economy. The idea of economic growth was incomprehensible to much of the medieval and early modern world. Also influential was the manner in which Roman law treated the question. According to Roman law, one could not charge interest on the 'personal' loan – the *mutuum* (Sohm, 1892: 372–3). This could be anything fungible (a *res fungibilis*): something measurable in both quantity and quality which was consumed in use and thus not capable of creative use. If borrowed, it could be restored only in the exact kind and quantity: one apple for one apple. Because Roman law treated money as a means of exchange with no potential future lasting value of its own, it was considered fungible. It was therefore 'sterile' – unable to bear fruit. It was consequently impermissible to charge interest on a loan of money (Charles, 1998: 203).

As western Europe moved from static to wealth-creating economic arrangements, the inadequacies of Roman law's understanding of money began to be understood. Aquinas played a major role in helping people to see that money was capable of transcending its character as simply a means of exchange by focusing on how people could use money. There were, Aquinas noted, two general types of charges that could be levied for giving others the use of our money. Noting that a *mutuum* excluded the possibility of charging interest that was *intrinsic* to the loan itself, Aquinas established that there were at least two *extrinsic* titles on a loan.

One was recompense or indemnity (*interesse*) for losses. It was, Aquinas argued, legitimate for the lender to levy a charge on the borrower that compensated the lender for any losses or expenses incurred for making the loan (1975: II-II, q.78, a.1). This could include, Aquinas suggested, a charge payable to the lender if the borrower failed to repay the principal of the loan as scheduled, and which compensated the lender for any losses incurred as a result. The second extrinsic title was that of shared profits in joint enterprises. According to Aquinas, the person who lends money to another on the basis of sharing in any profits or losses resulting from the enterprise is entitled to part of the profits as well as the return of his capital (ibid.: II-II, q.78, a.2).

Several intellectual breakthroughs occur here. First, there is an implicit recognition that money is not always sterile. Given certain conditions (i.e. those of the free market, transparency in transactions, and economic growth), money acquires its own productive character. Second, Aquinas implicitly underlines a willingness to take risks by lending capital in the form of money to others as an activity worthy of financial compensation. Third, he recognises the factor of time as influencing the relative productivity of money. Fourth, Aquinas seems not to limit his view of money to the medium of coinage, as suggested by some commentators (Langholm, 1984: 80–86). Finnis observes that much of what Aquinas says about usury assumes that the principal can take more abstract forms such as bonds, stocks and shares (Finnis, 1998: 207, 217–18).

Over time, these observations had a powerful effect upon the legal and moral treatment of lending. It was not, for example, difficult for scholars such as Bernardino of Siena to observe, on the basis of Aquinas's remarks, that '[m]oney has not only the character of money, but it has beyond this a productive character which we commonly call capital' (Pachant, 1963: 743). The Fifth Lateran Council (1512–17) was able to define usury as 'nothing else than gain or profit drawn from the use of a thing that is by its nature sterile, a profit acquired without labour, costs, or risk' (Gilchrist, 1969: 115). This meant that charging interest upon money-as-capital was permissible because money-as-capital was not sterile. Commenting on this and related texts, the historian Werner Sombart remarks:

> The very simple formula in which ecclesiastical authority expressed its attitude to the question of profit making is this: interest on a pure money loan, in any form, is forbidden; profit on capital, in any form, is permitted, whether it flows from commercial business, or from an industrial undertaking ... or from insurance against transport risks; or from shareholding in an enterprise ... or however else. (Sombart, 1967: 314)

The late Scholastics and the market

Scholasticism was not a static intellectual movement. This much is evident from observing how post-Aquinas scholars ranging from Joannis Gerson (1362–1444) to Cardinal Tomas Cajetan (1468–1534) continued to develop the insights of the tradition in response to new problems. The fruits were considerable, not least the establishment of the foundation of modern international law by sixteenth-century Scholastics such as Francisco Suárez, SJ (1548–1617), and Cardinal Robert Bellarmine (1542–1621).

Less well known is the contribution of Spanish Scholastic thinkers writing during the same period to the intellectual refinement of concepts and institutions important for free markets. The Austrian economist F. A. Hayek did not exaggerate when he indicated that the tradition of liberty under law – so strong in continental Europe during the Middle Ages – was kept alive:

> ... by the Schoolmen after it had received its first great systematization, on foundations deriving from Aristotle, at the hands of Thomas Aquinas; by the end of the sixteenth century it had been developed by some of the Spanish Jesuit philosophers into a system of essentially liberal policy, especially in the economic field, where they anticipated much that was revived only by the Scottish philosophers of the eighteenth century. (Hayek, 1978: 123)

The specific contributions to economic thought of the 'late Scholastics', as they have become known, many of whom were associated with Spain's University of Salamanca in the sixteenth and seventeenth centuries, have become better known as a consequence of the work of scholars such as Alejandro Chafuen (2003), Marjorie Grice-Hutchinson (1973), H. M. Robertson (1973) and Jesús Huerta de Soto (2006). The inquiries of the late Scholastics embraced practices as varied as taxation, coinage, foreign exchange, credit, prices, value, interest and banking.

On subjects such as private property, late Scholastic thinkers such as Juan de Mariana, SJ (1535–1624), Domingo de Soto (1493–1560) and Leonardo Lessio (1554–1623) largely elaborated upon the foundations established by Aquinas's analysis of the subject. Some late Scholastics emphasised the problems arising from common ownership by underlining the fact that the fallen nature of man, or original sin, made it extremely difficult for people to practise complete detachment from temporal goods (Chafuen, 2003: 37). Other late Scholastics contributed to developing the discussion of usury, most notably by identifying more extrinsic titles upon loans (Cruz, 1637).

There are, however, two areas in which late Scholastic thinkers made distinctive contributions to the development of contemporary free markets which reflect not simply the exegesis of Aquinas but also responses to issues confronting Spanish society at the time. The late Scholastics wrote in a period when Spain not only acquired a world empire but also experienced the economic costs of the almost continuous wars that accompanied and followed many such acquisitions. While Aquinas's treatment of the state is one that notes its limits, several late Scholastic writers focused upon its limited competence in the economic realm. Domingo de Soto, for example, emphasised how the state's excessive intervention in economic life deeply damaged the common good: 'Great dangers for the republic spring from financial exhaustion; the population suffers privations and is greatly oppressed by daily increases in taxes' (1968: Bk 3, q.6, a.7).

Reacting to the financial privations visited upon Philip II's Spain as the king struggled to suppress rebellion in the Netherlands, ward off Muslim invaders from the Mediterranean and maintain order throughout his ever-expanding dominions, Juan de Mariana argued that public law and government should protect private property rather than usurp it. While taxation, he argued, was necessary if government was to perform its essential functions, he observed that the state's tendency is to move beyond such boundaries very quickly and to increase taxation accordingly (1950b: 23–7). Mariana also noted how government-sponsored currency debasements and excessive expenditures (and subsequent tax increases) effectively amounted to the slow but sure violation of private property (Mariana, 1950a: 548). Writing in response to the same problems, Pedro de Navarra outlined a range of criteria to help establish whether or not a tax was just. This went beyond simply the tax being legislated according to due process. It involved using classic Scholastic analysis to establish criteria to judge whether the need for a tax was genuine and whether the amount levied was excessive (Navarra, 1597: 135).

The second area in which late Scholastic natural-law theory contributed significantly to the development of free markets concerned the area of price and value. The late Scholastics did not adhere to a labour theory of value, as suggested by R. H. Tawney (1937: 36). Instead, they drew upon a growing body of consensus among natural-law thinkers including Aristotle, Aquinas, Bernardino of Siena, Antonio of Florence and Cajetan (not to mention St Augustine) (Chafuen, 2003: 80–81) to develop the idea that the value (and therefore price) attached to goods and services depended upon the utility attached to them by people. They often employed the phrase 'common estimation' to describe this. In doing so, they developed a sophisticated theory of pricing.

The late Scholastics generally identified three elements that determined the prices of saleable goods. These were a good's *virtuositas* (objective use in value), *raritas* (scarcity) and *complacibilitas* (desirability or common estimation) (ibid.: 81). As Scholastic thinking on this subject continued to develop, it rapidly moved towards the conclusion that the just price was the value of the good as determined by common estimation in the market. Francisco de Vitoria (1483–1546), for example, wrote that wherever there is a marketable good, the price is not determined by the nature of the good or the labour employed to create it. 'If', he wrote, 'according to common estimation, the bushel of wheat is worth four silver pieces and somebody buys it for three, this would constitute an injustice to the seller because the common estimation of a bushel of wheat is four silver pieces' (Vitoria, 1934–36: Bk 2, q.2, a.1). Likewise, Luis de Molina (1535–1600) insisted that:

> ... it should be observed that a price is considered just or unjust not because of the nature of things in themselves ... but due to their ability to serve human utility. Because this is the way in which they are appreciated by men, they therefore command a price in the market and in exchanges. (Molina, 1981: 167–8)

Molina then, however, specifies that he understood utility as subjective utility: 'the nature and the need of the use given to them determined the quantity of price ... it depends on the relative appreciation which each man has for the use of the good' (ibid.: 168).

Conclusion

Many of the ideas outlined above may be obvious to those living in the relatively free economies of the developed world, but they were not so obvious to people living in classical Greece or medieval and early modern western Europe. Indeed, many of the analyses outlined above were undertaken in the context of detailed discussion of other questions, such as the nature and authority of the political community, to the attainment of quite different ends, most notably the devising of confessional manuals. Even closer to our own time, much intellectual reflection studied from the standpoint of natural law tends to relegate economic issues to the periphery, though there are some important exceptions, such as the nineteenth-century Italian priest-philosopher Antonio Rosmini (2007).

In part, this reflects the fact that natural law is not prescriptive in a detailed sense when it comes to either economics or economic systems. Certainly, neither anarchism nor communism is reconcilable with classical natural-law theory. But between these poles, natural-law theory recognises a range of possibilities as just and meeting the demands of practical reason. Nonetheless, at particular points of history, the natural-law tradition has made significant – and, in some instances, decisive – intellectual contributions to practices and ideas that have positively shaped the development of the habits and institutions required by free markets. For a tradition not focused on economic questions per se, this is a considerable achievement.

References

Aquinas, T. (1929), *S. Thomae Aquinatis Ordinis Praedicatorum Doctoris Communis Ecclesiae Scriptum super Libros Sententiarum Magistri Petri Lombardi Episcopi Parisiensis,* Paris : Sumptibus P. Lethielleux.

Aquinas, T. (1954), *In Duo Praecepta Caritatis et in Decem Legis Praecepta. Prologus: Opuscula Theologica*, II, no. 1129, Paris: Ed. Taurinen.

Aquinas, T. (1975), *Summa Theologiae*, London: Blackfriars.

Aquinas, T. (1992), *Sententia Libri Ethicorum, in Thomae Aquinatis Opera Omnia cum Hypertextibus*, CD-ROM, Milan: Editoria Elettronica Editel.

Aristotle (1988), *The Politics*, ed. Stephen Everson, Cambridge: Cambridge University Press.

Atiyah, P. S. (1995), *An Introduction to the Law of Contract*, 5th edn, Oxford: Clarendon Press.

Berman, H. (1983), *Law and Revolution*, vol. 1: *The Formation of the Western Legal Tradition*, Cambridge, MA: Harvard University Press.

Chadwick, H. (1988), *The Cambridge History of Medieval Political Thought*, Cambridge: Cambridge University Press.

Chafuen, A. (2003), *Faith and Liberty: The Economic Thought of the Late-Scholastics*, Lanham, MD: Lexington Books.

Charles, R. (1998), *Christian Social Witness and Teaching*, vol. 1: *The Catholic Tradition from Genesis to Centesimus Annus*, Leominster: Gracewing.

Crespo, R. (1998), 'Is economics a moral science', *Journal of Markets and Morality*, 1(2): 201–11.

Cruz, F. de la (1637), *Tratado unico de interreses*, Madrid: Francisco Martinez.

De Soto, D. (1968), *De Iustitia et Iure*, Madrid: IEP.

Finnis, J. (1998), *Aquinas: Moral, Political, and Legal Theory*, Oxford: Oxford University Press.

Finnis, J., J. Boyle and G. Grisez (1990), 'Incoherence and consequentialism (or proportionalism) – a rejoinder', *American Catholic Philosophical Quarterly*, 64: 265–76.

Gilchrist, J. (1969), *The Church and Economic Activity in the Middle Ages*, London: Macmillan.

Giuseppi, J. (1966), *The Bank of England: A History from its Foundation in 1694*, Chicago, IL: Henry Regnery.

Gordley, J. (1991), *The Philosophical Origins of Modern Contract Doctrine*, Oxford: Clarendon Press.

Grice-Hutchinson, M. (1973), *Early Economic Thought in Spain 1177–1740*, London: Allen & Unwin.

Hayek, F.A. (1978), *New Studies in Philosophy, Politics, Economics and the History of Ideas*, Chicago, IL: University of Chicago Press.

Hobbes, T. (1996), *Leviathan*, ed. J. Gaskin, Oxford: Oxford University Press.

Huerta de Soto, J. (2006), *Money, Bank Credit, and Economic Cycles*, trans. M. A. Stroup, Auburn, AL: Ludwig von Mises Institute.

Jackson, R. (1947), 'Closing Speech', in *Trial of the Major War Criminals before the International Military Tribunal*, vol. xix, Proceedings, 7/19–29/1946 [official text in English language], One Hundred and Eighty-Seventh Day: Friday, 7/26/1946: Morning Session: Part 2, Nuremberg: IMT.

Langholm, O. (1984), *The Aristotelian Analysis of Usury*, Bergen: Universitetsforlaget.

Langholm, O. (1998), *The Legacy of Scholasticism in Economic Thought: Antecedents of Power and Choice*, Cambridge: Cambridge University Press.

Mariana, J. de (1950a), *Del Rey y de la institución real*, Madrid: Editions Atlas.

Mariana, J. de (1950b), *Tratado sobre la Moneda de Vellon*, Madrid: Editions Atlas.

Molina, L. de. (1981), *La Teoria del justo precio*, Madrid: Ed. Nacional.

Navarra, P. de (1597), *De Restitutione*, Toledo.

Newman, W. L. (1951), *The Politics of Aristotle*, Oxford: Clarendon Press.

Pachant, M. (1963), 'St Bernardin de Sienne et l'usure', *Le Moyen Age*, 69: 740–53.

Robertson, H. M. (1973), *Aspects of the Rise of Economic Individualism: A Criticism of Max Weber and his School*, Clifton, NJ: A. M. Kelly.

Rosmini, A. (2007), *The Constitution under Social Justice*, trans. A. Mingardi, Lanham, MD: Lexington Books.

Shawcross, H. (1947), 'Opening Address', in *Trial of the Major War Criminals before the International Military Tribunal*, vol. iii, Proceedings, 12/1/1945–12/14/1945 [official text in the English language]: Twelfth Day, Tuesday, 12/4/1945, Part 1, 91–4: Part 6, Nuremberg: IMT.

Sohm, R. (1892), *The Institutes: A Textbook of the History and System of Roman Private Law*, Oxford: Clarendon Press.

Sombart, W. (1967), *The Quintessence of Capitalism*, trans. M. Epstein, New York: Howard Fertig.

Tawney, R. H. (1937), *Religion and the Rise of Capitalism*, New York: Harcourt, Brace.

Vitoria, F. de (1934–36), *De Justitia*, Madrid: Publicaciones de la Asociación Francisco de Vitoria.

Weisheipl, J. A. (1967), 'Scholastic method', in *New Catholic Encyclopaedia*, New York: McGraw-Hill.

4 THE COMMON LAW AND WEALTH

Cento Veljanovski[1]

Introduction

Laws and institutions affect a nation's wealth. This is an obvious but neglected claim. Fortunately, as concerns over the adverse impact that the growth of regulation on productivity, competitiveness and economic growth have increased, interest in the efficiency of different laws and legal systems has been rekindled.[2] One fundamental area which warrants serious research is which legal system – common or civil law – contributes most to the wealth of a nation.[3]

Views on the relative economic efficiency of these two legal systems differ sharply. F. A. Hayek (1973) advanced the view that the common law contributed to greater economic welfare because it was less interventionist, less under the tutelage of the state, and was better able to respond to change than civil legal systems. Indeed, it was for him a legal system that led, like the market, to a spontaneous order. Judge Richard Posner (of the US Federal Court of Appeals) achieved notoriety in the 1970s by claiming, and then adducing evidence based on an analysis of specific legal doctrines, that the hidden logic of the common law was and is wealth maximisation (Posner, 1971).

On the other hand, there is general hostility to the untidiness of the

---

2 The law and development literature is also relevant: Schafer and Raja (2007); Dam (2006); Joireman (2004); Fullerton (2001).

3 The terms wealth maximisation and efficiency are used interchangeably. This is defined in the Kaldor-Hicks sense of an efficient allocation of resources which maximises producer and consumers' surplus or simply the cost–benefit test of economic benefits exceeding costs. For a general introduction to these concepts see Veljanovski (2006).

common law and a preference for codes, rules and public enforcement. Jeremy Bentham, the founder of utilitarianism, argued that the common law lacked coherence and rationality – a repository of 'dead man's thoughts' and 'dog law' similar to beating a dog after it has disobeyed its master – and was less effective and authoritative law than a legal code (Bentham, 1777). Gordon Tullock, a founder of the economics of politics (public choice) school, argued that the common-law method of adjudication is inherently inferior to the continental European civil-law system because of its duplicative costs, inefficient means of ascertaining the facts, and its scope for wealth-destroying judicial activism (Tullock, 1980, 1997; Zywicki, 2007). Many lawyers in common-law countries have also supported its erosion, beginning with workers' compensation laws, no-fault schemes and replacement by statute on the grounds that these are more certain, cheaper and fairer methods of enforcing rights and resolving disputes. Many of these claims have, however, never been empirically verified, and run against the grain of the growing view that statutory law (regulation) in practice is not efficient.

The common law, it is true, is an enigma – claimed by some to be an engine of wealth maximisation and economic freedom while at the same time opaque and shrouded in ambiguity. It is in the eyes even of many lawyers incoherent, irrational and frequently 'unfair'. In this, some say, it shares many of the attributes of the marketplace. Here the nature of common-law adjudication and evidence of its relative efficiency compared to other legal systems are examined.[4]

A tale of two laws

Two major legal systems vie with one another in non-socialist countries – the common or judge-made law; and civil or code-based law exemplified by France's Napoleonic Code but which includes the German and Scandinavian legal systems. Owing to the imperial ambitions of Britain,

4 The discussion is based on Veljanovski (2007: ch. 1).

France and Germany, these legal systems have been 'exported' across the world – today 54 countries have a common-law legal system and 94 civil-law legal systems. It must be stressed, however, that within these broad categorisations there are major differences.

These two legal systems differ in origin, development and structure. The common law's origin is the customary law of England developed after the so-called tyranny of the Norman Conquest and is reputed to have taken hold under the reign of Henry II. It is judge-made law evolved through case-by-case decisions of a judiciary independent of the state. Civil-law systems are based on written codes handed down by the state.

There are also procedural differences. The common law is based on the private enforcement of rights by those affected by a breach of the law, adversarial trials and, originally, juries. In civil-law systems there is often a prosecutor; the system is inquisitorial, with a greater role given to judges, who are less independent.

The other major difference is the interaction between the judiciary and the executive. In England, since the Magna Carta, the courts have not been beholden to and controlled by the sovereign or the executive. At the heart of the common-law system is the 'rule of law'. To quote Dicey (1885: 194):

> In England no man can be made to suffer punishment or to pay damages for any conduct not definitely forbidden by law; every man's legal rights or liabilities are almost invariably determined by the ordinary Courts of the realm ... These principles mean that there can be no punishment or taking of property without an explicit law, and all persons (including officers of the government) are subject to the power of the courts.

The position in France after the French Revolution was radically different – a war (literally) ensued between the judiciary and the executive, with the latter appointing judges and blocking them from controlling the actions of the state. While this is a controversial statement, French-based civil-law systems are more dirigiste and have less respect for the rule of law.

Table 1 **Common-law countries**

Africa	*Asia*	*Australasia*	*Caribbean*	*Europe*	*North America*	*South America*
Botswana	Bangladesh	Australia	Anguilla	Cyprus	Canada	Falkland Islands
Ethiopia	Hong Kong	Fiji	Bahamas	Ireland	United States	Guyana
Ghana	India	New Zealand	Barbados	England		
Kenya	(Iran)	Papua New Guinea	Belize	Wales		
Lesotho	Israel	Samoa	Bermuda			
Malawi	Malaysia	Solomon Islands	British Virgin Islands			
Namibia	(Nepal)		Cayman Islands			
Nigeria	Pakistan		Dominica			
Sierra Leone	(Saudi Arabia)		Grenada			
South Africa	Singapore		Jamaica			
Tanzania	Sri Lanka		Montserrat			
Tonga	Thailand		St Kitts & Nevis			
Uganda	(United Arab Emirates)		St Vincent & Grenadines			
Zambia	(Yemen)		Trinidad & Tobago			
(Zimbabwe)			Turks & Caicos Islands			

Note: Countries in brackets have mixed legal origins but which include elements of the common law
Sources: World Bank (2004: 115–18); Reynolds and Flores (1991)

Structure of the common law

The first step to understanding common-law adjudication is to describe its main features.

First, it relies on private enforcement. That is, the parties to dispute must litigate their claims, and fund the costs of litigation and out-of-court settlements.

Second, disputes are adjudicated by an independent judiciary in adversarial proceedings. The parties – known as the plaintiff but now called the claimant under recent reforms in England and Wales, and the defendant – must present their claim and defence respectively to the court. The burden of proof is placed on the claimant to establish that the alleged harm is a legal wrong on a balance of probabilities in civil actions; and it is for the defendant to counter these allegations. The proceedings are said to be adversarial, involving a legal 'contest' before a judge, and contrast with most other European civil legal systems, where the judge elicits the facts and questions the parties, the latter known as an inquisitorial system.

Third, the common law offers a limited range of remedies, which are confined to enforcing the parties' rights or compensating them for their losses. The typical remedy is compensatory damages, which aim to restore the claimant to the position in which he or she would have been had the wrong not occurred. In more limited circumstances, the courts may offer an injunction to prohibit or force a party to do something or, in contract disputes, determine a specific performance requiring the party to honour the contract. Courts cannot impose more general penal sanctions such as fines or imprisonment, and can only rarely impose damages in excess of a genuine pre-estimate of the claimant's losses (except where there is contempt of court).

Fourth, the common law often denies those harmed a remedy. It is generally based on a fault liability, or other judgemental standard governed by the conduct of both parties. The law also often provides the defendant with a number of defences or excuses which allow him or her to avoid paying compensation. This means that the common law does not operate as a general (universal) compensation or insurance scheme.

Finally, because of the costs and uncertainty of litigation, an overwhelming proportion of legal disputes and potential cases are settled out of court or abandoned. The proportion of cases coming to court of those that are meritorious probably numbers a few per cent. That is, litigation is a last resort, or, as is now often said, the common law encourages 'bargaining in the shadow of the law'.[5]

To the above features must be added the way common law evolves. Common law is often described as judge-made law. This is something judges would dispute, since they regard themselves as discovering already existing law which they apply to new fact situations. 'Childish fiction' or not, the common law has evolved over centuries through the decisions of judges in individual cases. These cases, or rather the legal precedents they set, create a body of law which must be distilled from the written decisions of judges, and when distilled must be applied to new cases with different facts. It is, to use a contemporary term, 'bottom-up law' created in an evolutionary and practical way to resolve disputes. This contrasts again with the civil-law systems of the rest of Europe, which are based on written legal codes devised by governments.

It is also the case that common-law judges rarely state general principles of law. It has been described as a system of law that places a particular value on dissension, obscurity and the tentative character of judicial utterances so that 'uniquely authentic statements of the rule ... cannot be made' (Simpson, 1986). The linguistic formulations used by judges, such as 'duty of care', 'reasonable foreseeability', 'proximity' and 'reasonable care', have a chameleon-like quality. They are frequently used interchangeably, confusing lawyer and layman alike. The result is that the general principles of English common law are open-ended. '[T]he conceptual structure of tort law', declared Patrick Atiyah (1980: 35–6), 'is a disorganised and ramshackle affair'.

Further, there is no general agreement as to the objectives of the

5 The expression was coined in Mnookin and Kornhauser (1979).

common law, and its specific branches. Among lawyers the common law is seen as having three often conflicting objectives – corrective justice, distributive justice (compensation) and deterrence.

At a formalistic level there can be little dispute that the common law appears for the most part to be concerned with corrective justice, i.e. 'rendering to each person whatever redress is required because of the violation of his rights by others' (Epstein, 1979: 50). But corrective justice is an empty shell, since it lacks a definition of rights or wrongs, although it does stress that much of the common law is concerned with reinstating those wronged to their original position.

Few would claim the common law is an effective method of redistributing wealth in society. Nonetheless, many legal scholars and reformers have seized on the fact that common-law remedies seek to give monetary compensation to those whose rights have been infringed. They have in turn sought to assess the law in terms of its ability to compensate accident victims and those 'wronged'. The view that the goal of the common law is compensation is a half-truth. While the routine remedy at common law is compensatory damages, this is provided only when there has been a violation of an individual's rights. Thus, as with corrective justice, this begs the question of how the rights and wrongs are determined.

Finally, deterrence is often discussed as a goal of the common law. This sees the law's primary function as influencing conduct and deterring avoidable accidents, interference with property, crimes and other harms. Most legal texts mention this objective only to dismiss it as unsupported in law, and unlikely in practice. In the economic approach, however, this view is central. Law is viewed as a system of rules, standards and constraints that guide individual and collective actions into desirable outcomes – it is an incentive system rather than a means of redress for an actionable wrong.[6] This is even so when the law does not seek to promote efficient outcomes, or express itself in economic terms.

6 For a full discussion of the differences and similarities between economic and legal reasoning, see Veljanovski (2006).

Why would the common law be efficient?

'Economic' views of the common law are not new or novel. Historians and legal scholars have claimed in different ways that the common law has been influenced by economic interests and power. Changes to the common law during the Industrial Revolution purportedly from strict to fault liability are claimed by some to have been motivated by the need to protect a nascent industry from the crushing costs of strict liability, which would have required factories to compensate an army of injured workers and a public choking on the fumes and smoke belching from iron foundries (e.g. Horwitz, 1977). The shift to fault-based liability was designed to relieve industry in its formative stages from these crippling 'external' costs, thereby promoting industrialisation and economic growth. It was, some argue, a judicial 'subsidy' justified on infant industry grounds. Why the judges should be interested in the welfare of an emerging class of merchants, coal-mine and mill owners, and railway companies is not satisfactorily explained.

Others see the development of the common law in nineteenth-century England as shaped by an intellectual elite that included judges influenced by the ideas of Scottish political philosophers and economists, such as Adam Smith and David Hume, who extolled the virtues of laissez-faire and freedom of contract. The legal judgments, extrajudicial views of judges and the historical record lend some support for this view in some areas of the common law (Atiyah, 1979). The claim that judges are 'intellectuals', however, especially judges and barristers in England, where the common law originated, is roundly ridiculed, and in jurisdictions where judges are more susceptible to grand social theories of the role of the law, such as the United States, this has led to an activist judiciary and, some argue, the decline of the efficiency of the common law.

The modern law and economics literature offers several other, admittedly not fully satisfactory, explanations as to why the common law might have an 'economic logic'.[7]

7 For an excellent review of this literature, see Rubin (2005).

Judge (then Professor) Richard Posner (1972), beginning with his paper 'A theory of negligence', advanced the radical and highly controversial thesis, refined in later articles and books (for example, Landes and Posner, 1987), that the fundamental logic of the common law was economic; that its doctrines and remedies could be understood 'as if' judges decided cases to encourage a more efficient allocation of resources, or simply to maximise wealth. This was posed not as a statement of fact but an economic hypothesis or theory to be tested against the empirical evidence. If this hypothesis were to be verified, it would be a finding of great legal and empirical significance.

The idea that economics could unlock the logic of the common law and its specific legal doctrines and remedies raised its profile among legal scholars, who were either attracted or repelled by the proposition. For many legal scholars the fact that judges do not use explicit economic reasoning and language in their decisions is sufficient to dismiss the claim that the common law has an economic purpose. This often reflected, however, no more than the lawyers' aversion to (or lack of understanding of) theory and social science approaches.

Posner's explanation of why the common law maximised wealth focused on the role of judges. He claims that common-law adjudication forces judges to restrict their attention to a narrow range of issues correlated with efficiency and wealth maximisation, making it a poor method for large-scale wealth redistribution. Judges are required to reinstate wronged individuals and firms to their prior position in a process of case-by-case adjudication (Posner, 1995: ch. 3). This necessarily implies acceptance of the pre-existing distribution of wealth, and places a severe constraint on the use of the common law to redistribute wealth.

On the other hand many view public or statute law as largely redistributing wealth despite its stated public interest objectives and the intention of Parliament. Stigler's (1971) 'capture theory' and the economic theory of regulation (Posner, 1974; Peltzman, 1976; Becker, 1983) have as their central hypothesis that the primary 'product' transacted in the political marketplace is wealth transfers. The demand for legislation comes from cohesive coordinated groups, typically industry or special interest groups; the supply side of legislation is less easy to define given the nature of the political and legislative process. The state has a monopoly over one basic resource, however – the power to legitimately coerce. This leads to the view that because the legislative process is skewed towards cohesive groups which can lobby effectively, it tends to overly favour these to the disadvantage of the public and is generally inefficient. Indeed, this view gave rise to a pessimistic assessment of the sustainability of a liberal and open society as politics and government become overwhelmed by special interest politics that undermine economic growth and social progress (Olson, 1982).

This 'theory' of regulation is not wholly satisfactory. While much statute law, especially during the heyday of the common law, supported monopolies and was redistributive, much was not. For example, the Factory Acts, which governed work conditions and safety, had a common-law character with their focus on liability based on the 'reasonably practicable' standard. More recently deregulation, market liberalisation, privatisation and other supply-side reforms have signalled not only the radical transformation to private property in most post-war mixed and socialist economies, but a political endorsement of markets and economic efficiency.

To explain the alleged efficiency of the common law others have looked not at the personal motivations, predilections and/or self-interest of judges and politicians but to evolutionary forces – that is, the supply-and-demand factors that would 'predict' institutional outcomes and their effects over time. This idea is not new, and in its modern form can be traced back to the early property rights literature of the 1960s (Demsetz, 1967). The economics of property rights 'predicts' that new property rights evolve as costs and benefits alter with changes in market conditions and technology. Thus, all things being equal, the more valuable prospective property rights, the more likely new ones will emerge.

One evolutionary approach has been to link the development of the common law to the litigation/settlement process, and the natural survival of efficient legal precedent.[8] These so-called demand-side models are driven by the self-interest of individual litigants in response to the prospect of succeeding in the courts, either to gain compensation or other remedies or to avoid them. The central hypothesis is that because inefficient laws by definition impose larger losses on the parties, they are litigated more often than efficient laws (Rubin, 1977). Thus, even if they are oblivious to economic efficiency as a legal goal, judges will have to adjudicate a disproportionate number of cases challenging inefficient laws, and over time the courts will tend to overturn inefficient laws more often than efficient laws. As a result the body of efficient legal precedent grows, even though at any one time a significant part of the law may be inefficient. That is, the efficiency of law evolves through a myriad of independent individual actions and not by design, as if, to use Adam Smith's metaphor, by some 'hidden hand'.

Subsequent work examining this hypothesis has found that not all roads lead to efficiency (Priest, 1977, 1980; Landes and Posner, 1979; Goodman, 1979; Cooter and Kornhauser, 1980; Eisenberg, 1990). Indeed, the original model was a special case, and private litigation is just as likely to lead to inefficient as efficient law (Fon and Parisi, 2003; Hylton, 2006).

Others have employed 'supply-side' models that focus on competition between different courts, and other forums for the business of litigants. During the formative period of the common law in England there was active competition between a large number of courts to attract litigants (Berman, 1983). This competition occurred between civil and ecclesiastical courts, and within civil courts between the royal (King's Bench, Exchequer and Court of Common Pleas), feudal, manorial, urban and mercantile law courts. All these vied for the business of litigants and their fees, and were free to adopt the remedies and rules of the others. Adam Smith, in the *Wealth of Nations* (Book V), offers one historical account:

8 The main articles are collected in Rubin (2007) and Cross (2005).

> The fees of court seem originally to have been the principal support of the different courts of justice in England. Each court endeavoured to draw to itself as much business as it could, and was, upon that account willing to take cognisance of many suits which were not originally intended to fall under its jurisdiction. The Court of King's Bench, instituted for the trial of criminal causes only, took cognisance of civil suits; the plaintiff pretending that the defendant, in not doing him justice, had been guilty of some trespass or misdemeanour. The Court of Exchequer, instituted for levying of the king's revenue, and for enforcing the payment of such debts only as were due to the king, took cognisance of all other contract debts: the plaintiff alleging that he could not pay the king because the defendant would not pay him. In consequence of such fictions it came, in many cases, to depend altogether upon the parties before what court they would choose to have their cause tried; and each court endeavoured by superior despatch and impartiality, to draw to itself as many causes as it could. The present admirable constitution of the courts of justice in England was, perhaps, originally in great measure formed by this emulation which anciently took place between the respective judges; each judge endeavouring to give, in his own court, the speediest and most effectual remedy which the law would admit for every sort of injustice.

Zywicki (2003) argues that this created an incentive for each court to provide unbiased, accurate and quick dispute resolution, and the evolution of efficient law.[9] Indeed, the adoption of the law of merchants (the law merchant) into the common law (Benson, 1989) was an important source of efficient law.

Is the common law efficient?

Two types of evidence have been examined to assess whether the

9 Benson (1990) takes issue with this claim, arguing that the common law differs from customary law as a result of the intervention of the king, who set up a subsidised court system and forced dispute resolution into the royal courts.

common law has or had an economic logic – the economics of specific common-law doctrines; and more rigorous statistical analysis of its and other legal systems' impact on economic growth.

The first is exemplified by the work of Posner. His evidence that wealth maximisation underlies the common law is based on his and others' findings that, in a large number of areas, common-law doctrines can be explained 'as if' they are efficient. This method of verification is based on looking at common-law doctrines and remedies and seeing whether they have a plausible economic rationale. The explanation and evidence used to support the theory are the law and cases rather than its verifiable effects on behaviour, economic growth and/or quantification of costs and benefits in a given case or over a run of decisions. This approach, while appealing to lawyers since they rarely have to stray beyond the law, is often no more than a plausible story rather than hard empirical analysis of the economic facts. Nonetheless, it has offered surprising confirmation of the common law's economic logic, and new genuine insights into the common law's doctrinal structure and coherence (Veljanovski, 2007: ch. 5). Others vigorously question the validity and evidence used to establish the efficiency of specific rules (Veljanovski, 1981).[10]

In many areas this model of law is plausible. Take one of the core concepts of the common law – fault liability. This is not treated in law as indicating moral culpability but as an objective standard of conduct based on the actions of the parties. One is 'at fault' if the care exercised falls below that regarded by the court as objectively required in the circumstances. That is, liability is tied to actions. It can be shown that there is an economic version of fault liability that leads to an efficient level of care and harm prevention, and that the system of defences and remedies that attach to fault liability can also be rationalised in terms of this model of efficient (victim) accident prevention (Landes and Posner, 1987). In other areas where there is strict liability, the link between

10 For a more sympathetic view based on experience teaching tort law, see Veljanovski (1985; 1986).

actions and legal outcomes seems absent. But often these pockets of strict liability are consistent with the view that the law can be explained as if it seeks to influence actions to promote a more efficient outcome.

The second approach is based on more objective empirical evidence of the efficiency of the common law. Beginning with the work of Barro (1991) and Scully (1992),[11] there have been a number of empirical studies of the impact of common law, civil law and other legal systems on economic growth. These have found that, after controlling for other factors, economic growth has been greater in common-law than in civil-law countries.

Scully's statistical analysis found that, on average, the 54 common-law countries in his sample gave much greater protection of civil liberties than the 94 civil-law countries, and that in politically open societies real per capita income grew at an annual compound rate of 2.5 per cent compared with 1.4 per cent for politically closed societies. According to Scully (1992: 179):

> ... societies where freedom is restricted are less than half as efficient in converting resources into gross domestic product as free societies. Alternatively, more than twice the standard of living could be obtained with these same resource endowments in these societies, if liberty prevailed.

Mahoney (2001) studied the legal systems of 102 non-socialist countries over the period 1960 to 1992. His empirical research found that economies in countries with common-law legal systems grew 0.71 per cent or one third faster, and the standard of living measured by real per capita income was 20 per cent greater, than in countries with civil-law legal systems. Mahoney attributes the higher economic performance to better-quality judiciary, as measured by their integrity and efficiency, and greater security of property and contract rights in common-law nations.

11 Other important recent contributions include Barro (1997); Hall and Jones (1999); Knack and Keefer (1997).

Heitger's (2004) empirical analysis, while not directly testing for the effects of the common law, finds that secure property rights and respect for the rule of law contribute significantly to economic growth. He used data for 84 countries from 1975 to 1995, and an index covering security of property rights (risk of confiscation), enforcement of contracts (risk of government repudiation) and rule of law (independence of judiciary) to represent the legal system. He found the impact on economic growth of his property rights index 'quite remarkable', even when compared with capital accumulation and other drivers of economic development – a doubling of the index more than doubled per capita income! Interestingly, Heitger's empirical research tested for the possibility that the causation ran the other way from economic growth to better protection of property rights/rule of law. Even adjusting for this, he found that law affects economic growth.

Other empirical research finds that common-law systems are more efficient in governing finance markets (La Porta et al., 1998), more efficient in settling disputes (Djankov et al., 2003) and have less interventionist laws which promote economic growth (World Bank, 2004). For example, the study by Djankov et al. of the court procedures required to evict a tenant for non-payment of rent and to collect a bounced cheque in 109 countries found that the procedures were more formal and complex in civil- than in common-law countries. On the other hand, judicial decisions took longer, were less consistent, honest and fair in civil-law countries – and there was more corruption.

Conclusions

The nature of legal processes and their effects remain poorly understood. Nonetheless, it is obvious that different legal and political systems generate different laws, remedies and enforcement which affect the behaviour of individuals and organisations, and the wealth of nations. Some laws are more efficient or more conducive to facilitating economic activity and growth than others. It appears that the common law may do this better than civil-law systems, at least in some areas and in some jurisdictions. It must also be recognised, however, that common-law systems vary considerably, not only in terms of the law, but also in terms of procedures, the appointment of the judiciary and the legal culture, all of which will affect the performance of the legal system and its economic effects.

References

Atiyah, P. S. (1979), *The Rise and Fall of Freedom of Contract*, Oxford: Clarendon Press.

Atiyah, P. S. (1980), *Accidents, Compensation, and the Law*, 3rd edn, London: Weidenfeld and Nicolson.

Barro, R. (1991), 'Economic growth in a cross-section of countries', *Quarterly Journal of Economics*, 106: 407–43.

Barro, R. (1997), *Determinants of Economic Growth: A cross country study*, Cambridge, MA: MIT Press.

Becker, G. (1983), 'A theory of competition among pressure groups for political influence', *Quarterly Journal of Economics*, 98: 371–400.

Benson, B. (1989), 'The spontaneous evolution of commercial law', *Southern Economic Journal*, 55: 644–61.

Benson, B. L. (1990), *The Enterprise of Law: Justice without the State*, San Francisco, CA: Pacific Research Institute.

Bentham, J. (1777), *A Fragment on Government*, London: T. Payne.

Berman, H. (1983), *Law and Revolution: The formation of the Western legal tradition*, Cambridge, MA: Harvard University Press.

Cooter, R. and L. Kornhauser (1980), 'Can litigation improve the law without the help of judges?', *Journal of Legal Studies*, 9: 139–63.

Cross, F. B. (2005), 'Identifying the virtues of the common law', University of Texas Law and Economics Research Paper no. 063, available at ssrn.com/abstract=812464.

Dam, K. W. (2006), 'The judiciary and economic development', University of Chicago Law and Economics Olin Working Paper no. 287, available at ssrn.com/abstract=892030.

Demsetz, H. (1967), 'Toward a theory of property rights', *American Economic Review*, 57: 347–59.

Dicey, A.V. (1885 [1950]), *Introduction to the Study of the Law of the Constitution*, 9th edn, London: Macmillan.

Djankov, S., R. La Porta, F. Lopez-de-Silanes and A. Shleifer (2003), 'Courts', *Quarterly Journal of Economics*, 118: 453–513.

Eisenberg, T. (1990), 'Testing the selection effect: a new theoretical framework with empirical tests', *Journal of Legal Studies*, 19: 337–58.

Epstein, R. A. (1979), 'Nuisance law: corrective justice and its utilitarian constraints', *Journal of Legal Studies*, 8: 49–102.

Fon, V. and F. Parisi (2003), 'Litigation and the evolution of legal remedies: a dynamic model', *Public Choice*, 166: 419–33.

Fullerton, S. J. (2001), 'Inherited legal systems and effective rule of law: Africa and the colonial legacy', *Journal of Modern African Studies*, 39: 571–96.

Goodman, J. C. (1979), 'An economic theory of the evolution of common law', *Journal of Legal Studies*, 7: 393–406.

Hall, R. and C. Jones (1999), 'Why do some countries produce so much more output per worker than others?', *Quarterly Journal of Economics*, 114: 83–116.

Hayek F. A. (1973), *Law, Legislation, and Liberty: Rules and Order*, London: Routledge.

Heitger, B. (2004), 'Property rights and the wealth of nations: a cross-country study', *Cato Journal*, 23: 381–402.

Horwitz, M. J. (1977), *The Transformation of American Law, 1780–1860*, Cambridge, MA: Harvard University Press.

Hylton, K. (2006), 'Information, litigation, and common law evolution', *American Law and Economic Review*, 8: 33–61.

Joireman, S. J. (2004), 'Colonization and the rule of law: comparing the effectiveness of common law and civil law countries', *Constitutional Political Economy*, 15: 315–38.

Knack, S. and P. Keefer (1997), 'Does social capital have an economic pay-off? A cross-country investigation', *Quarterly Journal of Economics*, 112: 1251–88.

La Porta, R., F. López-de-Silanes, A. Shleifer and R. Vishny (1998), 'Law and finance', *Journal of Political Economy*, 106: 1113–55.

Landes, W. M. and R. A. Posner (1979), 'Adjudication as a private good', *Journal of Legal Studies*, 8: 235–84.

Landes, W. M. and R. A. Posner (1987), *The Economic Structure of Tort Law*, Cambridge, MA: Harvard University Press.

Mahoney, P. (2001), 'The common law and economic growth: Hayek might be right', *Journal of Legal Studies*, 30: 503–23.

Mnookin, R. and M. Kornhauser (1979), 'Bargaining in the shadow of the law', *Yale Law Journal*, 88: 950–97.

Olson, M. (1982), *The Rise and Decline of Nations*, New Haven, CT: Yale University Press.

Peltzman, S. (1976), 'Toward a more general theory of regulation', *Journal of Law and Economics*, 19: 211–40.

Posner, R. A. (1971), *Economic Analysis of Law*, Boston, MA: Little, Brown.

Posner, R. A. (1972), 'A theory of negligence', *Journal of Legal Studies*, 1: 28–96.

Posner, R. A. (1974), 'Theories of economic regulation', *Bell Journal of Economics and Management Science*, 5: 22–50.

Posner, R. A. (1995), 'What do judges maximize?', in R. A. Posner, *Overcoming Law*, Cambridge, MA: Harvard University Press, ch. 3.

Priest, G. (1977), 'The common law process and the selection of efficient rules', *Journal of Legal Studies*, 6: 65–82.

Priest, G. (1980), 'Selective characteristics of litigation', *Journal of Legal Studies*, 9: 399–421.

Reynolds, T. H. and A. A. Flores (eds) (1991), *Foreign Law Current Sources and Legislation in Jurisdictions of the World*, Colorado: Fred B. Rothman & Co.
Rubin, P. H. (1977), 'Why is the common law efficient?', *Journal of Law and Economics*, 6: 51–67.
Rubin, P. H. (2005), 'Why was the common law efficient?', in F. Parisi and C. Rowley (eds), *The Origins of Law and Economics: Essays by the Founding Fathers*, Cheltenham: Edward Elgar, pp. 383–95.
Rubin, P. H. (ed.) (2007), *The Evolution of Efficient Common Law*, Cheltenham: Edward Elgar.
Schafer, H.-B. and A. V. Raja (eds) (2007), *Law and Economic Development*, Cheltenham: Edward Elgar.
Scully, G. (1992), *Constitutional Environments and Economic Growth*, Princeton, NJ: Princeton University Press.
Simpson, B. (1986), 'The common law and legal theory', in W. Twining (ed.), *Legal Theory and Common Law*, London: Blackwell, ch. 2.
Stigler, G. J. (1971), 'The theory of economic regulation', *Bell Journal of Economics and Management Science*, 2: 3–21.
Tullock, G. (1980), *Trials on Trial – the Pure Theory of Legal Procedure*, New York: Columbia University Press.
Tullock, G. (1997), 'The case against the common law', Durham, NC: Carolina Academic Press, reprinted in C. K. Rowley (ed.) (2005), *Law and Economics – the selected works of Gordon Tullock*, vol. 9, Indianapolis, IN: Liberty Fund.
Veljanovski, C. G. (1981), 'Wealth maximisation, law and ethics – on the limits of economic efficiency', *International Review of Law and Economics*, 1: 5–28, reprinted in K. Dau-Schmidt and T. S. Ulen (eds) (2002), *A Law and Economics Anthology 2002*, 2nd edn, Cincinnati, OH: Anderson Publishing.
Veljanovski, C. G. (1985), 'Economic theorising about tort', *Current Legal Problems*, pp. 117–40.

Veljanovski, C. G. (1986), 'Legal theory, economic analysis and the law of torts', in W. Twining (ed.), *Legal Theory and Common Law*, Oxford: Blackwell.

Veljanovski, C. G. (2006), *The Economics of Law*, 2nd edn, London: Institute of Economic Affairs.

Veljanovski, C. G. (2007), *Economic Principles of Law*, Cambridge: Cambridge University Press.

World Bank (2004), *Doing Business in 2004 – Understanding Regulation*, Washington, DC.

Zywicki, T. (2003), 'The rise and fall of efficiency in the common law: a supply-side analysis', *Northwestern University Law Review*, 97: 1151–1633.

Zywicki, T. J. (2007), 'Gordon Tullock's critique of the common law', George Mason Law and Economics Research Paper no. 07–13, available at http://ssrn.com/abstract=964781.

5 ECONOMICS AND THE DESIGN OF REGULATORY LAW

Anthony Ogus

Introduction

For a book entitled *The Legal Foundations of Free Markets* it may seem somewhat perverse to write a chapter on regulation. Arguably, regulated markets are the very opposite of 'free markets'.[1] Nevertheless, an understanding of why and how governments regulate and the interaction between regulatory law and market activity is of the greatest importance.

'Regulatory law' is an imprecise term. Here I use it to refer to legal instruments used by governments to induce economic actors to outcomes that would not have been reached if they had been allowed to engage freely in market activity (Ogus, 2004a: 1–4). During the last fifty years or so, there have been immense changes in the substance of this area of law; even more importantly, perhaps, there have been immense changes in the way this area of law has been perceived by economists and in their influence on the design of it.

A quick glance at the pronouncements of some of the greatest economists might suggest a uniform hostility to, and distrust of, regulation. The arguments are at times couched in the language of freedom (for example, Hayek, 1960); others (for example, Friedman, 1962) have focused on the inefficiencies, both allocative and productive, to which regulation typically gives rise. The degree of conviction with which these views are held should not, however, be allowed to distort the more constructive role that economics has played in relation to regulation, and

1 I refer, of course, to markets regulated by government rather than through private mechanisms.

that from a variety of perspectives and with a variety of methodologies.

The task I have set myself in this chapter is to review different economic approaches to regulation and to speculate on how these approaches have, or might have, influenced the design of regulation. Since my own background is in law, I shall focus on the legal dimensions of regulation: the legal forms that are used to achieve regulatory ends, and the legal institutions and procedures that govern the process. Although my approach will not be chronological, I nevertheless take a historical perspective, because economic approaches to regulation have evolved over time.

Public interest analysis

Someone seeking to gain an impression, during the 1960s and 1970s, of the key features of economic and social regulation[2] in the United Kingdom, or other western European countries, would have observed the following:

- *With regard to economic regulation:* Important branches of public law concerned to authorise and control economic activity of the state in the form either of public enterprise or of public institutions investing in, or directing, private enterprise – what the French call *le droit public de l'économie* (Delvolvé, 1998) – and a relative absence of public law and public institutions to encourage and maintain the competitiveness of markets.
- *With regard to social regulation:* A solid core of principles and processes administered by public agencies concerned to protect citizens, particularly employees, against risks to health and safety and a fast-developing array of rules protecting consumers against inadequate quality in goods and services purchased.

2 For the distinction between the two types of regulation, see Ogus (2004a: 4–5).

The focus of this chapter is on social regulation, but it cannot be disassociated from economic regulation, which reflected both strong ideological trends, prevalent in Europe in the post-World War II period, and the continuing strengths of Keynesian macroeconomic theory (Robson, 1960). Microeconomic theorists may have had less of an impact on regulatory policymaking, but the lines of orthodox reasoning were clear (Skuse, 1972).[3] Market failure was assumed to be widespread. Technological change had generated large-scale externalities (primarily risks to public health and safety); it had also widened the information gap between supplier and consumer. It was assumed that interventionist, regulatory measures were both necessary and adequate to deal with these phenomena and hence overcome market failure.

Legal theorising about the British regulatory state during this period was weak[4] (public lawyers were obsessed with constitutional arrangements and the power of the courts to constrain the executive) and intellectual links with economic analysis are hardly discernible. It is, nevertheless, striking that such legal literature as did exist on general regulatory institutions and strategy reveals some interesting parallels with economic theorising. The key author was the German émigré Wolfgang Friedmann. In his classic text *Law in a Changing Society* (1959; see also Friedmann, 1971), he chronicled the rapid growth of public-law incursions on private law, including land-use planning on private property rights; state welfare provision on family-law entitlements; social insurance on tort liability; and health-and-safety regulation and consumer protection on contract. The justification for much of this was articulated in terms of what economists call transaction costs

3 Institutional economics, with its focus on the 'power' behind market and other institutions, and represented particularly by the work of John Commons (1924), was apt to support interventionist policies but had been largely neglected, at least on this side of the Atlantic.

4 With the possible exception of publications emanating from the London School of Economics (e.g. Laski et al., 1935), there had been nothing in the UK to match analysis like that of Ernst Freund in the USA, particularly his *Standards of American Legislation* (1917) and *Legislative Regulation* (1932).

and information costs, as these affect the capacity of the private law to address the problems of industrialisation. But there was also recognition of redistributional goals, the need for governments to overreach disparities of wealth and bargaining power, as well as some concessions to paternalism (although this word was studiously avoided), that governments should make decisions for individuals where the latter cannot be relied on to make wise decisions in their own best interests.

In retrospect, it is surprising that the analysis, which was so copious on market (or private-law) failure, paid such little heed to the possibility of government failure (Demsetz, 1969). True, there were concerns about the effectiveness of the implementation of regulatory programmes, but these were seen to arise from weaknesses in the institutional frameworks, rather than from any limitation in the capacity of governments to address the problems.

The theoretical input for challenging this capacity could have been sought in two major contributions to the economic literature. The first, by Hayek, had grown out of the Austrian tradition, with its subjectivist notion of information and hence suspicion of attempts to meet social preferences by centralised institutions. In the three-volume *Law, Legislation and Liberty* (1973–79), Hayek drew a sharp contrast between two systems of social organisation: 'spontaneous order', largely dependent on decentralised information and in which guiding principles evolve gradually over time in response to changes in that information; and 'rational constructivism', in which centralised rule-makers attempt to dictate outcomes on the basis of the (limited) information available to them. The pricing system of the market and the common law epitomise the first; a planned economy and regulatory law the second.

The other, if less obvious, theoretical input was that of Ronald Coase. His 'Problem of Social Cost' (1960) contained two insights relevant to the design of regulatory law. The first is the perception that conflicts in resource use can be, and will be, resolved by negotiation between the affected parties, provided that transactions costs and the law allow them to do so. The normative implication of this is that public centralised and coercive interventions to resolve such conflicts are likely to be less effective than private consensual approaches. The second insight was to expose the fallacy that misallocations arising from negative 'externalities' should always be corrected by internalising the costs to the actors 'responsible' for them, because other solutions may resolve the conflict at lower cost. I discuss the legal implications of this at length elsewhere (Ogus, 2006: ch. 6). Suffice it here to observe that, for this reason, regulatory interventions may not always be optimal.

Private interest analysis

In the late 1970s and early 1980s the expression 'regulatory failure' gained currency (Sunstein, 1990). Many regulatory regimes were perceived to be unduly complex, excessively burdensome and poorly targeted. Why should this have occurred? Political scientists had suggested that regulatory agencies were vulnerable to 'capture' by the regulated industries (Bernstein, 1955). Some economists developed this into an 'economic theory of regulation'. Regulation was a commodity made available in the political 'marketplace' and 'supplied' by politicians and bureaucrats by reference to the demand of those who would benefit from its promulgation, the price being some form of political, generally electoral, support (Stigler, 1971; Peltzman, 1976). While different groups could furnish political support, the transaction was most likely to be secured by those groups that could coordinate their influence at lowest cost, thus tending to favour, for example, producers over consumers (Olson, 1965).

Private interest economic theory was adept at showing how interventionist measures that were ostensibly designed to protect consumers (or other largely dispersed groups, such as environmentalists) in fact served to protect specific producer interests. This was generally achieved by restricting the entry of newcomers. The obvious example is a licensing system that purports to restrict supply to 'safe' or 'reliable' producers, but which, because of the barrier to entry, often serves simply to enhance the profits of incumbents (Maurizi, 1974). This is so also where a regulatory regime decrees by means of a so-called 'grandfather clause' that certain standards should apply only to new producers (Breyer, 1982: 115). A third example occurs where the regime adopts measures the compliance cost of which does not vary with output, thereby discriminating against small firms and removing competitive pressure from larger firms (Ogus, 2004a: 172).

Of course, not everyone is prepared to accept the assumption that politicians and bureaucrats are driven exclusively or even predominantly by self-seeking motives; ideology and altruism may be equally important (Farber and Frickey, 1991). Nevertheless, private interest theory has had a profound impact on the way we think about regulation and the regulatory processes, not least because, as the Virginia School of Public Choice has made clear, it has important normative implications (Tollison, 1982). Their main point is that the resources devoted to the campaigns to acquire regulatory wealth transfers – what Virginians refer to as 'rent-seeking' – are, from society's point of view, entirely wasted: they do not contribute to a wealth-enhancing activity (Tullock, 1967).

Clearly, to the extent that private interest analysis is sustainable and that rent-seeking behaviour leads to adverse consequences, regulatory policymaking processes should be designed to minimise such behaviour (Ogus, 1998: 490). More than this, the analysis underlines the importance of the availability of information as to the distributional consequences of regulatory measures. 'We need to know who wins and who loses and by how much, when thinking about public policy. Not only is this a necessary part of strategic public management, it is crucial to a normative consideration of whether the legislation is in the public interest' (Mashaw, 1989: 145).

Renewed public interest analysis

An observer returning to the United Kingdom (or western Europe) during the last 25 years would have been struck by the fundamental changes to economic and social regulation (OECD, 1992).

- *With regard to economic regulation:* The primary model of economic regulation, involving public ownership of monopolistic services, has been replaced by one in which the majority of those services have been privatised, but subject to price and quality regulation, at least for so long as the relevant market remains insufficiently competitive. A more vigorous competition law has impinged on other markets.
- *With regard to social regulation:* There has been some shift away from traditional command-and-control instruments, replacing some of them with financial incentives, and setting more general objectives, leaving it to the industry or individual firms to devise particular rules to meet these objectives, hence the notion of 'co-regulation'.[5] Some form of regulatory impact analysis is generally undertaken as part of the policymaking process.

Mainstream economic theorists have both contributed to, and fed on, these changes. Understandably, this has been most marked in relation to economic regulation, which is concerned with the desired degree of competition within markets and, where necessary, the appropriate principles for price control. Economic analysis was at the forefront both in revealing the weaknesses of the public ownership model (Swann, 1988) and in devising appropriate principles and processes for price controls (Littlechild, 1983). Even more significant, perhaps, has been its contribution to the debate on the liberalisation of energy markets, showing how it would be possible to segment the supplying industries in order to minimise the dimension, normally the transporting of the product, for which it was economically beneficial to retain a monopolistic undertaking (Vickers and Yarrow, 1988).[6]

Some economists use language that suggests that for them 'regu-

5 A system in which public regulators oversee rule-making by associations representing private regulatees: Gunningham and Rees (1997).

6 The so-called 'natural monopoly' conditions, where very large-scale economics prevail.

lation' is only concerned with prices and competition.[7] But if the interaction between economic theory and social regulation has been less pronounced, it has not been unimportant. Most influential, perhaps, has been a group of scholars whose work is described in Susan Rose-Ackerman's paper 'Progressive law and economics – and the new administrative law' (1988). The epithet 'progressive' is intended to distinguish them from other economists, notably those emanating from Chicago, whose analysis has led them to condemn as inefficient most forms of regulation, and instead to adopt a more constructive approach to interventionist measures. As Rose-Ackerman observes, the group is:

> ... similar to Chicagoans in recognising the value of markets in promoting efficiency and the importance of economic incentives in both the private and public sectors. They are trying to get the economic incentives right, not eliminate them. (Ibid.: 344)

We can here briefly survey different features of this work.

Comparison of instruments

Central to the revitalised public interest analysis of social regulation has been an exploration of the cost-effectiveness of different regulatory instruments (Dewees, 1983). With the regulatory objective, such as the level of safety for an activity or product as a given, how can the costs of achieving that goal be minimised? The important dimensions to this inquiry extended beyond the compliance costs to industry, which, in terms of British regulatory policy, were for political reasons given undue prominence (Froud et al., 1998). They included also the costs of obtaining the information necessary for the formulation of standards and other rules and the costs of administering the system, including notably monitoring for compliance and enforcement. Equally important, though less easy to appraise, are indirect costs – for example, the welfare losses from

7 A survey of 'regulatory economics' in the previous twenty years in Crew and Kleindorfer (2002) does not even mention social regulation!

inhibiting technological development and restricting competition (Ogus, 2004a: 152–5).

Institutional arrangements

Analysis of this kind has had a major influence on the developments to social regulation, most significantly as regards the substitution of more general principles for specific rules and the absorption of co-regulatory systems, both of which reflect in particular an appreciation of the information costs attendant on the more traditional approaches. Questions concerning the institutional arrangements for implementing more general principles have been, perhaps, less well treated in the economic literature. The problem here has been that although there has been economic modelling of the principal-agent problem as it applies within a public bureaucratic context (Spiller, 1990), exponents of it have been almost exclusively American and their work is heavily influenced by the separation-of-powers constitutional arrangements that are to be found in that jurisdiction (Spiller, 1998).[8]

Regulation at a European or a national level?

In contrast, the ever-continuing debate, within the European Union, on the extent to which regulation should be made, or perhaps harmonised, at a European level, rather than at the level of member states, has been subjected to penetrating economic analysis (Sun and Pelkmans, 1995), derived from Tiebout's seminal paper on the economics of federalism (1956). The starting point is the recognition that local decision-makers can best meet local preferences regarding regulatory objectives and that, assuming some degree of mobility of individuals and firms, competition

8 With a more pronounced constitutional separation of powers, regulatory agencies must seek to satisfy three 'principals': the legislature, the executive and the courts. Under a 'Westminster' approach, the legislature is largely controlled by the executive and the courts play a more passive role in relation to judicial review.

between regulatory systems can broaden choice and stimulate innovation. While, obviously, for the purposes of trans-boundary trade there are economies of scale in having a single set of rules, experience has shown that it might be very costly to establish such rules, particularly between jurisdictions with different legal cultures (Teubner, 1998). Moreover, any barriers to trans-boundary trade may be surmounted by a system of mutual recognition,[9] whereby the authorities in one jurisdiction accept compliance with the other jurisdiction's legislation as being equivalent to compliance with its own (Pelkmans, 1987).

It has not been difficult to invoke other arguments for European legislation overreaching localised diversity, but whether, in aggregate, they are powerful enough to justify this solution depends on their relative strength, which may vary from sector to sector, and on whether solutions other than harmonisation are available at lower cost. So, the fact that one jurisdiction's legislation – for example, that on environmental protection – may generate externalities in the sense that it has consequences for those in other jurisdictions does not necessarily mean that a pan-European measure imposing a common level of protection is optimal. The electorates in different jurisdictions may have different preferences regarding the level of protection, and where these collide a bilateral negotiated compromise may be more appropriate than a multilateral solution (Cohen, 1996).[10] Take, next, the assertion that regulatory competition will lead to a 'race to the bottom', meaning that member states will lower their regulatory standards in order to attract industry to their jurisdiction. Within the European Union, there is little evidence that diversity in standards has led to such consequences (for tax, Huizinga and Nicodeme, 2006; for employment, Dehejia and Samy, 2006; for the environment, Janicke, 2004). This should not be

9 This may be by legislation or by judicial practice, applying the familiar Cassis de Dijon [1979] ECR 649 principle.

10 The fact that in practice there will usually be some degree of negotiation and compromise between the jurisdictions involved in trans-boundary externalities suggests that the optimal arrangements might be some mixture of cooperation and competition – what Esty and Geradin (2001) call 'co-opetition'.

surprising. Location decisions are made by reference not only to regulatory compliance costs but also to considerations such as the quality of a jurisdiction's infrastructure and its labour force, and these are likely to be found in countries whose citizens have preferences for higher regulatory standards (Revesz, 2001).

In the 1970s and 1980s, the strength of ideological commitment manifestly adopted by some European politicians led to a programme of harmonisation that paid little heed to these arguments.[11] Some reversal to that policy is evident in the more recent adoption of the subsidiarity principle, and this has been influenced, or least underpinned, by the economic analysis (Van den Bergh, 1998).

Sanctions and enforcement

In the last decade, attention has focused on the incentive effects of regulation and on the methods of inducing compliance. At the time of writing, the Regulatory Enforcement and Sanctions Bill is before Parliament. Largely implementing Macrory's Cabinet Office review (2006), this will (if enacted) make radical changes to UK policy and practice of regulatory enforcement, including the widespread use of administrative financial penalties outside the ambit of the criminal justice system. Undoubtedly economic analysis has had a major influence in this area.

The economics of law enforcement, derived from Becker's classic (1968) paper, has provided the necessary input (Ogus, 2004b). This revealed the inadequacy of deterrence when a relatively modest criminal penalty was combined with a low rate of prosecutions, a consequence of the high cost to the prosecuting authorities of meeting the elevated evidentiary standards of the criminal process. A system of administrative penalties can solve the problem, given the higher rate of imposition,

11 Economic private interest theory can also be invoked to explain these developments, some key interest groups being stronger, relative to other groups, at a European level, compared to a national level, and thus applying pressure for a harmonisation policy on which they can exert their more powerful influence: Noam (1982).

although some trade-off must be made with the increased incidence of error costs that will arise, given the absence of the criminal justice standards of proof (Hylton and Khanna, 2007).

Regulatory impact assessment

The mode of economic analysis of regulation that has had the highest profile is undoubtedly regulatory impact assessment (RIA). In one form or another, it has been adopted by most industrialised countries as a mandatory bureaucratic investigation of the likely impact of regulatory proposals. In its most developed form, following the model established by Reagan's Executive Order 12,291, it is a full cost–benefit analysis (Heimann et al., 1990).[12]

The extent to which RIA has actually influenced regulatory policy, in the sense of leading to changes in the legislation made, remains unclear (Hahn et al., 2000). Furthermore, a cost–benefit analysis cannot provide a determinative judgement on whether a proposal should be implemented. This is not only because of the familiar difficulties of assigning a value to some of the key benefits of social regulation, such as the value of life or of a clean environment (McGarity, 1991); it is also because the mere fact that aggregate benefits exceed aggregate costs (the Kaldor-Hicks efficiency criterion) does not necessarily mean that the proposal is socially desirable (Ogus, 2006: ch. 7). Politically, or morally, it might be inappropriate to impose costs on some members of the community to improve aggregate welfare.

Nevertheless, RIA has become an important part of regulatory policymaking. Its primary value lies in its capacity to provide systematic information on important issues (Posner, 2001a), to render transparent the regulatory process and to impose a discipline on officials preparing policy proposals, forcing them to address key questions in a coherent manner (Froud et al., 1998).

12 For a survey of national developments, see Radaelli (2004).

Behavioural law and economics

The final area of economic input into regulatory policymaking to which I wish to refer should certainly be considered public interest analysis. I treat it separately from other types of that analysis because, drawing on social psychology, it distances itself from the assumptions of conventional microeconomics. Indeed, its very *raison d'être* is to predict consequences where individuals do not behave rationally (Sunstein, 2000). Although this obviously has important implications for regulatory policy, the analysis seems, so far, to have made little impact on policymakers. Here I shall deal with two questions on which, nevertheless, it has potentially much to offer: irrational attitudes to risk; and paternalism.

Risk management

A major dimension of modern social regulation involves risk management and control. Much of it is controversial, as there are difficult questions, such as how to value life and limb (Jones-Lee, 1989) and how to respond to phenomena such as climate change and terrorism, which are both uncertain in their incidence and fraught by political considerations (Sunstein, 2002). Clearly, these events can impose huge costs on society if, and to the extent that, they materialise. But, equally clearly, stringent regulatory measures taken to constrain them – for example, those taken to implement the so-called 'precautionary principle'[13] – are also very costly, particularly if governments aim at a level of protection that significantly exceeds what is socially optimal.

Determination of what is socially optimal involves targeting regulatory measures to the level of protection at which the marginal costs approximate to the marginal benefits, the latter involving principally reduced damage costs. That determination is often weakened by inadequate data, but the principle remains clear – that it should involve an objective, scientific assessment of the nature of the risk and of the means

13 On which see Majone (2002) and Sunstein (2005).

of controlling it, on the basis of such evidence as is available at reasonable cost.

The crucial difficulty here is that lay perceptions of risk often differ widely from the objective assessment made by experts. Behavioural economics, drawing on social psychology empirical studies (Noll and Krier, 1990), indicates that ordinary people will, in particular:

- overestimate risks identical, or analogous, to those arising from events receiving much media attention ('availability heuristic');
- overestimate risks that have already materialised ('hindsight bias');
- overvalue the benefit of preventing (or reducing) risks from new activities or technologies ('status quo bias').

By way of topical illustration, empirical studies have shown that, relative to what is suggested by objective evidence, Americans attribute a high value to the probability of a terrorist attack[14] and a low value to the possibility of climate change (Sunstein, 2007). Such phenomena give rise to a delicate policy question: to what extent should policymakers adjust safety regulation upwards from optimal safety standards as reflecting expert assessments to meet the preferences implicit in the lay perceptions?

Mainstream welfare economics would seem to give a straightforward answer to this question. Lay perceptions can be treated simply as examples of risk aversion. The object of economic decision-making is to maximise utility. Even if the lay perceptions of risk outlined above are 'irrational', they cause disutility, and those who are risk-averse will pay more than those who are risk-neutral to alleviate the disutility, by reducing the risk or engaging in self-insurance (Cicchetti and Dubin, 1994). Assuming that regulatory policy aims at mimicking the market transactions that would have taken place without heavy coordination

14 In the period after 9/11, 88 per cent of Americans believed that it was 'likely' or 'somewhat likely' that another terrorist attack would occur within the next few months: Sunstein (2007: 516).

costs, there is therefore a justification in making safety policy meet standards higher than those required by expert assessments.

Adopting this approach meticulously would, however, lead to disproportionate responses to flawed and irrational risk perceptions and seriously inhibit technological development (Viscusi, 1998). Nor does economic reasoning ineluctably lead to such a conclusion. As we have already seen, Coase's 'social cost' paper (1960) teaches us to be sceptical of normative propositions that the *active* creators of risks should always be expected to modify their conduct; in some situations the potential 'victim' is the cheaper cost-abater. If, and to the extent that, attitudes to risk are based on inadequate information or fallacious understanding, it can be argued that the disutility to which these give rise may more easily and cheaply be contained by the better informing and educating of public opinion (Ogus, 2004c). Take, for example, terrorism (Ogus, 2007). A different regulatory strategy can be adopted, the focus shifting from attempts to control the risk of terrorist acts to alleviating fear, which is the consequence of such risk (Posner, 2002). The strategies might include not only the provision of information and public reassurances but also efforts to 'normalise' the risk of terrorism, for the psychological evidence shows that the longer people are exposed to a risk the better they adapt to it and the less the fear that it engenders (Posner, 2001b).

Paternalism

Paternalism, the overriding of individual choice on the ground that individuals cannot be trusted to make decisions wisely, would seem to lie behind a large number of regulatory measures, including social insurance; the compulsory wearing of seat belts and safety helmets; and 'cooling-off periods' enabling consumers and investors to withdraw from contractual undertakings. They also include, more generally, prohibiting or controlling certain risk-generating products and services, as an alternative to providing information and risking leaving it to consumers to decide whether they wish to purchase the product or service. Yet, perhaps because of political correctness, the topic is rarely discussed openly and analysis of when paternalistic justifications for regulation should be invoked are hard to find.[15] This is to be regretted and, in this final section of the chapter, I seek to show how such analysis can make a valuable addition to regulatory policymaking.

We should note, in the first place, that many apparently interventionist measures, overriding individual preferences, can be rationalised economically without reference to paternalistic arguments. Most obviously and importantly, some unwise individual decisions generate negative externalities. Thus, insistence that a safety helmet or an equivalent protective device be worn by those at risk may reduce injuries and thus also the healthcare costs borne by taxpayers and health insurance contributors. Alternatively, it can be justified on grounds of information asymmetry; this is conceptually distinct from paternalism, which can apply even where these is perfect information.

Genuine paternalistic arguments are founded on presumed irrationality and, as we have seen, the work of behavioural economists provides some rich insights as to when this is likely to occur. With the aid of this evidence, it is possible to identify situations in which many, perhaps most, individual decision-makers select options that would not reflect their preferences if they had been responding rationally to the information available. The benefit of a legal intervention forcing an individual to adopt the rational choice may then be expressed as the difference between the utility gained from complying with the legal requirement and the utility that would have been gained from exercising the preferred option. The social benefit of the measure would then be the aggregate of such increases in utility for all those subject to the requirement – though some deduction would have to be made for imperfect enforcement of the law – and these can then be compared with costs of the regulatory measure (Zamir, 1998).

15 Exceptions are Zamir (1998) and Camerer et al. (2003), in addition to my own paper (Ogus, 2005) on which this section is based.

Of course, these variables cannot be quantified with any precision, but policymakers could on this basis adopt an analytical framework for reviewing paternalist measures, taking the following steps (Ogus, 2005):

- Are there plausible traditional justifications (externalities, information failure, inadequate competition) for the measure, operating independently of paternalism?
- If not, and taking account of the insights of behavioural economics, is the regulated activity one with regard to which a significant proportion of the agents make decisions that are unlikely to reflect their real preferences?
- If so, are the likely costs of the regulatory measure proportionate to the likely benefits and/or could the same outcome be reached at lower cost by an alternative instrument?

Conclusion

This chapter reaches no simple, or provocative, normative conclusions regarding the level or character of regulation. My principal mission has been to convince my readers not only that economic analysis has a large and critical function in relation to regulatory law, but also that this function is positive as well as negative.

For a variety of reasons, economic and non-economic, we will always have regulation. Public interest economic analysis provides us with guidance on how regulatory law might be designed at minimum cost to society; private interest analysis alerts us to the dangers of regulatory goals being subverted and how we should respond to this risk. Finally, behavioural economics responds to the problems of 'bounded rationality' and indicates how regulation might adapt to them.

References

Becker, G. S. (1968), 'Crime and punishment: an economic approach', *Journal of Political Economy*, 76: 169–217.

Bernstein, M. H. (1955), *Regulating Business by Independent Commission*, Princeton, NJ: Princeton University Press.

Breyer, S. (1982), *Regulation and its Reform*, Cambridge, MA: Harvard University Press.

Camerer, C. F., S. Issacharoff, G. Loewenstein, T. O'Donoghue and M. Rabin (2003), 'Regulation for conservatives: behavioral economics and the case for "asymmetric paternalism"', *University of Pennsylvania Law Review*, 151: 1211–54.

Cicchetti, C. J. and J. Dubin (1994), 'A microeconometric analysis of risk aversion and the decision to self-insure', *Journal of Political Economy*, 102: 169–86.

Coase, R. H. (1960), 'The problem of social cost', *Journal of Law and Economics*, 3: 1–44.

Cohen, M. (1996), 'Commentary', in E. Eide and R. Van den Bergh (eds), *Law and Economics of the Environment*, Oslo: Juridisk Forlag.

Commons, J. R. (1924), *Legal Foundations of Capitalism*, London: Macmillan.

Crew, M. A. and P. R. Kleindorfer (2002), 'Regulatory economics: twenty years of progress?', *Journal of Regulatory Economics*, 21: 5–22.

Dehejia, V. H. and Y. Samy (2006), 'Labor standards and economic integration in the European Union: an empirical analysis', CESifo Working Paper Series no. 830, Munich.

Delvolvé, P. (1998), *Le Droit public de l'économie*, Paris: Dalloz.

Demsetz, H. (1969), 'Information and efficiency: another viewpoint', *Journal of Law and Economics*, 12: 1–22.

Dewees, D. N. (ed.) (1983), *The Regulation of Quality: Products, Services, Workplaces and the Environment*, Toronto: Butterworth.

Esty, D. C. and D. Geradin (2001), 'Regulatory co-opetition', in D. Esty and D. Geradin (eds), *Regulatory Competition and Economic*

Integration: Comparative Perspectives, Oxford: Oxford University Press, pp. 30–46.

Farber, D. A. and P. P. Frickey (1991), *Law and Public Choice: A Critical Introduction*, Chicago, IL: University of Chicago Press.

Freund, E. (1917), *Standards of American Legislation*, Chicago, IL: University of Chicago Press.

Freund, E. (1932), *Legislative Regulation*, New York: Commonwealth Fund.

Friedman, M. (1962), *Capitalism and Freedom*, Chicago, IL: University of Chicago Press.

Friedmann, W. F. (1959), *Law in a Changing Society*, London: Stevens.

Friedmann, W. F. (1971), *State of Law in a Mixed Economy*, London: Stevens.

Froud, J., R. Boden, A. Ogus and P. Stubbs (1998), *Controlling the Regulators*, Basingstoke: Macmillan.

Gunningham, N. and J. Rees (1997), 'Industry self-regulation: an institutional perspective', *Law and Policy*, 19: 363–414.

Hahn, R. W., J. K. Burnett, Y. H. I. Chan, E. A. Mader and P. Moyle (2000), 'Assessing regulatory impact analyses: the failure of agencies to comply with Executive Order 12,866', *Harvard Journal of Law and Public Policy*, 23: 839–78.

Hayek, F. von (1960), *The Constitution of Liberty*, Chicago, IL: University of Chicago Press.

Hayek, F. von (1973–79), *Law, Legislation and Liberty*, London: Routledge.

Heimann, C. M. et al. (1990), 'Project: the impact of cost–benefit analysis on administrative law', *Administrative Law Review*, 42: 545–654.

Huizinga, H. and G. Nicodeme (2006), 'Foreign ownership and corporate income taxation: an empirical evaluation', *European Economic Review*, 50: 1223–44.

Hylton K. N. and V. Khanna (2007), 'Toward a public choice theory of criminal procedure', *Supreme Court Economic Review*, 15: 61–118.

Janicke, M. (2004), 'Lead markets for environmental innovations: a new role for the nation state', *Global Environmental Politics*, 4: 29–46.

Jones-Lee, M. (1989), *The Economics of Safety and Physical Risk*, Oxford: Blackwell.

Laski, H. J., W. I. Jennings and W. A. Robson (1935), *A Century of Municipal Progress, 1835–1935*, London: Allen & Unwin.

Littlechild, S. C. (1983), *Regulation of British Telecommunications' Profitability*, London: HMSO.

Macrory, R. (2006), *Regulatory Justice: Making Sanctions Effective*, London: Cabinet Office.

Majone, G. (2002), 'What price safety? The precautionary principle and its policy implications', *Journal of Common Market Studies*, 40: 89–109.

Mashaw, J. L. (1989), 'The economics of politics and the understanding of public law', *Chicago-Kent Law Review*, 65: 123–60.

Maurizi A. (1974), 'Occupational licensing and the public interest', *Journal of Political Economy*, 82: 399–413.

McGarity, T. (1991), *Reinventing Rationality: The Role of Regulatory Analysis in the Federal Bureaucracy*, Cambridge: Cambridge University Press.

Noam, E. (1982), 'The choice of government level in regulation', *Kyklos*, 35: 278–91.

Noll, R. G. and J. E. Krier (1990), 'Some implications of cognitive psychology for risk regulation', *Journal of Legal Studies*, 19: 747–90.

OECD (1992), *Regulatory Reform, Privatisation and Competition Policy*, Paris: OECD.

Ogus, A. (1998), 'Law-and-economics from the perspective of law', in P. Newman (ed.), *The New Palgrave Dictionary of Economics and the Law*, London: Macmillan, vol. 2, pp. 486–92.

Ogus, A. (2004a), *Regulation: Legal Form and Economic Theory*, Oxford: Hart Publishing.

Ogus, A. (2004b), 'Enforcing regulation: do we need the criminal law', in H. Sjogren and G. Skogh (eds), *New Perspectives on Economic Crime*, Cheltenham: Edward Elgar.

Ogus, A. (2004c), 'Risk management from an economic perspective', in E. Vos and G. van Calster (eds), *Risico en voorzorg in de rechtsmaatschappij*, Antwerp: Intersentia, pp. 229–38.

Ogus, A. (2005), 'Regulatory paternalism: when is it justified?', in K. J. Hopt, E. Wyrmeesch, H. Kanda and H. Baum (eds), *Corporate Governance in Context: Corporations, States, and Market in: Europe, Japan and the United States*, Oxford: Oxford University Press, pp. 303–20.

Ogus, A. (2006), *Costs and Cautionary Tales: Economic Insights for the Law*, Oxford: Hart Publishing.

Ogus, A. (2007), 'Responding to threats of terrorism: how the law can generate appropriate incentives', *Journal of Interdisciplinary Economics*, 19: 35–55.

Olson, M. (1965), *The Logic of Collective Action*, Boston, MA: Harvard University Press.

Pelkmans, J. (1987), 'The new approach to technical harmonization and standardization', *Journal of Common Market Studies*, 25: 249–69.

Peltzman, S. (1976), 'Towards a more general theory of regulation', *Journal of Law and Economics*, 19: 211–40.

Posner, E. A. (2001a), 'Controlling agencies with cost-benefit-analysis: a positive political theory perspective', *University of Chicago Law Review*, 68: 1137–99.

Posner, E. A. (2001b) 'Law and the emotions', *Georgetown Law Journal*, 89: 1977–2012.

Posner, E. A. (2002), 'Fear and the regulatory model of counterterrorism', *Harvard Journal of Law and Public Policy*, 25: 681–97.

Radaelli, C. M. (2004), 'The diffusion of regulatory impact analysis – best practice or lesson-drawing', *European Journal of Political Research*, 43: 723–47.

Revesz, R. (2001), 'Federalism and regulation: some generalizations', in D. Esty and D. Geradin (eds), *Regulatory Competition and Economic Integration: Comparative Perspectives*, Oxford: Oxford University Press, pp. 3–29.

Robson, W. (1960), *Nationalized Industry and Public Ownership*, London: Allen & Unwin.

Rose-Ackerman, S. (1988), 'Progressive law and economics – and the new administrative law', *Yale Law Journal*, 98: 341–68.

Skuse, A. (1972), *Government Intervention and Industrial Policy*, 2nd edn, London: Heinemann.

Spiller, P. T. (1990), 'Politicians, interest groups and regulators: a multiple-principals agency theory of regulation', *Journal of Law and Economics*, 33: 65–101.

Spiller, P. T. (1998), 'Agency discretion and accountability in regulation', in P. Newman (ed.), *The New Palgrave Dictionary of Economics and the Law*, London: Macmillan, vol. 1, pp. 30–34.

Stigler, G. J. (1971), 'The theory of economic regulation', *Bell Journal of Economics*, 2: 3–21.

Sun, J. M. and J. Pelkmans (1995), 'Regulatory competition in the single market', *Journal of Common Market Studies*, 33: 67–89.

Sunstein, C. R. (1990), *After the Rights Revolution: Reconceiving the Regulatory State*, Cambridge, MA: Harvard University Press.

Sunstein, C. R. (ed.) (2000), *Behavioral Law and Economics*, Cambridge: Cambridge University Press.

Sunstein, C. R. (2002), *Risk and Reason: Safety, Law, and the Environment*, Cambridge: Cambridge University Press.

Sunstein, C. R. (2005), *Laws of Fear: Beyond the Precautionary Principl*e, Cambridge: Cambridge University Press.

Sunstein, C.R. (2007), 'On the divergent American reactions to terrorism and climate change', *Columbia Law Review*, 107: 503–57.

Swann, D. (1988), *The Retreat of the State: Deregulation and Privatisation in the UK and US*, Brighton: Harvester.

Teubner, G. (1998), 'Legal irritants: good faith in British law or how unifying law ends up in new divergences', *Modern Law Review*, 61: 11–32.

Tiebout, C. M. (1956), 'A pure theory of local government expenditure', *Journal of Political Economy*, 64: 416–24.

Tollison, R. D. (1982), 'Rent seeking: a survey', *Kyklos*, 35: 575–602.

Tullock, G. (1967), 'The welfare costs of tariffs, monopolies and theft', *Western Economic Journal*, 5: 224–32.

Van den Bergh, R. (1998), 'Subsidiarity as an economic demarcation principle and the emergence of European private law', *Maastricht Journal of European and Comparative Law*, 5: 129–52.

Vickers, J. and G. Yarrow (1988), *Privatization: An Economic Analysis*, Cambridge, MA: MIT Press.

Viscusi, W. K. (1998), *Rational Risk Policy*, Oxford: Clarendon Press.

Zamir, E. (1998), 'The efficiency of paternalism', *Virginia Law Review*, 84: 229–86.

6 ECONOMIC RIGHTS

Norman Barry

Introduction

It is noticeable that in all the febrile debate about rights which has emerged in recent years there has been little discussion about economic rights – that is, the right to property, contract and all the other procedural requirements that go to make up a market society. The *civil* rights to non-discrimination, free discussion, religion and so on have been to the fore in political and philosophical argument. It is true that in America certain economic liberties have emerged as almost accidental by-products of these concerns, such as the right to advertising, which has been protected as a necessity for the right to free expression, guaranteed by the First Amendment to the Constitution, but for most of the time, in all countries, economic rights have been at the mercy of legislatures throughout this and the last century, with little or no protection from the courts or written constitutions.

This is partly due to philosophical reasons, the shift in the meaning of liberalism away from economic freedom towards a more socially oriented doctrine that permits redistribution and excessive liberty-reducing regulation, and also involves a redefinition of liberty. This last point has involved the abandonment of the essential *unity* of liberty, in which economic liberty flows directly from an all-embracing concept of freedom, towards the promotion of particular *liberties.* In that taxonomy economic rights have not been regarded as of overwhelming importance, or of any real value at all. There is scarcely any recognition of the intimate connection between economic rights and all the other more fashionable notions.

Of equal importance is the way that *representative* democracy works. Political parties find it easy to secure parliamentary majorities by offering favours (bribes) to significant interest groups. This invariably involves redistribution and over-regulation, which are to the detriment of the community as a whole, of which the members of interest groups are also members. Indeed, as the example of Switzerland shows, at the cantonal and federal levels, where government decisions are subject to nationwide referenda, economic liberty is better protected. So far from encouraging mob rule, as Edmund Burke thought, direct democracy turns out to be rather conservative.

In all legal systems throughout the world economic rights, especially property, have been poorly protected. In common-law countries certain remedies have developed through judicial decision-making which protects property, but this tends to be limited to harms caused by other private persons, especially in cases of externalities. Thus if a neighbour causes an obnoxious smell you can go to a common-law judge and get an *injunction* forbidding the action. Then, the perpetrator can in effect 'buy' the right, by way of an enforceable contract, to continue his action. This is not so easy in civil-law systems, which try to establish the absolute 'separateness' of property titles so that you would have to establish that you owned the property. This might involve excessive costs and prevent a Pareto solution emerging through bargaining by the respective parties. But neither system has proved at all effective in preventing invasions of property by the state. It is true that eminent domain exists, which allows such invasion by the state subject to the establishment of a public good argument for the violation of property and, importantly, to the payment of compensation to the aggrieved party, but since the collapse of communism this had not been the main threat to property. The threat to property rights comes more from excessive regulation, e.g. through 'zoning laws' that prevent a person embarking on a possible profitable use of his property, and in most legal systems, with the partial exception of America's in recent years, little compensation is paid to a property holder adversely affected by government action. Civil- or code-law systems normally have grandiose statements about the right to property but the codes have been modified over time to gradually whittle down this right. It is also true that the European Convention on Human Rights, in Article 1 of its First Protocol, talks of the right 'to the peaceful enjoyment of ... possessions', but this has been of little use in the prevention of the value-reducing actions of government intervention (see below).

Protection of economic rights in America

In the USA there is some formal constitutional protection for economic liberties in the Fifth and Fourteenth Amendments to the Constitution, but these relate exclusively to property; and other economic liberties are not specifically enumerated and depend entirely on controversial constitutional decisions of the courts. The economic right to free contract was established (temporarily) in the notorious *Lochner* v. *New York* (1905) case (see Siegan, 1980). A New York statute had severely restricted the hours per week that bakers could work. Free market critics argued that the law was designed to protect large established bakers against competition from smaller immigrants prepared to work long hours, and a case was brought; the Supreme Court ruled that the statute was unconstitutional. The court read into the First Amendment the right to free contract. In a famous dissent, Justice Holmes said that the Constitution did not enact Herbert Spencer's *Social Statics* and that the legislature, using the 'police power' (incidentally not in the Constitution), had the authority to regulate working conditions as it had done elsewhere. But the court found for the plaintiff, and it was a decision followed by others that struck down regulatory statutes at state and federal level, though it did uphold some.

But in fact the court was not implementing a free market agenda (indeed, it upheld many regulatory statutes) but was simply interpreting the Constitution. It used the doctrine of 'substantive due process' (ibid.: ch. 2), which authorises the court to interpret the Constitution in terms of its overall aims and purposes rather than according to the strict wording of the various clauses. And though historically and philosophically the US Constitution was designed to protect private property and free enterprise, US liberals, who have vastly extended civil liberties, have used precisely the doctrine of substantive due process to validate, for example, the court-created right of abortion. Certainly the *Lochner* decision was consistent with the US free enterprise tradition that welcomes immigrants into the life of free contracting, the key to economic progress. The statute would have impeded the prospects of immigrants who were fully prepared to work long hours to compete with established businesses.

Yet *Lochner* has provoked tremendous obloquy: even the distinguished economist of law, and now Court of Appeals judge, Richard Posner has described Holmes's dissent as 'magnificent' (see Posner, 1997). This is largely a consequence of his famed 'pragmatism', i.e. a reluctance to admit any absolute principles into judicial interpretation.

But as the Great Depression progressed throughout the 1930s there was an increasing demand for government action, and not just at the state level. Roosevelt's New Deal was vastly increasing the regulatory power of the federal government. But the New Deal was upheld by the Supreme Court, which struck down many of Roosevelt's early measures. The court, in defending economic liberties, became the target of the interventionist state, and Roosevelt eventually announced a plan to 'pack' the court; i.e. increase its size with his supporters. It turned out that this was not required and would probably have failed in Congress. In fact, the court switched in the *West Hotel* v. *Parrish* (1937) case: a Washington state statute that regulated the wages of female hotel workers was upheld, thus bringing about the end of the 'free market' court. After this decision, every statutory infringement of economic liberty was upheld (see Siegan, 1980: chs 2–5). Indeed, in the case of *US* v. *Carolene Products* (1938) the Supreme Court drew a clear distinction between economic and civil liberties. The court said it would subject laws in the latter to much greater scrutiny than the former on the ground that legislatures were more subject to the democratic will here, so that minorities were not endangered. This has been the standard view of the judiciary and the American intelligentsia: economic rights are not worth protecting. Perhaps the most egregious case was *Williamson* v. *Lee Optical* (1955), in which the court upheld an Oklahoma statute that reserved spectacle work for ophthalmologists and optometrists, thus severely restricting the work of opticians who had been doing the work satisfactorily for years. Posner strongly opposed this decision (Posner, 1977: 502), but is there any real distinction between it and *Lochner*?

All this goes along with the rejection of the unity of liberty. In American social liberalism, rights and liberties can be divided up and defended separately or, in the case of economic liberty, not at all. At least Posner objected to *Lee Optical*, but there were other decisions equally damaging for American economic rights. *Euclid* v. *Ambler Realty* (1926) constitutionally validated zoning so that certain areas were reserved for certain developments. This was designed to preserve the value of certain properties against developers, but it seriously undermined the rights of property owners who lost money. There is, of course, a market solution to the problem. Owners could design restrictive covenants that would limit the rights of newcomers who might damage the area so that the value of the properties could be preserved. Houston has preserved its pleasant environment without zoning.

Another constitutional provision designed to protect economic liberty is the Commerce Clause. The power to regulate interstate commerce was originally included to guarantee free trade between the states: one of the reasons for the abandonment of the Articles of Confederation in 1789 was the fact of states putting up barriers preventing the free import of goods and services across state lines. With the centralisation of economic power, however, this authority to regulate has become the regulation of *intrastate* commerce. National standards must apply everywhere. In 1942 Roscoe C. Filburn, who raised a small amount of wheat for his own private use, was fined for violating the Agricultural Adjustment Act 1933 (upheld in *Wickhard* v. *Filburn*), which limited wheat production. Apparently his action had an effect nationally since without it he would have purchased wheat on the open market. If everything affects everything else then there really is no limit to the powers of Congress.

With regard to *Lochner,* that case belongs to a different era entirely. The court today seems to be oblivious to the needs of a free and flexible market and the imperishable rights on which it depends. Minimum wage laws and the Americans with Disabilities Act 1990 are obvious examples of the violation of simple rules of economic liberty. The Supreme Court has been supine before these aberrations. It is one of the virtues of a genuine federal system that it permits exit from national standards in taxation and regulation. The US Constitution has the Tenth Amendment, which says that apart from the responsibilities formally allocated to Congress all other legislative powers belong to the states. We have seen how Congress has repeatedly usurped the responsibilities, but the final death knell to competitive federalism came with *Garcia* v. *San Antonia Transit Authority* (1985), in which the court ruled that federalism meant merely that the states had equal representation in the Senate with no mention of the specific constitutional provisions, such as the Tenth Amendment, that guarantee their freedoms.

Of course, the main method by which the state exercises economic power over the individual is through its regulation of private property, and here the outlook in the USA is not quite as bleak as elsewhere in economic matters. US governments had always been able to take private property under eminent domain, 'takings'. But the taking had to be for a public purpose and had to be accompanied by 'just compensation'. There had to be a physical taking of private property before the above procedures could take effect, but it was obvious to everyone that there were takings, especially via regulation, without any actual physical possession. The Constitution may say, somewhat grandly, that 'private property shall not be taken into public use without just compensation', but often the public use was dubious and the compensation non-existent.

In the 1980s things changed significantly in a few cases that challenged the political authorities' land-use planning powers. In *Nollan* v. *California Coastal Commission* (1987) Mr and Mrs Nollan applied for a permit to convert some property and the commission agreed subject to the condition that they dedicate a public easement across it. On appeal to the Supreme Court it was ruled that the regulation did not advance public goals and the Nollans won. But the most famous case was *Lucas* v. *South Carolina Coastal Commission* (1992). David Lucas had spent a million dollars on a beach property which he planned to convert into vacation homes. Unfortunately, the Coastal Commission later introduced environmental regulations that rendered the Lucas purchase worthless. A lot of issues were involved: was there a claim against retroactive laws and, most importantly, were claims for partial takings admissible (early commentators seemed to think not), and was there protection for investment-backed expectations? (Barry, 2000: 28–9).

Mr Lucas won in the Supreme Court and was duly compensated, indicating that the judiciary would be more searching in its inquiries into the rationale of regulation where property was concerned. But he suffered a total wipeout, and some questions left unsettled in *Lucas* were answered in *Dolan* v. *City of Tigard* (1994). Florence Dolan wanted a permit to extend her business but the grant of this was dependent on her dedicating a part of her land to public use in the form of flood abatement. Dolan appealed against this and other conditions and won in the court, and the decision provided the rationale for compensation for partial takings.

While all this is encouraging it would be foolish to imagine that the economic constitution has been rehabilitated. There are vast areas of commercial life that get no protection from the law, and government at all levels has pretty much a free hand. Contract law is subject to endless statutory depredations (whatever happened to 'employment at will'?) and arbitrary anti-discrimination law has removed the market from the resolution of the most contentious disputes – and this is ignoring anti-trust and other economic anomalies. But a measure of shift in the debate can be gauged in Chief Justice William Rehnquist's opinion in *Tigard*:

'[we] see no reason why the Takings clause … as much a part of the Bill of Rights as the First or Fourteenth Amendments should be relegated to the status of a poor relation'.

Common and civil law[1]

Britain is a common-law country with no written constitution and has little formal protection of economic rights. The USA is also a common-law country but has a kind of code, the Constitution, superimposed on it. As we have seen, the Constitution provides whatever protection there is for property and economic rights. Of course, common law is always subservient to statute law, but it has provided a minor protection for property, at least in comparison with European codes. The latter tend to have grandiose statements protecting property but, in practice, often perform worse than common law. The common law from time immemorial has protected property in a case-by-case manner and is very efficient at protecting individually owned possessions from invasion by others. The main weapon here is the *injunction*: if an individual feels that his property right is being undermined he can sue the alleged perpetrator, and if that is proved to be so by the court, the judge can order the perpetrator to desist from the action or to perform one. At that point the two parties may get together and reach a Pareto-efficient solution by a legally enforceable contract. Civil law does not have such procedures and all property disputes are settled by definitive actions for damages. In effect, at common law, the judge determines the property right. All this is very important in externality questions, which can be settled between the parties. In civil law such matters have to be settled by endless alterations to the code and excessive use of public law.

An important feature of common law is the development of the law of nuisance. In the English case of *Rylands* v. *Fletcher* (1868) Lord Codsworth ruled: 'For when one person, in managing his own affairs causes,

1 See Barry (2004).

however innocently, damage to another, it is obviously only just that he should be the party to suffer.' Thus this is part of the law of torts and developed entirely spontaneously. Interestingly, the law of nuisance can be used against the state. Under the rule of law the state cannot be exempt from legal action. In a recent case (*Dennis* v. *Ministry of Defence* (2002)), Mr Dennis sued the government, under the law of nuisance. Dennis had bought an expensive house in Cambridgeshire but, soon after, the Royal Air Force established a jet fighter training school at Wittering near by and the training of the pilots ruined the Dennises' previously quiet amenities. The court recognised that there was a public good of defence but said that in this case it should give way to the private economic right. Dennis was not granted an injunction but was awarded damages of close to £1 million.

The really important thing about the law of nuisance is that it provides a remedy when one is not available from statute. A claim has occurred recently in California where in the light of the current scare about 'global warming' the state has taken action against the major automakers under the law of nuisance. Apparently, no remedy was available under the various federal clean air acts. No equivalent remedies are available in civil-law regimes, but tentative moves are being made in that direction in several European countries.

The state and economic rights

It is still the case that no legal regime anywhere provides protection against a government determined to seize private property in its desire to socialise the country. Of course, even market theorists, anarcho-capitalists apart, recognise the need for the state to provide public goods and to solve other problems of market failure. But how do we stop governments acting oppressively and going beyond public good requirements? The experience of communism tells us that we cannot rely on goodwill. Even if there were any it would never be enough. Yet while there has been outrage at the state's violation of human or civil rights there is no equivalent protest at the regular breaches of economic rights. Indeed, the intimate connection between the two is rarely recognised. And, of course, there can be violations of economic rights without communism – for example, under the Labour governments in Britain during 1945–51 and under François Mitterrand's government in France in the early 1980s. The welfare states that advanced countries have developed all involve breaches of economic rights: the right to dispose of one's income, the right to property and all the rights that derive from trade.

Britain, with its unwritten constitution, sovereign parliament, absence of significant judicial review and heavily centralised form of government, provides the least formal protection for economic rights of any advanced country: it has very much depended on goodwill and an inefficient democratic system to prevent the complete socialisation of the economy. It might be thought that the addition to the European Convention on Human Rights of the First Protocol guaranteeing the protection of the 'peaceful enjoyment of … possessions' would lead to improvements. After all, the admission of the convention directly into British law is a significant dent in the sovereignty doctrine. The courts have the authority to refer a law suspected of being in breach of the convention back to Parliament for reconsideration. But the courts do not have the authority to strike it down, so sovereignty formally remains. Still, there have been signs that the protocol will make little difference to governments' anti-economic rights strategies. A Viennese lady failed to get an Austrian rent control law struck down and the Duke of Westminster protested against a British law that allowed leaseholders to buy out their freeholds at very favourable prices to no avail. The difficulty is that the law is not favourable to individual economic rights. The full reading is as follows: 'The preceding provisions shall not, however, in any way impair the right of a State to enforce such laws as it deems necessary to control the use of property in accordance with the general interest or to secure the payment of taxes or other contributions or penalties.'

In other words, *there are no economic rights.*[2] The point of an individual right is that it is held *against* the general interest: that is the way civil rights are understood. The Duke of Westminster had the disadvantage of being Britain's richest person, and there is no reason to assume that the judiciary is immune from current fads. But the Viennese lady was not rich: her only source of income was a rent-controlled apartment she let.

Only the US Constitution provides feasible protection for economic rights and, as we have seen, even that applies seriously only to property. Even here, however, a new problem has emerged. This is the increasing practice of granting eminent domain powers to private persons, normally companies. Local governments, anxious to attract business to their areas, have found this new economic power irresistible. The most famous and notorious example was *Poletown* v. *City of Detroit* (1981). Here General Motors wanted to buy out a residential area to develop a new plant. The company had, of course, brought much employment and prosperity to that part of Michigan. The trouble was that Poletown was a thriving ethnic community whose inhabitants were reluctant to sell. General Motors were granted eminent domain powers. Of course, there were good utilitarian reasons for this. No doubt there was the possibility of a hold-out problem if the decision had been left to the market, but these issues are not insoluble through free market exchange, and in this case the residents and General Motors could have reached an agreement in which they could have shared the surplus. Of course, the company wanted to obtain the property cheaply and it had great political influence.[3] It might be thought that civil law, with its formal reasoning from written rules, would have been a better protection for property than the 'creative powers' of the common law, but the trouble is that civil-law regimes have not been solicitous in the protection of private property in the face of eminent domain.

2 While the Human Rights Act 1998 makes this statement not as literally true as before the Act, it does not change the position substantively for reasons that are not fully discussed in this chapter.

3 See also *Kelo* v. *New London* (2005).

Conclusion

Despite the collapse of communism and all the talk about rights these days there is very little protection of economic rights against government oppression. Except, that is, the claim for welfare rights from the state – the granting of which involves the violation of the economic rights of the taxpayer. But the crucial thing about proper economic rights is that they do not require any financing from the state; their proponents simply ask the state to withdraw from the peaceful activities of law-abiding citizens, i.e. trade. Although claims to economic rights lack the glamour of civil rights there is a close connection between them. Where would the right to free expression be without the right to own a printing press and publishing company? And the exercise of economic rights is a great contributor to progress and prosperity. But this is not to base economic rights entirely on utility, for, as we have seen from the Poletown example, economic rights can be held against general utility.

Naturally we look to the law to find protection of our rights but here we should be aware of Hayek's famous distinction between *law* and *legislation*. In the past 100 years we have seen a vast increase in legislation, in welfare, tax and general economic planning, but a decline in the significance of the common law, where this refers to the spontaneous development of those general rules which make exchange possible. In common-law countries contract and tort developed spontaneously, and no new law, in the sense of legislation, is needed. Law that develops in this way is likely to be superior to designed statutes precisely because it emerges from the context of exchange and trade. To restore economic rights would not require much in the way of government activity. It mainly requires the removal of all the statutory restraints on free contract and a promise by government that all future interventions should be abandoned. A huge advance for economic liberty would occur if government withdrew from welfare and left decisions about health and wellbeing to individuals. Of course, that would release tax money for investment in the real economy.

It would be most important if government fully recognised economic rights and intervened less through regulation. This would include, for example, the regulation of financial transactions such as those through the stock market with onerous, counterproductive rules about, *inter alia*, insider trading and takeovers (see Barry, 1999). All the moral problems here can be resolved by a careful application of the law of contract, and any policy problems can be analysed with the principles that emerge from the basic right to trade.

References

Barry, N. (1999), *Business Ethics*, London: Macmillan.

Barry, N. (2000), 'Constitutional protection of economic liberty', *Ideas on Liberty*, 50.

Barry, N. (2004), 'Property rights in common and civil law', in E. Colombatto, *The Economics of Property Rights*, Cheltenham: Edward Elgar.

Posner, R. A. (1977), *Economic Analysis of Law*, 2nd edn, Boston, MA: Little, Brown.

Posner, R. A. (1997), 'The Constitution as an economic document', in R. A. Posner and F. Parisi (eds), *Law and Economics*, Cheltenham: Edward Elgar.

Siegan, B. (1980), *Economic Liberties and the Constitution*, Chicago, IL: University of Chicago Press.

7 BREACH OF CONTRACT AND THE EFFICIENCY OF MARKETS

David Campbell[1]

Introduction

Developments in the English law of remedies for breach of contract, which may be traced back to *Wrotham Park Estate Co Ltd* v. *Parkside Homes Ltd* in 1974,[2] but which received enormous impetus from the House of Lords' 2001 decision in *AG* v. *Blake (Jonathan Cape Ltd Third Party)*,[3] have posed fundamental questions about the current structure of that law. In *Blake*, that structure was described as 'seriously defective',[4] and, in the important subsequent *Experience Hendrix LLC* v. *PPX Enterprises Inc., Edward Chalpin*, the Court of Appeal commended *Blake* as the 'new start in this area'[5] which was necessary to begin the essential redesign of that structure. No informed commentator on the law of contract (certainly not myself, if I may be included in this set) would deny that the law of contract is marked by many shortcomings which should be eliminated, and the law of remedies for breach is no exception to this. But, in a textbook (Harris et al., 2002: chs 16–17)[6] and in

1 This chapter is based on a paper given as one of the Law 125 Distinguished Speakers Public Lectures to mark the 125th anniversary of the Law School of the University of Adelaide, Australia. I am grateful to Kevin Dowd, John Gava and the editor of this collection for their comments on the chapter. The law is as stated at 31 December 2007.

2 [1974] 1 W.L.R. 798.

3 [1997] Ch. 84 (Ch. D.); [1998] Ch. 439 (CA) and [2001] 1 A.C. 268 (HL(E)).

4 Ibid., (CA) at 457E.

5 [2003] EWCA Civ. 323 at para. [16].

6 The subsequent case law is discussed in Campbell and Wylie (2003), Campbell (2004) and Campbell and Devenney (2006).

a number of papers[7] published over the last decade, I[8] have sought to defend the fundamental structure of the law of remedies as far superior to the novel alternatives being proposed; indeed, I believe it is the best fundamental structure of which, given certain ineluctable characteristics of economic action, it is possible to conceive.

In this chapter, I will briefly restate this defence, but only as the foundation of an analysis of the, as it were, nature of the criticism being made of the law of remedies that has made that defence necessary. That criticism is based on the perceived failure of the current law to bring about desirable goals derived from abstract reasoning about the 'law', in this case the 'justice' of 'correcting' the 'wrong' of breach. But, though in its essentials codified in 1893,[9] the current law is the common-law institutionalisation of commercial practice, and the default rule governing breach of contract is that rule which competition over the terms of the sale of goods has identified as the most efficient. It is my principal aim in this chapter to show just how ill advised it is to purport to improve on this practical economic wisdom by abstract legal reasoning, for the proposed alternative to the current law cannot possibly be enforced unless competition over the terms of the sale of goods is prevented; that is to say, unless choice is replaced by fiat.

The structure of the law of remedies for breach of contract

To one who comes to the study of the English law of remedies for breach with conventional ideas about the enforcement of contracts, the remarkable feature of that law, and of the corollary laws of all those jurisdictions that have a law still based on the English law, is

7 See particularly Campbell and Harris (2002) and Campbell (2005).

8 Much of my thinking on the topic of this chapter has been formed in the course of joint work with Hugh Collins, James Devenney, Roger Halson, Donald Harris and Philip Wylie.

9 The Sale of Goods Act 1893, pt 5; now the Sale of Goods Act 1979, pt 6.

that it cannot be said usually to seek to prevent breach from taking place. The law rather seeks to regulate the terms on which breach is allowed to take place. The 'default' remedy is not the compulsion of performance but rather compensation of the claimant by compulsory payment of money damages. With the misleading exception of actions in debt (which can be ignored here because the exception they present is more apparent than real; Harris et al., 2002: ch. 11), compulsory performance is an uncommon remedy, available only if a special case is made out for it, one part of that case being that compensatory damages are 'inadequate'. It is normally the case, then, that if the defendant is willing to pay the damages, he can breach the contract and successfully refuse to perform. The defendant is, as Mr Justice Holmes seminally put it, 'free to break his contract if he chooses' (Holmes, 1881: 301).

What is more, compensatory damages are:

- Quantified on the basis of a 'net expectation' view of the claimant's protected interest, so that compensation aims to protect only the claimant's net profit.
- Subject to rules of causation that effectively require the claimant to prove that the defendant reasonably could have clearly foreseen (and so be able to negotiate about) his liabilities when he agreed the contract.
- Subject to a requirement that the claimant take reasonable steps after breach to minimise or 'mitigate' his loss. Quantification of compensation on this basis strongly tends to keep the defendant's costs of breach to a minimum, which can often be zero.

A law of remedies with this fundamental structure will of its nature give the defendant an incentive to breach when he encounters difficulties in performing, for whenever the costs of compensation are smaller than the costs of performance, the defendant has an incentive to breach, and this law typically keeps the costs of breach low.

Let us take what is intended to be an absolutely typical example.[10] A seller agreed to sell 2,000 tonnes of steel to a buyer for £1 million, delivery to be made six months hence. At the time of agreement, the seller's projection of his cost price for making the steel was £900,000, and he therefore expected to realise a net profit of £100,000 from the sale. During performance, he encountered unanticipated difficulties, and, one month into that performance, the projected cost of making the steel rose to £1,500,000. At the point where the cost of performance becomes larger than the sum of the cost of his own lost net profit, the cost of his wasted expenditure and the cost of his liability to the claimant, the defendant seller will have an incentive to breach. This incentive can arise only because compulsory performance will not normally be awarded, and the cost of liability for the claimant's losses is kept to a minimum. It is kept to a minimum in one of two main ways.

If the breach causes the claimant to abandon future plans that were dependent upon delivery of the steel, he will suffer a 'consequential loss'. The 'special' or 'consequential' damages he may claim are limited to compensation of the lost net profit of the abandoned plans (plus out-of-pocket expenses, or 'reliance' losses, already incurred, if any). But the claimant will suffer consequential loss only if he cannot 'cover' by buying substitute steel on the market, and continue production using the substitute. If, as is usually the case, the steel is a 'generic' good in that it is available in competitive supply on the market, the claimant will be confined to 'normal, 'direct' or 'market' damages, quantified as the difference between the contract price and the market price of the substitute at the time of the breach. If the market price is higher than the contract price, the claimant can claim the difference.[11] If the contract price and the market price are the same, or the latter is lower than the former, the claimant's damages are 'nominal', in effect zero, and no legal

10 For the sake of brevity, I will discuss only the case of the relatively complex, longer-term contract, where the issues are particularly clear. The analysis can readily be extended to simple, quickly performed contracts.

11 Obverse rules govern buyer's breach.

proceedings will arise. Such costless breach is, I repeat, a very common case indeed in commercial law. In fact, the most common response of commercial parties to breach is not to seek a legal remedy at all, but to forbear from legal action and deal with the problem by adjusting their positions, to the point where empirical studies show the 'non-use' (Macaulay, 1963) of formal legal remedies to be the defining characteristic of empirical contracting behaviour. But though the law in the sense of the involvement of lawyers in dispute resolution is not used, it is crucial to recognise that the law provides the institutional framework in which the parties resolve the problem by non-use of the formal legal remedies.

The key to understanding the law of remedies is to recognise, as we will see the law itself does, that the legal contract is *not* the essential component of the commercial relationships that contract regulates. What is essential is the economic exchange between the parties. The contract is merely the legal institution which is to facilitate that exchange. There is no necessity for the parties to express their exchange in the legal form of a contract, and the main reason they do so is to seek security against the possibility of non-performance. That security is provided by the defendant's liability to provide the remedy in the event of non-performance which the contract stipulates, which the state ultimately will compel the defendant to provide.[12] The terms of the economic exchange constitute the 'primary obligations' under the contract, which, saving fraud,[13] the parties intend to perform. The fact that these are expressed in a contract means, however, that, from the time of the agreement, there also arises a liability to provide a remedy in the event of non-performance, which crystallises into the 'secondary obligation' to provide a remedy upon breach of contract.

12 Though sometimes, of course, enforcement fails.

13 Fraud will be ignored here as, in the developed, 'high trust' market economies, this is a much less important problem than dealing with mistaken agreements, and the ways of dealing with it are incidental to the basic structure of the law of remedies, and, indeed, of contract in general.

This fundamental distinction between primary and secondary obligations makes possible a range of remedial 'choices', for while, of course, one such choice could be to identify the primary and secondary obligations so that the remedy is always compulsory performance of the primary obligation, this need not be the case, and if another remedy better serves the function of the legal contract, which is to facilitate the economic exchange, it can, should and, under competitive pressures, will be adopted. Commercial parties enter into contracts to realise a net profit. By directly focusing on the claimant's net profit, the net expectation view of the claimant's protected interest allows the possibility of minimising the costs of dealing with breach. In our steel example, if the market price (of the substitute) and the contract price (of the steel) are equivalent, the damages are zero. If the market price were higher than the contract price, damages would protect the claimant's net profit by compensating him for the rise in price, but typically this is a relatively small marginal adjustment. Though I do not have space to go through all of the increasingly complicated examples with which one has to deal when explaining this to law students, I can say that compensatory damages typically protect the expectation interest in a way that minimises the defendant's costs of breach. In the famous words of Farnsworth, the central feature of the law of remedies is that it 'shows a marked solicitude for men who do not keep their promises' (Farnsworth, 1970: 1216).

The current criticism of the law of remedies

A law of remedies of this nature is obviously repugnant to those who subscribe to the conventional view captured in the maxim *pacta sunt servanda*, which is usually translated as 'agreements should be kept'. The academic thinking that lay behind *Blake* was a commitment to what Professor Friedmann has felicitously called 'the performance interest':

> The essence of contract is performance. Contracts are made in

> order to be performed. This is usually the one and only ground for their formation ... This interest in getting the promised performance ... the performance interest ... is the only pure contractual interest. (Friedmann, 1995: 629)

The main tactic that has been advocated to give effect to the performance interest has been the wider use of 'restitutionary' or 'disgorgement' damages, so that the defendant has to make restitution of, or disgorge, any benefit he gains by breach. *Wrotham Park* has been interpreted as authority for partial disgorgement of this benefit; *Blake* as authority for its total disgorgement; and *Hendrix* is an attempt to unite them both in a 'sliding scale' of disgorgement damages. If the total disgorgement which is logically required for the purposes of a 'corrective justice' which seeks to prevent the 'wrong' of breach is available to the 'innocent' claimant, then breach becomes pointless or meaningless, for, *ex hypothesi*, the defendant can gain nothing from it. I have argued in the academic legal literature that there is a very great deal of unavoidable doctrinal incoherence in the idea of these disgorgement damages, but let us leave this aside and ask outright what, in the end, is the question which must be answered: why not seek to prevent breach?

Why the law of remedies works the way it does; or, why not prevent breach?

In one or two of my contributions to the academic literature, I have, as I said at the time, invited considerable risk of exposing myself to ridicule by quoting a passage from some of the work of John von Neumann, which has proved to be the foundation of modern computing, and which I attempted to read when trying to come to terms with game theory. The passage runs:

> Error is viewed ... not as an extraneous and misdirected or misdirecting accident, but as an essential part of the process under consideration – its importance ... being fully comparable to that of

> the factor which is normally considered, the intended and correct logical structure. (Von Neumann, 1956: 43)

Most of von Neumann's work in computing (or in game theory, for that matter) is quite incomprehensible to me, but, insofar as my understanding is correct, one of his contributions to the conceptualisation of computing problems was to recognise that error is ineliminable,[14] and therefore that the goal of eliminating error from calculation was illusory. One should first be aware of this, and so not put excessive faith in one's results, and then try to manage the inevitable failure. In computing, von Neumann's basic strategy was to duplicate the calculation on various computers (or parts of computers) and work from some sample of the multiple results.

Without wishing to put any great weight on what is intended purely as a heuristic device, I submit that an analogue to this happens in the market economies. It is obvious that in those economies, composed of countless numbers of exchanges of varying degrees of complexity, dealing with the inevitably occurring contracts in which one party finds his costs of performance growing in an unanticipated way, telling him he made a mistake by agreeing this contract, is a major issue. It is a problem which cannot be eliminated. Given the positive transaction costs that are present in any empirical situation, parties must contract on the basis of bounded rationality, and so agreements to perform primary obligations which turn out to be mistaken are inevitable, and, indeed, are bound to be a significant proportion of all agreements made. The mechanism for handling this problem is central to the efficiency of the market economy. The fundamental mechanism is adjustment of obligations by the parties without recourse to legal action, which is encouraged by limiting the extent to which performance can legally be insisted upon. This means that we should readily allow (regulated) breach. Breach allows flexibility

14 The mechanical reliability of the computing machines available to von Neumann was very much poorer than that of contemporary computers, but the basic point still holds, of course.

in the system of exchanges,[15] allowing parties relief from obligations that are more expensive than anticipated when further performance would merely be wasteful as the claimant can be compensated in damages. In this sense, *the major function of the law of contract is to allow breach*, but on the right occasions and on the right terms: in essence, on terms that encourage claimants to cover in the knowledge that the defendant will compensate lost net expectation.

All this, of course, assumes that it is usually possible for the claimant to cover by buying a substitute. But this is usually possible for commercial parties because the market economies are characterised by the ready availability of goods in competitive supply, including a margin of excess capacity which allows a buyer faced with breach to cover. This margin functions *inter alia* as the space in which inevitable misallocations of resources through contract are adjusted through breach, or by adjustment by the parties which makes it unnecessary for the party experiencing difficulty to breach. Much economic theory that views 'excess capacity' in the economy as a sign of malaise simply fails to take on board this vital function of such capacity in making the taking of cover widely possible. Maintaining such a view follows from the difficulty of integrating the competitive process of continual discovery in imperfect market conditions into conventional conceptions of equilibrium. But the difficulties of economic theory are greatly exaggerated by legal theories of the performance interest. These simply have no inkling of the economic difficulties to which the pursuit of the goal of the general prevention of breach will lead. This approach would require the terms of agreements to be so often right as to eliminate the necessity of breach. To set the prevention of breach as the goal of the law of remedies is ultimately to imagine that mistaken agreements can be eliminated. Of course, they cannot.

It would be wrong to say that theories of the performance interest and disgorgement damages do not recognise that some breaches cannot

15 Comparative legal studies have revealed an extremely important contrast with the damaging rigidity of plan fulfilment in the command economies (and the emergence of an extensive informal market economy in an inadequate attempt to mitigate this damage).

be prevented. In the academic literature it is allowed that there may be situations in which disgorgement of the proceeds of wrongdoing is impractical and has to be given up, and similar caveats have been entered about the extent to which the performance interest should be protected. But this is, however, merely accepting a situation that one would put right if one could. There is no concession of a positive role for breach, merely an acknowledgement that it cannot be wholly eliminated, for reasons that are casually and, on examination, implausibly attributed to the moral delict of the wrongdoer. This is theoretically unsatisfactory. Breach, a central feature of commercial contracting, is being treated as a mere exception to the law of contract, and this is so because it is not understood by approaches to the law of contract which divorce formal legal principle from the underlying economic action. It is regrettable that, during a period in which transaction cost and institutional economics have stressed the importance of the law for economic policy formulation, major shifts in the English case law of remedies are taking place, and are possible only because they take place, on the basis of abstract reasoning about principle which, albeit unbeknown to those engaged in this reasoning, postulates an unrealisable goal of exchange without error, and allows the extremely misleading identification of the function of contract as the prevention of breach.

Choice over levels of precaution

Reflection on the nature of the market economy would, then, show the goal of the prevention of breach to be absurd. Fortunately, the intentions of commercial parties reflected in the common law of contract are too sophisticated to be formed by reference to this goal. Faced with the inevitability of breach as a practical commercial reality, parties have not fruitlessly attempted to eliminate it, but have contracted on terms that set the optimal level of precaution against it, and the wisdom of their spontaneous order is institutionalised in the common law of remedies. This would be swept away by the current criticism of that law, which therefore cannot respect the intentions of the parties. The most telling criticism of the performance interest and disgorgement damages is that the stress they place on performance could not be pursued as a goal unless freedom of contract in respect of choice of remedies were abolished.

The institutionalisation of economic choice in freedom of contract requires the law to refrain from imposing its own terms on contracts, and instead to strive to give effect to the intentions of the parties. That this requires, for example, ensuring that the price of goods, such as the £1 million for our steel, is the product of the parties' voluntarily agreed bargain is widely understood (though this is a much more complex matter than is usually appreciated, involving the state in much more than merely refraining from setting prices). What is much less widely understood is that freedom of contract also requires that the terms of the contract stipulating liability should also be the product of the parties' agreement, for this is essential to rational price formation and the efficient functioning of markets in general. For the 'fully contingent' price of goods includes not merely the cost of, as it were, the physical production of the goods, but also, *inter alia*, the cost of bearing the liability that the parties undertake by agreeing the contract, with its latent secondary obligation to provide a remedy.

Our argument now requires us to look at one aspect of the way this works in the developed system of commercial law, which turns on the concept of a 'default rule'. I have earlier described compensatory damages as the 'default' remedy for breach of contract. By the default remedy we mean the implicit term stipulating the remedy that will, in the absence of explicit agreement otherwise, apply by default. In the common law, these implicit terms are the product of the institutionalisation of commercial practice in cases guided by precedent. Subject to some important (but by no means always defensible) limits, which need not be mentioned here, the law does not make it mandatory that compensatory damages are the remedy for breach, but allows the parties to 'contract out of' or 'oust' this default rule by stipulating their own 'bespoke' rule governing remedies.

We can see the significance of this if we imagine that the steel in our example was not a generic good readily available in competitive supply, but a specially commissioned 'specific' good with special qualities, and no substitute was readily available for this steel. The seller's failure to deliver could not, in these circumstances, be met by covering, and the buyer would be faced with consequential loss. The causation rules could well pose the claimant serious difficulty in obtaining compensatory damages. Without entering into a discussion of the law, one can get a sense of the issues if we assume that, without the steel, the buyer is obliged to cancel construction of a new shopping centre, and so face loss of the net profit from retail sales. One might well concede that the buyer's ultimate net profit was, except in unusual circumstances, going to be positive, but imagine the problems of quantifying the loss in a way that allowed the court to, subject to the rules of causation mentioned above, compensate the claimant. The very same rules that allow compensatory damages to work so well in the relatively easy quantification of market damages make those damages generally inappropriate to the quantification of 'idiosyncratic' losses of this nature. The potential claimant who negotiates in ignorance of this can well be left with a very substantial uncompensated loss.[16]

A competent potential claimant faced with possible uncompensated loss under the default rule will (having reviewed other possibilities, such as obtaining insurance from a third party) negotiate to oust the default rule and replace it with one that imposes a liability on the potential defendant in which the potential claimant has confidence. Within the limits imposed by the law, he may, for example, require the potential defendant to post a bond that will be forfeited on breach, or stipulate a fixed sum which the potential defendant will pay on breach regardless of what the other party would have had to pay as compensatory damages, or try to make compulsory performance the remedy regardless

16 An excellent recent example, in which the issues were fully discussed by the Court of Appeal and the House of Lords, is *Co-operative Insurance Society Ltd* v. *Argyll Stores (Holdings) Ltd* [1996] Ch. 286 (CA); [1998] A.C. 1 (HL(E)).

of whether the special case normally required for this could have been made out. There are many other possible devices for securing 'real', rather than merely 'legal', remedies, which constitute a most important branch of advanced commercial law.

The device that concerns us here, which certainly is open to the potential claimant, is to stipulate disgorgement rather than compensatory damages as the remedy. But, of course, to get this into the contract, the potential claimant has to get the potential defendant to agree to it, and herein lies the problem for the potential claimant, and the source of the wisdom of spontaneous order. For the reason we have seen, compensatory damages are normally cheaper for the defendant than compulsory performance, and in negotiations in which this is an issue, *ex hypothesi* this is so, otherwise the defendant would be indifferent between compulsory performance and compensatory damages. The potential claimant may wish to get the extra security of primary performance that comes from making disgorgement damages the remedy, but the potential defendant will want payment for this as he is incurring extra liability, and so will have to take extra precautions against breach. He may, in our steel example, contract with two suppliers for the necessary iron ore, thereby greatly reducing the chance of failure of supply, even though he will incur avoidable costs in, for example, warehousing the consignment of ore he does not use making the steel for this contract. The range of means of taking extra precaution is very large, but the point is that all will impose extra cost. Though the physical steel will be the same, the price will be higher if disgorgement damages are the remedy because the liability will be higher.

Now, if the risk of idiosyncratic loss is high, the potential claimant may pay the higher price for steel, because the extra security, and ultimately extra precaution, will be of value to him. But when the exposure is to merely market damages in the normal way, the potential claimant will not pay the extra price, because the extra security, and ultimately extra precaution, has no value to him, as he can obtain a satisfactory substitute for undelivered goods on the market. In our steel example, if the steel is generic steel available on the market, then adequate security is provided by the ready availability of a substitute, and extra precaution is pointless. Depending on the extent of his exposure to idiosyncratic loss, the potential claimant will be prepared to pay for extra precaution, and negotiation between the parties will fix the optimal level of precaution. In extremely high-value contracts involving a high level of exposure to idiosyncratic loss, such as if special steel were required for shielding a nuclear power installation, the potential claimant may be prepared to pay for as near as possible absolute precaution, because this is the optimal level of precaution. But in normal cases in which cover is readily possible, such precaution would be a senseless waste for which no one would voluntarily pay, because the optimal level of precaution is much lower.

The absurd mistake made in the current criticisms of the law of remedies is to think that the law is unilaterally generous to the defendant. It is nothing of the sort. It is as generous (if this terminology may be used) to the defendant as the claimant and defendant have agreed. The claimant can avail himself of a lower price if he contracts on the basis of compensatory damages. This effectively requires him to cooperate in dealing with the mistaken agreement by providing his own remedy by taking cover, which keeps the defendant's liability, and therefore the price he will agree, low. If the claimant wants to impose heavier liability on the defendant, he can do so by negotiating with the defendant to do so, and paying for this. The law establishes a sophisticated cooperative basis on which competition and choice over the terms of the contract stipulating the remedy take place, and a spontaneous order coordinating optimal levels of precaution emerges.

The extent of the absurdity of seeing the current rules as unilaterally generous to the defendant emerges if we speculate on the consequences of changing the law to make disgorgement damages the default remedy. The potential defendant contracting on this basis would incur the higher level of liability and so would have to charge a higher price for the goods. Competition would quickly lead to sellers offering to sell on terms that explicitly ousted this default and replaced it with a bespoke compensatory damages clause, and, in the normal case, buyers would contract on these cheaper terms. There would be the extra transaction cost of having to contract away from a default that is unsuitable in the normal case (which is why compensatory damages now are the default), but the ultimate result would be the same. The only way to prevent this would be to make the disgorgement remedy mandatory by imposing it on the parties, so making it impossible for them to contract out of that remedy. The contradiction between the abstract legal criticisms of the current law of remedies and the law of contract that institutionalises choice as freedom of contract could not be more marked.

Conclusion: the complexity of spontaneous order and the morality of competition

This chapter has demonstrated, by reference to the important 'case study' of the fundamental questioning of the current law of remedies, that it is most ill advised to attempt to supplant the practical economic wisdom of spontaneous order with the products of abstract ratiocination about legal principle. Yet again, the pursuit of 'justice' as a goal is proving fruitless or damaging, as it is not appreciated that justice in the allocation of economic goods is not a goal but the quality of a process: '[i]n a free society the state does not administer the affairs of men. It administers justice among men who conduct their own affairs' (Lippmann, 1937: 267).

But I have another aim, one which, though subsidiary to the main argument, raises more important issues. It is obvious that my argument is a defence of spontaneous order. In this case, however, as in so many others, spontaneous order needs this defence because its nature is misunderstood. The questioning of the current law of remedies has gained its basic strength from its ability to depict the position in which the defendant can choose to breach if he pays the price of doing so as unacceptably amoral or immoral. At root, this is a criticism of what is taken to be pure economic action, with the breaching defendant portrayed as committing a wrong because his economic self-interest drives him to do so, in defiance of his legal, and therefore moral, obligations. As Professor Friedmann, whose formulation of the performance interest has been mentioned, has put it in criticising Mr Justice Holmes's analysis of paying for breach: 'such a taking of an entitlement, for the sake of private gain, runs counter to the very basis of private law' (Friedmann, 1989: 23). But the abstract, legal approach surely rests on a basic mistake. For economic action within the parameters of the common law is by no means immoral or amoral; and its value lies in the fact that it is neither.

Though there is an acknowledgement among all those committed to market ordering, save complete anarchists, that the legal 'enforcement' of contracts has a role in such ordering, this is put forward as a rather simple matter which should, indeed, be minimised by a state that conforms to liberal principles. But though we have looked only at the bare essentials of the law of remedies for breach of contract, it is obvious that the laissez-faire rhetoric of simplicity and minimalism will be found implausible by those who know the law of contract, for even those bare essentials involve, as we have seen, numerous complex 'choices' between remedial alternatives. If we follow Coase's definition of economic regulation as 'the establishment of the legal framework within which economic activity is carried out' (Coase, 1977: 5), then it becomes clear that the negativity of the typical liberal attitude towards the state's role in such regulation is far too sweeping. For though the point is to regulate *for* choice, not to regulate *for* the imposition of a pattern, the vital work of 'framework setting' or 'institutional direction' necessary for choice must be approached with a positive attitude, for inevitably it is a complex matter requiring extensive regulatory effort (Campbell and Klaes, 2005).

One particularly important aspect of the negativity of the typical liberal attitude to the role of law in the economy is its moral minimalism. Save anarchists, all those committed to market ordering acknowledge the role of the state in channelling maximising behaviour into productive lines to the extent of insisting that goods may legitimately be acquired only by exchange, rather than by force or fraud. But the difficulties of reconciling the other-regarding aspect of the exchange *relationship* with the explanation of economic action in terms of pure individual maximisation cannot be dealt with in this way, for we have seen that the law of contract establishes a fundamentally cooperative relationship between the parties within which competition about price takes place, and the optimum levels of precaution and liability, and therefore a rational price, are set. Without this cooperative relationship, rational price determination is impossible.

In sum, analysis of the basic legal framework for the sale of goods, the paradigm case of exchange envisaged in microeconomics at all levels of sophistication, from the high theoretical to the common practical, teaches us two things. First, that welfare-enhancing competition must be based on an ontologically prior cooperation between the parties to particular exchanges, and between economic actors in the market economy in general. And, second, that the framework for such cooperation, and therefore for defensible market ordering, has to be provided by more or less complex regulation in Coase's sense.

References

Campbell, D. (2004), 'The extinguishing of contract', *Modern Law Review*, 67(5): 817–43.

Campbell, D. (2005), 'The relational constitution of remedy: co-operation as the implicit second principle of remedies for breach of contract', *Texas Wesleyan Law Review*, 11(2): 455–80.

Campbell, D. and J. Devenney (2006), 'Damages at the borders of legal reasoning', *Cambridge Law Review*, 65(1): 207–25.

Campbell, D. and D. Harris (2002), 'In defence of breach: a critique of restitution and the performance interest', *Legal Studies*, 22(2): 208–37.

Campbell, D. and M. Klaes (2005), 'The principle of institutional direction: Coase's regulatory critique of intervention', *Cambridge Journal of Economics*, 29(2): 263–88.

Campbell, D. and P. Wylie (2003), 'Ain't no telling (which circumstances are exceptional)', *Cambridge Law Journal*, 62(3): 605–30.

Coase, R. H. (1977), 'Advertising and free speech', *Journal of Legal Studies*, 6(1): 1–34.

Farnsworth, E. A. (1970), 'Legal remedies for breach of contract', *Columbia Law Review*, 70(7): 1145–216.

Friedmann, D. (1989), 'The efficient breach fallacy', *Journal of Legal Studies*, 18(1): 1–24.

Friedmann, D. (1995), 'The performance interest in contract damages', *Law Quarterly Review*, 111: 628–54.

Harris, D. et al. (2002), *Remedies in Contract and Tort*, 2nd edn, Cambridge: Cambridge University Press.

Holmes, O. W., Jr (1881), *The Common Law*, Boston, MA: Little, Brown.

Lippmann, W. (1937), *The Good Society*, Boston, MA: Little, Brown.

Macaulay, S. (1963), 'The use and non-use of contracts in manufacturing industry', *Practical Lawyer*, 9(7): 13–40.

Von Neumann, J. (1956), 'Probabilistic logics and the synthesis of reliable organisms from unreliable components', in C. E. Shannon and J. McCarthy (eds), *Automata Studies*, Princeton, NJ: Princeton University Press, pp. 43–97.

8 LIMITED LIABILITY AND FREEDOM

Stephen F. Copp[1]

... the fact of a company being established on the principle of limited liability, does not strengthen the case in favour of ... restraints and safeguards ... It is not a question of privilege; if anything, it is a right ... The principle is the freedom of contract, and the right of unlimited association – the right of people to make what contracts they please on behalf of themselves, whether those contracts may appear to the Legislature beneficial or not, as long as they do not commit fraud, or otherwise act contrary to the general policy of the law. It is easy to make anything a privilege. Any right, the exercise of which is denied, becomes a privilege, the very term privilege arising from the negation of a natural right ... My object at present is not to urge the adoption of limited liability. I am arguing in favour of human liberty – that people may be permitted to deal how, with whom they choose, without the officious interference of the State ...

Robert Lowe, Hansard HC, vol. 140, cols 129–31 (1 February 1856)

Introduction

The concept of the limited liability company has become one of the most important legal foundations of a free market economy. There are sound economic reasons why. Limited liability may reduce the cost of capital, for example by encouraging investors to diversify rather than monitor and incentivising management to act efficiently (Easterbrook

---

1 This chapter is based on, and further develops, my doctoral research (Copp, 2003) and related papers (for example, Copp, 2004). I am grateful for the comments of the anonymous referees.

and Fischel, 1985: 93–101). It may enable risk to be allocated efficiently (Posner, 1976: 508–509) and facilitate organised securities markets (Halpern et al., 1980: 129–31, 147). Inevitably, there are detractors. Some criticise its role in the context of questioning big business, globalisation and economic growth (see, for example, Korten, 1995: 37–50, 53–68, 91–3, 99, 307–24). Some see limited liability as offending a moral principle that people should take personal responsibility for their debts (see, for example, Schluter, 2000). Some think limited liability is too widely cast, either because it can enable shareholders to evade tort liabilities (Hansmann and Kraakman, 1991: 1881), or is inappropriate for small businesses (Hicks, 1997: 104), or because it encourages undue risk-taking at creditors' expense (ibid.: 119; Freedman, 2000: 353). The policy implications of such arguments are very serious – should the availability of limited liability be restricted?

The formation of a limited liability company as a matter of right for most types of business activity (but not initially for banking and insurance companies; Hunt, 1936: 133, 136) first became possible with the Limited Liability Act 1855 (the '1855 Act'). It was a short piece of legislation, a mere nineteen sections. It simply amended and supplemented the existing and deeply unsatisfactory Joint Stock Companies Act 1844 (the '1844 Act'), which had enabled most types of unincorporated company to obtain incorporation by registration, but not limited liability. The introduction of general limited liability came only after considerable debate and discussion in a number of official committees over the best part of twenty years, involving some of the leading academic, professional and business figures of the day.[2] It was also a source of considerable press discussion.[3]

2 The Bellenden Ker Report (1837); a Select Committee on Investments for the Savings of the Middle and Working Classes (1850) (to which John Stuart Mill had given evidence); a Select Committee on the Law of Partnership (1851); and the First Report of the Royal Commission on the Mercantile Laws and the Law of Partnership (1854): it received only slight coverage in the well-known Gladstone Committee Report (1844).

3 See, for example, Lord Stanley's comments, Hansard HL, vol. 139, col. 1896 (7 August 1855).

The immediate pressure for the Limited Liability Bill (the 'Bill') appears to have resulted from the Board of Trade ceasing to take decisions on charters to create companies,[4] combined with the impact of the Crimea War.[5] There was strong popular feeling in favour of it, with Cardwell referring to 'the almost uniform feeling of the House and the country'.[6] The Marquess of Clanricarde noted, perhaps more accurately, that the great mass of the *middle classes* were in favour of the Bill because they were prevented from using their capital as they wanted.[7] It was regarded by the new prime minister, Viscount Palmerston, as being of the 'utmost interest and importance'.[8] The Bill had a rocky ride through Parliament: for example, on its second reading in the House of Lords there was a formal protest against the speed with which it had been 'forced' through Parliament.[9] Eventually, it was passed with the reluctant inclusion of some draconian amendments insisted upon by the House of Lords, receiving royal assent on 14 August 1855.[10]

The 1855 Act was the only occasion in this country's history when the liability regime has been substantially changed. This chapter seeks to answer the question why, by examining the records of the parliamentary debates (including those in committee) covering the Bill (the

4 This appears also to have extended to private Acts of Parliament for this purpose from the resolution subsequently put to the House of Lords: see Hansard HL, vol. 139, cols 1895–6 (7 August 1855).

5 Ball, Hansard HC, vol. 139, col. 1384 (26 July 1855); Earl Granville, Hansard HL, vol. 139, col. 1903 (7 August 1855); Lord Stanley, ibid., col. 1921 (7 August 1855); John Bright, who opposed the war, claimed in 1856 that the Palmerston administration rushed it through so it could say something had been done other than voting for the war (Davies, 1997: 44 n. 50).

6 Hansard HC, vol. 139, col. 340 (29 June 1855). See also Lord Stanley, Hansard HL, vol. 139, col. 1896 (7 August 1855); Laing, Hansard HC, vol. 139, col. 1392 (26 July 1855); and Cairns, ibid., col. 1397 (26 July 1855). Butler (1986: 181) thought Parliament was reacting to public demand, influenced by appreciation of the benefits of limited liability.

7 Hansard HL, vol. 139, col. 1910 (7 August 1855), author's emphasis.

8 Cairns, Hansard HC, vol. 139, cols 1396–7 (26 July 1855).

9 Hansard HL, vol. 139, col. 1918 (7 August 1855). Well-respected peers, such as Lord Overstone, who opposed limited liability, were missing: ibid., col. 1914 (7 August 1855).

10 Hansard HC, vol. 139, cols 2123–31 (11 August 1855); Hansard HL, vol. 139, cols 2141–2 (14 August 1855).

'1855 debates'). The arguments have been organised for convenience into the headings below (put in contemporary language and not reflecting the order in which issues arose):

- Limited liability was an integral characteristic of companies.
- Unlimited liability was impracticable to enforce.
- Contractual limited liability was unsatisfactory.
- Unlimited liability resulted in disproportionately high risk for investors and a suboptimal level of investment.
- Unlimited liability resulted in disproportionately low risk for creditors and led to an above-optimal level of credit being allocated to unmeritorious business activities.
- Limited liability would remove disincentives to enterprise, working-class investment and diversification.
- Limited liability was irrelevant to the incidence of incompetence/fraud.
- A right to limited liability would discourage the loss of company formations to more competitive jurisdictions.
- A right to limited liability would avoid the delay, inconsistencies and costs associated with discretionary government control and the influence of vested interests.
- Statutory limited liability was not inconsistent with freedom of trade and freedom of contract.
- Experimenting with limited liability was desirable to ascertain the most effective rule.
- *But* concessions were necessary over size and solvency regulation.

Limited liability was an integral characteristic of companies

Limited liability was seen as an integral characteristic of a company, not as something that could be separated from it. The importance of this can be seen from the prominence it received in Bouverie's speech, moving the second reading of the Partnership Amendment Bill. He criticised the 1844 Act for being injurious to completely registered joint-stock companies, by making their shareholders personally liable for debts for three years after ceasing to be members, despite limited liability being 'the grand characteristic of a corporation'.[11] The law was objectionable in recognising the merit of such companies but deterring those needed from joining them, i.e. those with large means and judgement.[12] He stressed the 'substantial distinction' between joint-stock companies that were technically partnerships but had been subject to statutory regulation, and private partnerships that were based on the common law.[13] Key factors were the transferability of shares at will, the limited voice of shareholders in management, and the lack of mutual knowledge and confidence between shareholders and directors, so that shareholders could be bound to an unlimited extent by the acts of a new set of directors despite not knowing them.[14] This is consistent with Easterbrook and Fischel's view (1985: 93) that limited liability, rather than being a benefit bestowed by the state, is a 'logical consequence' of the difference in forms of conducting economic activity.

Unlimited liability was impracticable to enforce

The law faced substantial difficulties under unlimited liability in coping with the number of parties potentially involved with large unincorporated joint-stock associations, i.e. promoters, shareholders, scrip holders, directors, trustees and creditors. In the event of a dispute, or failure, the matrix of potential litigation could be vast, combined with acute institutional and technological obstacles.

The first issue, identified in 1837 by the Bellenden Ker Report, was that relief could often not be obtained in legal proceedings involving large trading associations because they were usually regarded as partnerships

11 Hansard HC, vol. 139, col. 321 (29 June 1855).

12 Ibid.

13 Hansard HC, vol. 139, col. 310 (29 June 1855).

14 Ibid., cols 319–20 and 323–4 (29 June 1855).

at common law and, therefore, all partners had to be joined as defendants.[15] The absurdity of this was explained in George's (1825: 19–21) early practitioner text, *A View of the Existing Law Affecting Unincorporated Joint Stock Companies*. This explored the number and complexity of actions that might flow with a hypothetical association of 2,000 partners, a party who had bought goods on 25 different occasions, during which time there had been 300 changes in partners and six partner deaths leading to the admission of ten personal representatives, including the need to ascertain the exact time of each. Such concerns were not theoretical as *Van Sandau* v. *Moore*,[16] cited in the report, showed. As a consequence, such associations achieved a measure of de facto limited liability, which at the time led to them being regarded as a public nuisance on the fringes of legality. The risk of shareholders being party to litigation should have reduced as companies (new and old) gained incorporation under the 1844 Act, though the greater ease of litigation against companies may have increased the possibility of winding up.

The second issue related to the technical difficulties of winding up a substantial unlimited company with a large number of members, despite the introduction of various Winding-Up Acts in 1844, 1848 and 1849 (see generally Formoy, 1923: 73–76, 88–108). Some difficulties were institutional and capable of resolution – for example, conflict between court jurisdictions; others, however, were inherent to the exercise itself, given the numbers of creditors, shareholders and the multiplicity of proceedings required. Kostal (1994: 53) has described 'A Hurricane of Litigation', in which a 'sizeable proportion of the entire monied classes became participants in a vicious cross-fire of lawsuits'. What is surprising is that these problems were not used to justify limited liability, except for a cryptic remark by Lord Stanley, who based the urgency of the measure on how the law of unlimited liability had been found to be 'impracticable', if an attempt was made to enforce it with 'utmost vigour'.[17]

15 The Bellenden Ker Report (1837), p. 3.

16 (1825) 1 Russell's Reports 441.

17 Hansard HL, vol. 139, col. 1896 (7 August 1855).

Contractual limited liability was unsatisfactory

The question of whether companies needed state intervention to achieve limited liability has been controversial (see, for example, the criticisms by Mark (2000: 9–16) of Anderson and Tollison (1983)), yet seems to have preoccupied contemporaries less. As Earl Granville stated in the 1855 debates, referring to how limited liability could be achieved by contract: 'They had no right to consider that in passing this Bill they had discovered anything new.'[18] Language such as 'discovery' used by Butler, president of Columbia University in 1911 (Diamond, 1982: 42), to describe the emergence of limited liability would imply that the doctrine was new and the process swift. In contrast, the doctrine appears older than the mid-Victorian era, though its use may have been rare (DuBois, 1938: 223) and its meaning undoubtedly changed over time (see, for the seventeenth, eighteenth and early nineteenth centuries respectively, Scott, 1910: 270; DuBois, 1938: 94–104; and Harris, 2000: 127–32).

Evidence has been found of efforts to contract out of unlimited liability in the 1840s (Hunt, 1936: 99–101). The two methods adopted were either to place such a clause in the deed of association; alternatively, in every contract (insurance business particularly lent itself to this possibility). Each method was tested in the 1850s in the courts but only the latter proved acceptable. The constitutional method fell down because third parties could not have notice of it;[19] the contractual approach succeeded essentially because there was no reason to invalidate it.[20] Bouverie also drew attention to the specific example of mines in Devon and Cornwall conducting business on a limited liability basis because it had been decided at common law that the directors did not have the power to bind shareholders.[21]

The views of MPs in the 1855 debates show some confusion over the

18 Ibid., col. 2126 (11 August 1855).

19 *Re Sea, Fire & Life Assurance Co, Greenwood's case* (1854) 3 De G.M. & G. 459.

20 *Hallett* v. *Dowdall* (1852) 21 L.J. Q.B. 98. Butler (1986: 182) thought this decision explained the timing of Parliament giving up its monopoly control over limited liability.

21 Hansard HC, vol. 139, col. 326 (29 June 1855).

exact legal position. Palmerston and Lord Stanley clearly believed that limited liability could be achieved.[22] Bouverie, Cardwell, Spooner and Lord Stanley thought insurance companies could gain limited liability.[23] Spooner thought insurance companies enjoyed limited liability through their deed, but was informed by the Solicitor-General that that was not so.[24] The Solicitor-General proceeded to explain that limited liability was not new, liability arose only because every partner was considered the general agent of his partners, so if it were possible to limit that agency to make every person they dealt with aware of it, there would be no general liability.[25] These discussions focused on contractual liabilities. It is interesting that towards the end of the debates, Lord Redesdale asked about 'the nature of the liability' of manufacturing companies from which revenue had to be collected, i.e. excise duties; Lord Campbell responded that 'the managers' would be liable for any pecuniary penalties for any offence against the revenue, but the Earl of Harrowby argued that the company's own property would be sufficient security to the revenue.[26]

It is clear that companies could obtain some measure of limited liability by contract. This should not surprise us – attempts by companies and others to restrict their own liability (as opposed to shareholders') through exclusion clauses and other mechanisms are the staple diet of contract-law studies today. The lack of discussion on limiting liability for other risks does now seem surprising, especially given the legal literacy of those involved. It may reflect the undeveloped state of tort liability; on the other hand, Baker (1990: 467) has observed that 'By the beginning of Victoria's reign, actions for negligence were sufficiently numerous for some writers on the law to put them into a separate compartment', with the first specific example of such a collection of cases being published in 1843. From the vigour with which the arguments were pursued it can

22 Ibid., col. 356 (29 June 1855).
23 Ibid., cols 320 and 343 (29 June 1855), 1450 (27 July 1855) and Hansard HL, vol. 139, col. 1920 (7 August 1855).
24 Hansard HC, vol. 139, cols 1450–51 (27 July 1855).
25 Ibid.
26 Hansard HL, vol. 139, cols 2102–3 (10 August 1855).

only be concluded that contractual limited liability was not regarded as adequate.

Unlimited liability resulted in disproportionately high risk for investors and a suboptimal level of investment

There is a natural tendency to see the harsh state of English law governing personal financial failure as a likely contributor to the development of limited liability (see, for example, Harris, 2000: 131), because of the scale of risk to which it gave rise. Thanks to literary reformers, such as Charles Dickens, this area of law lives on in popular imagination. At the beginning of the nineteenth century, two systems governed personal financial failure – bankruptcy law, which applied only to traders with more than a minimum value of debt, and the law applicable to other debtors (Tolmie, 2003: 9). Opinion differs as to which system was more favourable.[27] Initially, debtors could be imprisoned for debt even before judgement, with no limit on the length of imprisonment (ibid.: 9). According to Stephen (1841–45: vol. 2, 214), 'the debtor might be left to languish, for an indefinite period of time, in hopeless confinement', a remedy described in the Cork Report (1982: 17) as 'the English equivalent of the slave trade'. It affected as many as 10,000 individuals annually, whose prospects were poor, with disease rampant (Harris, 2000: 131).[28] Reforms followed, however, with imprisonment after judgement for debt being abolished in 1869 (Tolmie, 2003: 9–10). Yet it is hard to find any strong criticism of the legal regime in the 1855 debates. Bouverie did not consider the changes would make any difference to the number of insolvencies or bankruptcies, since there would always be those incapable of managing their affairs.[29] Two MPs, Glyn and Mitchell, tried to use the need for bankruptcy law reform to delay consideration of limited

27 Contrast the Cork Report (pp. 16 and 17) and Tolmie (2003: 9), with Harris (2000: 131).

28 Unfortunately, the source is not cited. The period under discussion was generally 1721 to 1810.

29 Hansard HC, vol. 139, col. 1449 (27 July 1855).

liability.[30] But Lord Denman thought US and French bankruptcy law 'exceedingly severe' by comparison with English law.[31]

A key part of Bouverie's rationale for limited liability was that unlimited liability deterred 'men of prudence and capital', who were most likely to make a success of a company, from investing.[32] Strong feelings were expressed as to the plight of shareholders in unlimited companies, with Malins pointing to the collapses of the Newcastle Bank and the Monmouth and Glamorganshire Bank, which he claimed had been 'the ruin' of hundreds of families, and to the Australian Banking Company, which was being wound up, where probably more than 100 to 150 families 'would be utterly ruined'.[33] He contrasted the disproportionate effect of unlimited liability on investors, where a person had to risk the full extent of their fortune regardless of how small their real stake might be, referring to a 'morbid sensibility for the creditors', posing the question, 'Why should not the creditors be left to take care of themselves?'[34]

The consequence of investors being subjected to a disproportionate level of risk would be expected to be a suboptimal level of investment and it is, therefore, unsurprising that the need to encourage investment has featured highly in traditional accounts of the introduction of general limited liability. Shannon (1930–33: 291) thought Parliament reacted to the amount of capital not most productively employed. Hunt (1936: 32) cited evidence of 'masses of money' thrown away in South America because investors did not dare risk investing in England, implying both a demand for less risky investment and evidence of investors making a jurisdictional choice. There had been a Select Committee on Investments for the Savings of the Middle and Working Classes as recently as 1850.

Experience, especially with railway companies, indicated that limited

30 Ibid., cols 334 (29 June 1855) and 1391 (26 July 1855).

31 Hansard HL, vol. 139, col. 2050 (9 August 1855).

32 Hansard HC, vol. 139, col. 321 (29 June 1855). See also Lord Stanley, Hansard HL, vol. 139, col. 1920 (7 August 1855).

33 Hansard HC, vol. 139, cols 339–40 (29 June 1855).

34 Ibid.

liability did result in capital being attracted into economically desirable activities that might not otherwise have taken place. Bouverie showed how 914 companies had been completely registered under the 1844 Act, of which 723 were still in existence,[35] and how 136 limited liability companies, justified on the basis of public advantage, had been established in the previous five years by private Acts of Parliament.[36] The evidence supported his claim that limited liability should be extended because it was responsible for the immense capital raised for railways, docks and canals.[37]

Some, though, did not think it necessary to encourage more investment. Muntz claimed that the repeal of the usury laws had removed obstacles[38] and Hastie contrasted the position with the USA, where capital was extremely scarce.[39] Investment was demonised as 'speculation', an argument anticipated by Bouverie. Muntz argued that the real reason for the Bill was to induce those with capital to embark in speculations returning 5, 10 or 15 per cent rather than 3 per cent from funds or 4 per cent from land.[40] Bouverie, in contrast, thought speculation should not just mean rash and imprudent undertakings but could also mean the spirit of enterprise and progress.[41]

35 Hansard HC, vol. 139, col. 321 (29 June 1855). The main categories were 234 gas companies, 198 assurance companies, 99 mining companies, 78 public buildings companies, 74 manufacturing companies, 58 land and building (etc.) companies, 43 shipping companies, 40 public works companies, 18 railway companies and 14 trading companies.

36 Ibid., col. 324 (29 June 1855): 76 railway companies; 11 harbours, piers, docks, bridges or canals companies; 10 gas companies; 22 water companies; and 17 miscellaneous companies. Lord Stanley also emphasised this: Hansard HL, vol. 139, col. 1897 (7 August 1855).

37 Hansard HC, vol. 139, col. 325 (29 June 1855), giving the example of £285 million raised for railways. See also Malins, ibid., col. 339 (29 June 1855) and Laing, ibid., cols 1392–3 (26 July 1855). Russell, though, observed that such companies did not go to Parliament only for limited liability but also for powers over land: ibid., cols 1393–4 (26 July 1855).

38 Ibid., col. 1379 (26 July 1855).

39 Ibid., cols 1379, 1393 (26 July 1855). See also Strutt, ibid., col. 1385 (26 July 1855).

40 Ibid., col. 1381 (26 July 1855).

41 Ibid., col. 327 (29 June 1855).

Unlimited liability resulted in disproportionately low risk for creditors and led to an above-optimal level of credit being allocated to unmeritorious business activities

The belief 'that every man was bound to pay the debts he had contracted, so long as he was able to do so', described by Strutt as 'the first and most natural principle of commercial legislation',[42] emerged in the 1855 debates, as might be expected from an era so steeped in moral notions of personal responsibility. It led to a high degree of commitment, such that both Bouverie, who supported limited liability, and Muntz, who did not, thought that companies could not compete with private traders.[43] As Muntz put it, 'No Company could command that decision of purpose, that untiring exertion, and that concentrated power which an individual, whose sole interest was at stake, could always display.' This, combined with unlimited liability, could be expected to contribute to economic efficiency by ensuring the making of credible commitments. Such arguments were flawed, however: shareholders should not be morally responsible for the actions of others, i.e. directors, whom they could not control.

Experience showed that unlimited liability enabled undesirable businesses to raise capital – Bouverie commented on losses of £50 million involving companies with unlimited liability – and prevented '*bona fide* and beneficial undertakings' from doing so.[44] He argued that credit should be obtained because of how a company's business was conducted and what its objects were, rather than because of the size of the shareholders' combined fortune.[45] In contrast, such companies obtained an 'unfair and undue amount of credit'.[46] Malins blamed the collapses of the

42 Ibid., col. 1386 (26 July 1855).

43 Bouverie was influenced by Adam Smith, ibid., cols 328–9 (29 June 1855); Muntz, ibid., cols 1379–80 (26 July 1855).

44 Ibid., col. 1449 (27 July 1855); ibid., col. 322 (29 June 1855): Bouverie, citing the evidence of a London solicitor.

45 Ibid., col. 322 (29 June 1855). See also Lord Stanley, Hansard HL, vol. 139, col. 2038 (9 August 1855), who referred to them as 'decoy ducks' placed at the head of unsound undertakings.

46 Hansard HC, vol. 139, col. 322 (29 June 1855).

Australian Banking Company, the Newcastle Bank and the Monmouth and Gloucester Bank on precisely this problem.[47] In particular, had those who had lent £300,000 to the Australian Banking Company been forced to inquire as to its state and prospects, rather than merely seeing a list of shareholders whom 'they could pounce on', they would not have lent their money.[48] He contrasted railway companies, where money was invested or lent because people were satisfied with their position and administration as well as because of limited liability.[49]

Unlimited liability, it seems, increased the optimal level of risk-taking by creditors and led to an above-optimal level of credit being allocated to unmeritorious business activities, the mirror image of the criticism that limited liability increases the optimal level of risk-taking. This would seem inappropriate given the greater control creditors had over the extent of their exposure – for example, through the use of security. It might be expected that those supplying capital on the basis of unlimited liability would reflect the perceived risk in the price, rendering the cost of capital higher – needlessly, since not all companies would require the 'guarantee' implied by unlimited liability.[50] Equally, it might be expected that creditors dealing with a limited liability company would also reflect any perceived risk in the price and/or by taking security (but only where needed).[51] Limited liability, therefore, might be expected to lead to a more efficient allocation of resources.

47 Ibid., col. 340 (29 June 1855).

48 Ibid.

49 Ibid.

50 But see Anderson and Tollison (1983: 114–15), who argue that limited liability would not have altered the real cost of capital.

51 Halpern et al. (1980: 118– 19) note an argument from *The Economist*, 1 July 1854, that the liability issue was trite because parties could transact around it. The issue would only seem trite, however, if each liability regime could be contracted into/out of with equal ease, which may not have been so.

Limited liability would remove disincentives to enterprise, working-class investment and diversification

Bouverie's essentially free market argument was that 'legislators ought not to place any dam across the channels in which capital was disposed to run'.[52]

The need to remove disincentives to enterprise was recognised by Bouverie, who claimed in his speech on partnership law that Parliament had a duty to encourage inventors.[53] Palmerston asserted that there was a great quantity of small capital locked up which might be employed both for the benefit of those who possessed it and the community at large.[54] The consequences of restricting new ventures were well illustrated by his claim that Ireland's prosperity had been damaged by the inability of one group to work coal and iron because they had been refused a charter and were unprepared to give the security required by Glasgow or Liverpool speculators.[55] Muntz, though, queried the benefits for inventors, suggesting that under limited liability the work of Watt would have 'come under the control of a few ignorant donkeys, who knew nothing about his works, and ... all the inventions of that great man would have come to nothing'.[56]

Widening participation in limited liability companies might also enable the working classes to invest in, and attract capital into, businesses for which they provided the skills. John Mill had famously commented in evidence to a Select Committee that the great value of limited liability would not be so much to enable the poor to lend to the rich but the rich to the poor (Davies, 1997: 42). Collier claimed that limited liability might 'bridge over the gulf which divided capital and labour'.[57] Limited liability companies were considered by some, though,

52 Ibid., col. 329 (29 June 1855).

53 Ibid., col. 314 (29 June 1855).

54 Ibid., col. 1390 (26 July 1855). See also Lord Stanley, Hansard HL, vol. 139, col. 1921 (7 August 1855).

55 Hansard HC, vol. 139, col. 1456 (27 July 1855).

56 Ibid., col. 1381 (26 July 1855).

57 Ibid., col. 333 (29 June 1855). See also Malins, ibid., col. 340 (29 June 1855) and Mitchell, ibid., col. 1392 (26 July 1855).

to be unsuitable vehicles for working-class investment, either because the working class would be 'totally ignorant' of how to nurture them, or they would be used by lawyers floating companies simply to get long bills paid or by companies being established so paid officials could profit from their salaries.[58] Instead, Strutt thought working men should stick to a secure investment at an ordinary rate of interest or in a trade they could superintend personally.[59]

Unlimited liability would also have discouraged investment by discouraging diversification. McGregor appears to have understood this point, arguing for limited liability with the illustration that a man with £140,000 would not risk the whole of it in one ship, but would rather divide it up and invest in different ships.[60] In contrast, Strutt criticised limited liability for encouraging a limited chance of loss but unlimited chance of gain:[61] a point that is stressed in modern option-pricing approaches to the valuation of firms and also in relation to the incentives facing executives of modern banking institutions. Limited liability would damage trust by allowing a person to invest in several speculations, making a fortune in a number but failing in one while paying creditors a fraction of their debts.[62] This is interesting because it implies that limited liability and diversification would damage the making of credible commitments, potentially reducing economic efficiency. The benefits of enabling diversification would, however, appear to have been much more significant.

58 Muntz, ibid., col. 1379 (26 July 1855); Lord Redesdale, Hansard HL, vol. 139, col. 2042 (9 August 1855); and Lord Monteagle, ibid., col. 2041 (9 August 1855).

59 Hansard HC, vol. 139, cols 1387–8 (26 July 1855).

60 Ibid., col. 1388 (26 July 1855).

61 Ibid., col. 1385 (26 July 1855).

62 Strutt, ibid., cols 1385–6 (26 July 1855). As Bramley-Moore put it: 'a man might be a bankrupt in one street, and a wealthy merchant prince around the corner … this was irreconcilable with sound morality': ibid., col. 1447 (27 July 1855).

Limited liability was irrelevant to the incidence of incompetence/fraud

Strong cycles of boom and bust tend to reveal incompetence and fraud. The early nineteenth-century economy was subject to fairly dramatic cycles, with major harvest crises in 1815–16, 1829, 1838 and 1847, and depressions in basic industries in 1816, 1826–27, 1842–43 and 1848–49 (Mathias, 2001: ch. 7).[63] What is surprising now is the sheer crudeness of the methods of fraud. Many were analysed in the Gladstone Committee Report,[64] which led to the 1844 Act. Fraudulent means of seeking investment, for example, included using the names of distinguished, respectable or wealthy people without their authority and getting false newspaper reports published. But it seems that the cumbersome 1844 Act actually worsened the problem of fraud (Kostal, 1994: 35). Instead of deterring prospective bubble company promoters, it went disastrously wrong, giving speculators and swindlers a 'gloss of legality and legitimacy' with the opportunity to get a Certificate of Provisional Registration for little more than a £5 fee (ibid.). But it was not necessarily just government which was at fault – the difficulties may have been compounded by the courts' moral uncertainty as to who should bear losses (Lobban, 1996: 299–303).

Competence was central to Bouverie's rationale for limited liability because he blamed unlimited liability for companies falling into the hands of 'the reckless, thoughtless, and extravagant' and discouraging the prudent from investing[65] (though this would appear more a comment on investors than directors). Concerns were later raised by Muntz about directors' competence and the fear they would become masters rather than servants of the company[66] – nicely anticipating modern agency theory. But Bouverie's position was that it was not the duty of a legislator

63 See also Strutt's concerns regarding speculation and periodic crises, ibid., cols 1385–6 (26 July 1855).

64 'First Report of the Select Committee on Joint Stock Companies' (1844) ('the Gladstone Committee Report').

65 Bouverie, ibid., col. 321 (29 June 1855).

66 Ibid., cols 1381 and 1379 (26 July 1855).

to prevent imprudence, the real preventative for which was the resulting loss.[67] In other words, risk of failure was an important incentive.

Bouverie did not seek to deny that the Bill – which he was aware had been called 'a Bill to promote swindling' – might give rise to a great deal of fraud but observed how fraud took place in companies with unlimited liability too.[68] The point was that the public ignored the enormous mass of fair and honest transactions that took place.[69] While it was one of the 'great objects of the law ... to prevent fraud', this should be done by detecting and punishing fraud where it existed, rather than prohibiting a class of honest and advantageous transactions.[70] But no law would be able to prevent fraud because those who cheated would always find loopholes.[71] Earl Grey, for example, was unconvinced, claiming that even those most in favour of limited liability thought 'stringent precautions' were needed to guard against fraud, though his illustrations of the risks mainly involved small companies.[72]

How, though, might accountability be improved? Bouverie felt that the most effective way to secure shareholder and creditor interests in the long term was to call on them to protect themselves, in respect of both fraud and imprudence.[73]

A right to limited liability would discourage the loss of company formations to more competitive jurisdictions

Jurisdictional competition can lead to a Pareto-optimal (i.e. first-best) outcome if fairly rigorous assumptions are met – for example, if there is a perfectly elastic supply of jurisdictions (Trachtman, 2000: 338). We

67 Ibid., col. 327 (29 June 1855).
68 Ibid., cols 326 (29 June 1855) and 1449 (27 July 1855).
69 Ibid., col. 326 (29 June 1855).
70 Ibid., col. 326 (29 June 1855).
71 Ibid., col. 1449 (27 July 1855).
72 Hansard HL, vol. 139, cols 2032–4 (9 August 1855).
73 Hansard HC, vol. 139, col. 327 (29 June 1855). See also Earl Granville, Hansard HL, vol. 139, col. 2045 (9 August 1855).

can think of competition, in this context, as the process through which resources are allocated when prices are not distorted by monopoly: it does not imply rivalry, as it might in other contexts (Posner, 2003: 294). It might be tempting to conclude that the concept could have only a very restricted application in the context of the mid-nineteenth century as few jurisdictions offered any form of alternative corporate law, but the evidence suggests otherwise. We have already seen the influence of investors preferring overseas investment opportunities.

The arguments in the 1855 debates appear to have been between the realists, who recognised that an element of choice had arrived and could not be restricted, and those who were in denial. Bouverie saw that prohibiting limited liability companies resulted in those determined to have them forming companies abroad, while still carrying on business in England.[74] There was evidence from a London solicitor that such companies were 'frequently' being established in France (at least twenty in the previous two years) and the USA, despite the typical cost in France, for example, being between £400 and £500 per year, and in one case £4,000.[75] Lord Stanley claimed that a steam navigation company, refused a charter, obtained one in Canada, and that whole trades, carried on 30 years earlier by English houses, had been replaced by foreign branches.[76] MacGregor perhaps touched a raw nerve in saying that limited liability had made the USA one of the most powerful nations in the world, especially in naval power,[77] while Laing, commenting on how dividends paid by limited liability French and Belgian railway companies exceeded 10 per cent, warned that Paris could replace London as 'the great centre of European industrial enterprise'.[78]

The arguments of those in denial, however, were largely irrelevant to such immediate risks. Glyn noted that the reason for the introduction

74 Hansard HC, vol. 139, col. 322 (29 June 1855).

75 Ibid., col. 323 (29 June 1855).

76 Hansard HL, vol. 139, cols 1919 and 2037 (7 and 9 August 1855).

77 Hansard HC, vol. 139, col. 1388 (26 July 1855); he also raised the success of limited liability in other countries, such as the Hanse towns, Belgium and Holland (ibid.).

78 Ibid., col. 1393 (26 July 1855).

of limited liability in France had been different, aimed at countering the prejudices of the upper classes against investing in trade.[79] Cardwell cited evidence that the law did not always work well in other countries, mainly because of potential abuse and limited take-up.[80] Brown commented that limited liability damaged the credit of companies in France and the USA, and Hastie that countries with limited liability needed to come to England for credit.[81]

The existence of even a rudimentary level of jurisdictional competition renders the concession theory, that companies require government permission, meaningless, since a concession implies a monopoly. If states themselves are seen as rational actors, then it would be expected that they would act in a self-interested fashion, maximising their own welfare, and the introduction of a more competitive company law, with a right to limited liability, should be interpreted accordingly.

A right to limited liability would avoid the delay, inconsistencies and costs associated with discretionary government control and the influence of vested interests

Incorporation with limited liability could formally be achieved in three ways by 1855: private Act of Parliament, requiring a petition to Parliament; royal charter; or letters patent, requiring an application to the Crown, but referred to the Privy Council Committee for Trade and Plantations.[82] The use of discretionary routes to incorporation would be expected to give rise to problems. Governments are unlikely ever to

79 Ibid., col. 1382 (26 July 1855).

80 Ibid., col. 348 (29 June 1855). Hastie also noted that in France there were 2,000 partnerships without limited liability and only 400 with it; ibid., col. 357 (29 June 1855).

81 Ibid., col. 1384 (26 July 1855); ibid., col. 357 (29 June 1855). See also Bramley-Moore, ibid., cols 1448–9 (27 July 1855); Hastie, ibid., col. 1450 (27 July 1855); and Lord Monteagle, Hansard HL, vol. 139, cols 2040–41 (9 August 1855).

82 Chartered Companies Act 1837, s. 4, included an express power for members' liability to be restricted when incorporation privileges (but not actual incorporation) were conferred by letters patent. Limited liability could not be obtained under the better-known Joint Stock Companies Act 1844.

have sufficient knowledge or expertise to exercise such discretion, and it would be expected that delay, inconsistencies, cost and corruption would result, combined with vested interests seeking to gain influence.

Kostal (1994: 114–15) has graphically described how the private Bill process had hardly changed in 100 years, with pre-hearing documentation of 'labyrinthine complexity' and examination by select committees of both Houses of Parliament. Alleged delay on the part of the Board of Trade in dealing with a petition for a charter to set up a paper and textile manufacturing company based in the West Indies between October 1854 and March 1855 led to the formal statement by Lord Stanley that the Partnership Amendment Bill (with which the Bill was to be linked) would be forthcoming.[83] Bouverie used this to make the issue a matter of urgency.[84] Laing observed that delay in getting a charter was an even greater obstacle than cost.[85] Delay, coupled with discretion and requirements for public disclosure,[86] may also have provided vested interests with an opportunity for influence.

The problem of discretion affected both parliamentary and Board of Trade proceedings in different ways. In relation to Parliament, Bouverie made the perhaps obvious comment that if procedural changes could be made so that every company applying for a private Act was granted limited liability, legislation would be pointless.[87] He also attacked the Board of Trade for failing to approve applications for charters, arguing that it was not competent[88] and mocking the tests applied – for example, whether an undertaking was advantageous to the public – claiming that the true test of public advantage was a company's success or non-success.[89] More to the point, he criticised the power to determine

83 Hansard HL, vol. 137, cols 943–6 (22 March 1855).
84 Hansard HC, vol. 139, col. 1394 (26 July 1855). See also Lord Stanley, Hansard HL, vol. 139, col. 1897 (7 August 1855).
85 Hansard HC, vol. 139, col. 1393 (26 July 1855).
86 See, for example, Trading Companies Act 1837, s. 32.
87 Hansard HC, vol. 139, col. 324 (29 June 1855).
88 Ibid., col. 325 (29 June 1855).
89 Ibid. See also Cairns, ibid., cols 353–4 (29 June 1855) and Hunt (1936: 57–8).

limited liability according to the 'caprice' of who happened to be head of the department, as 'odious'.[90] The consequence of relying on government discretion, according to Bouverie, was the inconsistency of some companies in the same class, such as gas companies, having limited liability but others not.[91] This might be expected to have had competitive implications, with limited liability companies benefiting from government discretion having an unfair advantage over others.

Costs were more likely to have been a greater problem for smaller businesses than for large ones and, in the case of canal companies and railway companies after the 1790s and 1820s respectively, probably resulted from the introduction of requirements to submit detailed maps and plans with their petitions (Harris, 2000: 135).[92] This might explain the sort of charges cited by Todd (1932: 50) for incorporating railway companies such as the London and Birmingham Railway, ranging from £28,465 to £72,868, and Kostal's (1994: 126) estimate of £20 million spent by the railway industry by 1855 (which included the costs of preparing, promoting and *opposing* petitions). According to Laing, the 'enormous amount of Parliamentary expenses' was often enough to prevent a company starting where its capital was not large.[93]

Discretionary procedures with high monetary stakes would have provided the incentive for corruption (see, for example, Anderson and Tollison (1983: 112), who acknowledge that evidence of corruption would be 'understandably sparse') and enhanced the influence of vested interests. A detailed review by Harris (2000: 135) indicates the severity of problems caused by vested interests: for example, individuals who controlled sectors such as flour milling and brewing would unite to resist newcomers. There is, however, a fair amount of evidence from the 1820s of problems, generally of a conflict-of-interest nature (Hunt,

90 Hansard HC, vol. 139, col. 325 (29 June 1855). See also Lord Stanley, Hansard HL, vol. 139, col. 1897 (7 August 1855), and Cardwell, Hansard HC, vol. 139, col. 341 (29 June 1855).

91 Ibid., col. 324 (29 June 1855).

92 See also Lord Stanley, Hansard HL, vol. 139, col. 1897 (7 August 1855).

93 Hansard HC, vol. 139, col. 1393 (26 July 1855).

1936: 49 n. 103; Harris, 2000: 262–3). A not untypical example related to 1824, when sixteen MPs, who held shares of up to £30,000 each in a joint-stock company whose incorporation bill was pending, sat on the relevant committee (Harris, 2000: 263). Indeed, a motion put before Parliament in 1824 and 1825, which would have restricted voting by MPs with an interest in a Bill, was defeated (ibid.: 264). Closer to the period in question, the president of the Board of Trade, C. P. Thomson, who introduced the Trading Companies Act 1834, appears to have had 'various company interests' (Cooke, 1950: 125).

Vested business interests had long opposed private Acts to incorporate businesses with limited liability. This appears borne out by Lord Stanley's example of a large steam navigation company that had wanted limited liability to establish communication with Canada but had been refused a charter because of the opposition of Cunard and other existing companies.[94] Accordingly, a similar reaction against a Bill to allow incorporation with limited liability might have been expected. And so it was. Horsfall claimed that a majority of the commercial community opposed limited liability, citing several days' discussion at the Liverpool Chamber of Commerce, which decided against by a majority of about 200 to 100, with the strongest protest being in a petition from the Manchester Chamber of Commerce.[95] Malins observed how great capitalists with great power as a result were mostly opposed to the Bill because it could reduce their influence.[96] Ball came close to accusing another MP of hypocrisy, saying that he had amassed great wealth through competition but was refusing to others advantages he did not need.[97]

The presence of lawyers in Parliament might also have been a fertile source of vested interests, since lawyers had been very actively involved in company promotions (see generally Kostal, 1994: chs 1 and 3). Care

94 Hansard HL, vol. 139, col. 1919 (7 August 1855).

95 Hansard HC, vol. 139, col. 355 (29 June 1855).

96 Ibid., col. 340 (29 June 1855).

97 Ibid., col. 1383 (26 July 1855). See also MacGregor, ibid., cols 1388–9 (26 July 1855); Muntz, ibid., col. 1379 (26 July 1855).

must be taken, however, in rushing to conclusions, as by 1832 the proportion of lawyers had fallen below 10 per cent, though it did rise to 10.8 per cent after the 1841 election and 15.4 per cent after the 1852 election (Rush and Baldwin, 1998: 155–6). Also, such an interpretation would be inconsistent with the adoption of penal provisions targeted at lawyers (Kostal, 1994: 26, referring to s. 6 of the 1844 Act). Some of the leading figures in the 1855 debates were indeed lawyers. Bouverie, Cardwell, Collier and Laing were all qualified as barristers. Lowe had done well financially in Australia from a law practice before entering political life in England (Parry, 2004: 2). Muntz tried to argue that because lawyers favoured the Bill, it demonstrated that it would open a wide field for litigation.[98]

Exclusionary behaviour on the part of vested interests was anti-competitive in nature. The importance of competition was recognised by Bouverie, who argued that 'There ought to be no legal impediments in the way of competition'.[99] There was undoubtedly a fear of the potentially anti-competitive nature of limited companies, nicely expressed some years before the 1855 Act in *Kinder* v. *Taylor* by the Lord Chancellor,[100] who questioned whether the time was coming when people would not be allowed to eat, drink or wear clean linen except on terms that companies imposed. Glyn feared that shopkeepers in small towns would be injuriously affected by the Bill and that there appeared to be no security to prevent small companies being started in small towns to run down small traders.[101] Bouverie had anticipated such arguments, however, making the point that if limited liability enabled the public to be served more cheaply and better then it should be permitted.[102]

98 Ibid., cols 1381–2 (26 July 1855).

99 Ibid., col. 329 (29 June 1855). There was also debate as to whether banking, insurance companies, building societies and friendly societies should be excluded, which bears on issues of competition; see ibid., cols 320, 329–30, 339, 347 (29 June 1855), 1445–7, 1451 (27 July 1855).

100 (1825) 3 L.J. Ch. 68, cited in Hunt (1936: 39).

101 Hansard HC, vol. 139, col. 1518 (30 July 1855). There were similar warnings by Cardwell, ibid., col. 1454 (27 July 1855), Hastie, ibid., col. 1710 (2 August 1855) and Lord St Leonards, Hansard HL, vol. 139, col. 2029 (9 August 1855).

102 Hansard HC, vol. 139, col. 328 (29 June 1855).

Interestingly, the arguments moved beyond criticism of discretionary powers towards conceptualising limited liability as a right. Collier claimed that people had the 'right' to limit their liability without special Acts of Parliament or special favour from the Board of Trade.[103] Cardwell argued that the law should be available 'with perfect equality' to all persons and that officials should be 'ministers', implying servants, and not 'dispensers' of the law.[104] Bouverie stated that the decision should depend on some fixed and intelligible rule laid down by Parliament.[105] Cardwell objected to a high minimum capital because the law should be made equal for everyone 'whatsoever … the amount of their property' and not favour one class of the community over another.[106]

Government discretion, especially over significant economic activity, presents severe problems. The early Victorians discovered the limits of such control over economic activity. The choices are indeed simple: limited liability companies can be made illegal (suboptimal and likely to lead to black-market alternatives); made subject to a discretionary power (suboptimal as it increases transaction costs and decreases competition); or permitted as a matter of right (the eventual solution).

Statutory limited liability was not inconsistent with free trade and freedom of contract

On the face of it, the introduction of statutory limited liability might appear to have been the greatest act of state intervention in business of all time. It might, therefore, seem odd that this was justified on the basis of free trade, freedom of contract and freedom of association.

Free trade had been a rallying cry in the movement against the protectionist Corn Laws in the 1840s. Some, such as Palmerston, argued

103 Ibid., vol. 139, col. 333 (29 June 1855).
104 Ibid., col. 341 (29 June 1855).
105 Ibid., col. 1394 (26 July 1855).
106 Ibid., col. 1455 (27 July 1855).

that the introduction of limited liability was a question of 'free trade'.[107] Henley objected to a proposed £20,000 minimum capital and the exclusion of insurance companies and banks on the ground that these were inconsistent with free trade.[108] Collier praised the Bill for recognising the principle of freedom of contract, which he saw as a corollary of freedom of trade and freedom of navigation.[109] Limited liability, in Lowe's view, depended on: '... *freedom of contract* – that men might contract as they pleased, provided it was a contract in which each party had a perfect knowledge of the whole state of the case'.[110]

Bouverie expressed this differently, saying that it was the duty of a legislator to remove all impediments on commerce, provided that contracts were fulfilled and people left to ascertain the different ways of carrying on in business.[111] Lowe, significantly, linked limited liability not only to freedom of contract but also to 'the right of association'.[112]

These assertions attracted strong objections. Palmerston expressed surprise that the Bill was opposed by some of the most strenuous and successful advocates of free trade, arguing that it was a question of free trade against monopoly and that the 'contest lies between the few and the many'.[113] This link between limited liability and free trade was not unreasonable given the evidence that vested interests could obstruct market entry by opposing new charters. Strutt criticised the inconsistency of justifying limited liability as a matter of free trade, arguing that free trade would be violated by imposing restrictions in the terms of contracts.[114] Yet it is hard to see how the right to limited liability did this.

107 Ibid., cols 356–7 (29 June 1855). See also the Marquess of Lansdowne, Hansard HL, vol. 139, cols 2123–4 (11 August 1855).

108 Hansard HC, vol. 139, cols 1392 (26 July 1855) and 1446 (27 July 1855).

109 Ibid., col. 329 (29 June 1855).

110 Ibid., col. 352 (29 June 1855); emphasis added.

111 Ibid., col. 329 (29 June 1855).

112 Ibid., col. 352 (29 June 1855). The Circular to Bankers in 1855 put this nicely, claiming '... the liberty to associate for purposes of trade is undoubtedly a fundamental principle in the civil rights of nations' (Hunt, 1936: 123).

113 Hansard HC, vol. 139, cols 1390 (26 July 1855) and 1389 (26 July 1855).

114 Ibid., col. 1387 (26 July 1855). See also Dillwyn, ibid., col. 1395 (26 July 1855).

Malins pointed out that the Bill would give everyone fair notice that in dealing with a company they had nothing to look to but the company's assets, and it was a creditor's own fault if he were not paid,[115] and the Lord Chancellor that where people joined together and made only their stock liable then they had fulfilled their contract.[116] Pragmatically, Lowe commented that it was not necessary to trade with a limited company on a credit basis.[117]

The emphasis on freedom of contract may seem surprising, and limited liability now might perhaps be seen as being more important in supporting the establishment and maintenance of property rights in shares. As Ireland (2003: 462–4) has pointed out, from the 1830s onwards the way in which companies were being perceived was changing, with the decontractualisation of company law and the reconceptualisation of shares as 'autonomous and freely transferable forms of property', paving the way for the company to be seen as 'a separate, property-owning legal person'. While there was some recognition of this in how a partnership and company were carefully distinguished, it does not appear to have been an important consideration compared with liability issues. In contrast, Lord St Leonards saw limited liability as interference with property, taking away part of creditors' security.[118]

Experimenting with limited liability was desirable to ascertain the most effective rule

The willingness of those who supported limited liability in the 1855 debates to take legislative risks is striking. Bouverie, in closing his opening speech for the Bill, argued that it was necessary to make the experiment because otherwise it would not be possible to say what

115 Hansard HC, vol. 139, col. 1523 (30 July 1855).
116 Hansard HL, vol. 139, col. 2047 (9 August 1855).
117 Hansard HC, vol. 139, col. 1523 (30 July 1855).
118 Hansard HL, vol. 139, col. 2047 (9 August 1855).

the result would be.[119] Lord Stanley thought that objections to the Bill were influenced by a 'superstitious dread' of changing things thought to contribute to prosperity.[120] Associated with this was the ability of a leading figure, such as Bouverie, to refer to the work of prominent economists, including Adam Smith and Say.[121] But some were more cautious. Cardwell referred to John Mill as a man of 'very great eminence ... who had taken much interest in the subject' and whose views carried 'such weight', but added that they needed to know how far they were sustained by his authority.[122] Glyn, also referring to Mill, cautioned the House against hurrying 'into rash legislation upon mere abstract principles'.[123]

Adaptive efficiency, as North (1990: 80–81) has argued, is all about:

> ... the willingness of a society to acquire knowledge and learning, to induce innovation, to undertake risk and creative activity of all sorts, as well as to resolve problems and bottlenecks of the society through time ... The society that permits the maximum generation of trials will be most likely to solve problems through time.

In contrast, path dependence leads to inefficiency, where organisations and vested interests gain a stake in existing constraints and give rise to a supporting ideology and policies to reinforce them (ibid.: 99). The willingness to experiment here, supported by economic reasoning conducive to free markets, undoubtedly resulted in breaking with existing paths, in which vested interests had clearly gained a stake. The use of statutory intervention for this purpose was impossible to avoid by 1855, given the background of statutory intervention. As a consequence, however, the statutory character of the limited liability company became susceptible to political interference.

119 Ibid., col. 329 (29 June 1855). See also the Marquess of Lansdowne, Hansard HL, vol. 139, col. 2123 (11 August 1855).

120 Hansard HL, vol. 139, col. 1921 (7 August 1855).

121 Hansard HC, vol. 139, col. 315 (29 June 1855); ibid, col. 328 (29 June 1855).

122 Ibid., col. 345 (29 June 1855).

123 Ibid., col. 335 (29 June 1855).

... but concessions were necessary over size and solvency regulation

While the arguments in favour of limited liability proved persuasive, there were already many restrictions on gaining incorporation in the 1844 Act, which were temporarily to continue, and further regulation of the size and solvency of limited liability companies was included in the 1855 Act. Pragmatically, Palmerston thought it sensible to accept some restrictions as a sacrifice to get the Bill through.[124] Yet the debate over what restrictions should be attached demonstrated that the ancient legal doctrine that incorporation was a government concession was still alive and kicking.[125] While Lowe would have removed all restrictions, claiming that no MP who had addressed the House had ventured to follow his principles to their logical conclusion,[126] Cairns justified restrictions, arguing that:

> When Parliament was asked to confer a benefit, it had a right to impose such terms as it thought to be demanded by a regard to the *public interest* ... If the interference of the Legislature was not required, all the discussion that had taken place on the subject would be useless; but if the interference of the Legislature was required, then it was perfectly fair for Parliament to impose upon, as the condition upon which they would grant the benefit asked for, such terms as might ... promote the public interests.[127]

The concept of 'public interest' in company law is, of course, rather problematic (McGuinness et al., 1998: 291–2).

Various arguments were put forward to justify restricting limited liability companies to large associations, defined by reference to number of shareholders and minimum capital. Earl Grey thought it 'extremely ridiculous' that the whole machinery of companies' legislation requiring

124 Ibid., col. 356 (29 June 1855).

125 Despite powerful arguments against it – for example, Parkinson (1993: 25–30) – it remains influential.

126 Hansard HC, vol. 139, cols 350 and 352 (29 June 1855).

127 Ibid., col. 353 (29 June 1855). Author's emphasis.

directors, auditors and a secretary might be imposed for a company with £250 capital.[128] Lord Campbell thought the idea of two or three people keeping a chandler's shop as a limited liability company 'absurd' and Earl Granville that small companies would not inspire confidence in their shareholders.[129] Earl Grey suggested that convicts or uncertificated bankrupts might form small companies.[130] Cardwell feared fraud if there were no restrictions on the return of capital.[131]

Lowe argued passionately against any restrictions, saying they should leave people to do as they pleased, and restrictions gave an advantage to the rich over the poor.[132] Stanley thought small companies would not be a problem as the expense would be too great.[133] Malins commented on how easy it would be to evade a minimum shareholder requirement.[134] Cairns correctly anticipated that a minimum capital would not ensure there were assets when a crisis affected a company.[135] Bouverie objected to a proposal that would place an additional liability on shareholders because it would prevent trustees from holding shares.[136] But even Bouverie thought a minimum capital would provide a test of whether a company was 'established for *bona fide* purposes', and Palmerston that it could show whether a company was a 'real and *bona fide* body',[137] both meaningless concepts.

Conclusions

The purpose of this chapter has not been to give the Victorian legislators a pat on the back for the introduction of general limited liability (though

128 Hansard HL, vol. 139, col. 2102 (10 August 1855).
129 Ibid., cols 2031 and 2102 (9 and 10 August 1855).
130 Hansard HL, vol. 139, col. 2033 (9 August 1855).
131 Hansard HC, vol. 139, col. 1522 (30 July 1855).
132 Ibid., col. 352 (29 June 1855).
133 Hansard HL, vol. 139, col. 2102 (10 August 1855).
134 Hansard HC, vol. 139, col. 2128 (11 August 1855).
135 Ibid., col. 354 (29 June 1855), though using this to justify extra regulation.
136 Ibid., col. 1523 (30 July 1855).
137 Ibid., cols 1520 (30 July 1855) and 1455 (27 July 1855).

some may think they deserve this). There has to be a degree of caution in how we use parliamentary records. Then as now good arguments may fail to gain a hearing and bad arguments gain undue prominence. Their value lies in seeking to see what insights were possessed by those who had to grapple with the daily reality of conducting significant economic activity, often on an unlimited liability basis, albeit against a very different background than our own. There was no single or even small number of causes for general limited liability, but a complex web of overlapping and interacting moral, legal, economic and political factors.

It would not be possible in a short chapter to chart and address every objection to, or proposed restriction on, the right to form a limited liability company. There could indeed be issues that the Victorians failed to foresee or restrictions that might be desirable. Limited liability results in many behavioural changes, not all of which are desirable. The evidence suggests, however, that any significant return to an unlimited liability regime would be a disaster of unimaginable proportions. Many people would be condemned to poverty; the young and enterprising would struggle to address the risks in innovative business, the old would not be able to rely on a portfolio of investments for their pensions. Many companies would relocate offshore and investors follow them with their funds. The problems of winding up large unlimited liability companies with millions of shareholders would be daunting even with technological advances, compared with the thousands of the Victorian era, and would submerge such numbers of people in the ruin of litigation. Since there would always be a need for exceptions to an unlimited liability regime, government discretion might rear its ugly head again – would the men (and women) of the Department of Business, Enterprise and Regulatory Reform be wiser than their predecessors in the Board of Trade? Let us, therefore, defend the right to form a limited liability company as one of the foundations of a free market and perhaps our most important economic right.

References

Anderson, G. M. and R. D. Tollison (1983), 'The myth of the corporation as a creation of the state', *International Review of Law and Economics*, 3: 107–20.

Baker, J. H. (1990), *An Introduction to English Legal History*, London: Butterworth.

Butler, H. N. (1986), 'General incorporation in nineteenth century England: interaction of common law and legislative processes', *International Review of Law and Economics*, 6: 169–88.

Cooke, C. A. (1950), *Corporation, Trust and Company*, Manchester: Manchester University Press.

Copp, S. F. (2003), *The Early Development of Company Law in England and Wales: Values and Efficiency*, PhD thesis, Bournemouth University.

Copp, S. F. (2004), 'The origins of limited liability in England and Wales revisited', Paper delivered to the Relational Finance Group, London.

Cork Report (1982), *Insolvency Law and Practice*, Report of the Insolvency Law Review Committee, 1982 (Cmnd. 8558).

Davies, P. L. (1997), *Gower's Principles of Modern Company Law*, London: Sweet & Maxwell.

Diamond, A. L. (1982), 'Corporate personality and limited liability', in T. Orhnial (ed.), *Limited Liability and the Corporation*, London: Croom Helm.

DuBois, A. B. (1938), *The English Business Company after the Bubble Act 1720–1800*, New York: Columbia University School of Law.

Easterbrook, F. H. and D. R. Fischel (1985), 'Limited liability and the corporation', *University of Chicago Law Review*, 52: 89–117.

Formoy, R. R. (1923), *The Historical Foundations of Modern Company Law*, London: Sweet & Maxwell.

Freedman, J. (2000), 'Limited liability: large company theory and small firms', *Modern Law Review*, 63(3): 317–54.

George, J. (1825), *A View of the Existing Law Affecting Unincorporated Joint Stock Companies*, cited by Formoy (1923: 33–5).

Halpern, P., M. Trebilcock and S. Turnbull (1980), 'An economic analysis of limited liability in corporation law', *University of Toronto Law Journal*, 30: 117–50.

Hansmann, H. and R. Kraakman (1991), 'Towards unlimited shareholder liability for corporate torts', *Yale Law Journal*, 100: 1879–934.

Harris, R. (2000), *Industrialising English Law: Entrepreneurship and Business Organisation 1720–1844*, Cambridge: Cambridge University Press.

Hicks, A. (1997), 'Limiting the rise of limited liability', in R. Baldwin (ed.), *Law, Uncertainty and Legal Processes*, London: Kluwer Law International, ch. 6.

Hunt, B. C. (1936), *The Development of the Business Corporation in England 1800–1867*, Cambridge, MA: Harvard University Press.

Ireland, P. (2003), 'Property and contract in contemporary corporate theory', *Legal Studies*, 23(3): 453–509.

Korten, D. C. (1995), *When Corporations Rule the World*, Connecticut and California: Kumarian Press, Inc., and Berrett-Koehler Publishers, Inc.

Kostal, R. W. (1994), *Law and English Railway Capitalism 1825–1875*, Oxford: Clarendon Press.

Lobban, M. (1996), 'Nineteenth century frauds in company formation: Derry v. Peek in context', *Law Quarterly Review*, 112: 287–334.

Mark, G. A. (2000), 'The role of the state in corporate law formation', in F. Macmillan (ed.), *International Corporate Law Annual*, vol. I, Oxford: Hart, ch. 1.

Mathias, P. (2001), *The First Industrial Nation*, London: Routledge.

McGuinness, K., B. Rees and S. Copp (1998), 'Recent perspectives on company law: a review article', *Company Lawyer*, 19: 290–96.

North, D. C. (1990), *Institutions, Institutional Change and Economic Performance*, Cambridge: Cambridge University Press.

Parkinson, J. E. (1993), *Corporate Power and Responsibility*, Oxford: Clarendon Press.

Parry, J. (2004), 'Lowe, Robert, Viscount Sherbrooke (1811–1892)', *Oxford Dictionary of National Biography*, Oxford: Oxford University Press, online edn, January 2008, www.oxforddnb.com/view/article/17088, accessed 21 February 2008.

Posner, R. A. (1976), 'The rights of creditors of affiliated corporations', *University of Chicago Law Review*, 43: 499–526.

Posner, R. A. (2003), *Economic Analysis of Law*, New York: Aspen.

Rush, M. and N. Baldwin (1998), 'Lawyers in Parliament', in D. Oliver and G. Drewry (eds), *The Law and Parliament*, London: Butterworth, p. 145.

Schluter, M. (2000), 'Risk, reward and responsibility: limited liability and company reform', *Cambridge Papers*, 9(2): 1–6.

Scott, W. R. (1910), *The Constitution and Finance of English, Scottish and Irish Joint Stock Companies to 1720*, Cambridge: Cambridge University Press.

Shannon, H. A. (1930–33), 'The coming of general limited liability', *Economic History*, 2: 267–91.

Stephen, H. J. (1841–45), *Stephen's Commentaries on the Laws of England*, London: Henry Butterworth.

Todd, G. (1932), 'Some aspects of joint stock companies 1844–1900', *Economic History Review*, 4(1): 46–71.

Tolmie, F. (2003), *Corporate and Personal Insolvency Law*, London: Cavendish.

Trachtman, J. P. (2000), 'Regulatory competition and regulatory jurisdiction', *Journal of International Economic Law*, 3(2): 331–48.

9 UNILATERAL PRACTICES AND THE DOMINANT FIRM: THE EUROPEAN COMMUNITY AND THE UNITED STATES

Richard A. Epstein[1]

The two faces of competition policy

Unlike Gaul, all competition, or antitrust law, both in the United States and the European Community, is divided into two parts: one that covers cooperative activities and a second that covers unilateral practices. For these purposes, I shall confine my analysis to four provisions that address these practices. Two of the provisions, Sections 1 and 2 of the Sherman Act, are from the USA. The other two provisions are Articles 81 and 82 of the EC Treaty Establishing the European Community. The full text of these provisions is set out in the appendix at the end of this chapter. For the remainder of this chapter, I shall use the term 'antitrust law' to refer to US law on this topic, and the term 'competition policy' to refer to EC law. The two terms are meant to cover the same ground, but also to reflect their somewhat different origins. The term 'antitrust' refers to that body of law that was created in the late nineteenth century to counteract the business trusts which were used to house and organise the great American businesses formed during the last third of the nineteenth century. The term 'competition policy' refers less to the vehicle – the business trust was not used in Europe, except for England[2]

1 Richard Epstein has consulted extensively on the issues in this chapter for Microsoft and Visa and has recently published a book underwritten by Microsoft on the history of consent decrees (Epstein, 2007). Many of these controversial decrees flow out of Section 2 charges brought by the USA against large corporations on theories of market dominance; the views expressed are, however, entirely his own. He is grateful for comments that he received on an earlier draft of this paper at a workshop in the Department of Economics at Clemson University, and to Ramtin Taheri (University of Chicago Law School, class of 2009) for his usual excellent research assistance.

2 'Dating back to eighteenth-century England, a business trust is a business organisation

– but rather speaks to the close linkage between the competitive ideal and social welfare, independent of the choice of legal entity to house the basic business enterprise.

With these preliminaries completed, we can return to the two parts of this modern Gallic, or Byzantine, enterprise. The first part of competition or antitrust policy deals with cooperative activities, which are horizontal arrangements whereby a group of firms in the same market seeks to limit competition among its members by the creation of cartels on the one hand or through merger or acquisition on the other. On this occasion, I ignore the trade-offs between efficiency and restraint in the merger context (Hovenkamp, 2005: 26–7; Epstein, 2007: 40–41). Within the EC, the parallel provision to Section 1 of the Sherman Act is the more lengthy and detailed set of provisions in Article 81. Article 81 provides protection against a full range of horizontal arrangements, including agreements on prices, restrictions, output and much more. In most, but not all, of these cases Article 81 reflects the same consensus that underlies Section 1 of the Sherman Act on the harmful consequences of cartels and the possible dangers of mergers.

The second part of competition or antitrust policy deals with a set of problems in which the difficulties are inverted. The key question here in both the EC and US settings is what *unilateral* practices of individual firms, particularly those that occupy a 'dominant position', should be treated as inconsistent with sound competition policy. In these cases, the matters of proof are in general – hidden rebates are an exception – second-order problems because the competition policy attack is directed towards the explicit contractual terms and public business practices that a firm uses with all or some of its customers. The key question is the legality of these various contractual provisions and firm practices. The ostensible goal of

or entity created and formed in a written trust contract (agreement) that sets out the purposes, terms, and conditions of the trust. The business trust is a legal entity and an artificial individual, with rights almost equal to a natural person (a human being), able to own property and conduct business like a natural person.' (Internet Business Company: *Benefits, Formation, and Operation*, www.internet-business-company.com/business-trust-information.htm).

competition policy in this area is the same as that with respect to various collusive actions – the maintenance of a competitive equilibrium.

Nonetheless, at this point the similarities end, for the theoretical foundations that justify state intervention are far more tenuous, to say the least (Epstein, 2005a; Evans and Padilla, 2005; Rubinfield, 2005). This has led to extensive criticism of finding liability in bundling cases in both the USA and the EC where the defendant has neither priced below cost, nor tied goods, nor demanded exclusive relationships with customers.[3] Once outside the friendly confines of cartel theory, and the somewhat muddier waters of mergers and acquisitions, it is no longer possible to make any straightforward argument that the reduction in output and increase in price spells a decline in overall social welfare. Now it is necessary to develop sophisticated models of how these unilateral practices allow a firm to make a profit at the expense of the public at large.

Good luck. In dealing with this issue, the relevant statutory provisions are Section 2 of the Sherman Act and Article 82 of the EC Treaty Establishing the European Community. A quick inspection of the two documents reveals that they are drafted in very different fashion. The thin materials of Section 2 have become the point of departure of US judicial efforts to create a full body of law dealing with unilateral practices of firms that seem to occupy a dominant market position. There is, it should be stressed, no obvious reason why this provision has to be interpreted as addressing such key topics as tie-ins, bundling, exclusive dealing or predation. Any narrow reading of Section 2 does not, of course, accurately capture the complex history of statutory interpretation of this most controversial provision, which now covers all sorts of

3 For my general views, see Epstein (2005a). See also Evans and Padilla (2005); Rubinfield (2005). The source of many of these articles was the much-criticised decision on bundling, *LePage's, Inc.* v. *3M*, 324 F.3d 141 (3d Cir. 2003) (en banc), cert. denied, 542 U.S. 953 (2004). For the much-criticised EC equivalent, see Case 85/76, *Hoffman-La Roche* v. *Commission of the European Communities*, [1979] ECR 461, [1979] 3 CMLR 21, suggesting per se illegality under Article 82 rebate schemes that tend to reinforce exclusive dealing arrangements.

public unilateral practices said to result in an impermissible accretion of power. The most famous formulation of the test stresses:

1. the possession of monopoly power in the relevant market[;] and
2. the willful acquisition or maintenance of that power as distinguished from growth or development as a consequence of a superior product, business acumen, or historic accident.[4]

In general, this formulation is highly unsatisfactory because of the enormous weight that it attaches to the motivation of the antitrust defendant.[5] Virtually every firm that has a superior product will use business acumen to reap the highest possible reward for itself. It takes extraordinary mental gymnastics to distinguish this proper desire to obtain a decisive competitive advantage from the illicit desire to obtain a monopoly dominance, especially when the same techniques can be pressed into the service of either end.

Notwithstanding this conceptual breakdown, there is at least this silver lining to the US antitrust experience: the lack of an explicit statutory command to chase after various unilateral practices has, in my view, placed a modest obstacle to the rapid expansion of antitrust liability. The same modest interpretive strategy is not possible, however, with the language of Article 82, whose broad terms give it an extensive role in regulating the economic activities of ordinary business. Yet at the same time it does not contain any precise or detailed statement of the different practices that are denied to the dominant firm (itself a term that is left undefined). Instead the Article uses terms such as 'unfair' and 'indirect' to trigger liability. Thus 'directly or indirectly imposing unfair purchase or selling prices or other unfair trading conditions' is illegal. At this point there are both rule-of-law and substantive considerations that should be separately addressed.

4 *United States* v. *Grinnell Corp.*, 384 U.S. 563, 570–71 (1966), relying heavily on *United States* v. *Aluminum Co. of America*, 148 F.2d 416 (2d Cir. 1945).

5 Ibid. For discussion, see Hylton (2003).

The rule of law

The statutory language of Article 82 should make classical liberals blanch. One minimum condition for adherence to the rule of law requires the lawgiver to draw a clear and knowable line between conduct that is legal and that which is illegal. In saying this, I do not mean that it is the obligation of the basic code to make clear to individuals all of the detailed rules that govern their conduct. A prohibition that says 'thou shalt not kill' would be sufficient for the purposes of notice and guidance, even if it does not set out all of the details appropriate to the distinction between murder and manslaughter, the law of self-defence or of insanity. The primary object of that basic command is well understood, so that gaps can be filled in by the ordinary techniques of statutory construction to deal with such matters as provocation, self-defence or necessity.

Businesses do not have the same luxury with Article 82 (or, in lesser degree, Section 2 of the Sherman Act), which gives no clear indication of those everyday practices that it proscribes. The inevitable ignorance of this legal rule makes it difficult to meet the Lockean requirement that all individuals be judged by known and settled laws capable of coherent application.[6] Even with large resources, businesses are hard pressed to glean the needed information from a close textual dissection of the statute or from reliance on administrative interpretations of the text which are often no clearer, albeit much longer, than the original textual command. Furthermore, the delegation of administrative authority to a centralised agency, such as the Brussels bureaucracy, may well lead to a systematic expansion of the statutory command, such as that which has taken place under American law with such critical statutes as the Endangered Species Act or the Title IX of the

6 In a state of nature '[t]here wants an established, settled, known law, received and allowed by common consent to be the standard of right and wrong', and 'a known and indifferent judge, with authority to determine all differences according to the established law' (Locke, 1690: 124–5); for a modern expression of the same ideal, see Fuller (1964: 38–9).

Civil Rights Act (dealing with intercollegiate sports), which show that these extensions do take place.[7] Yet the judicial response to administrative overreaching in most cases is uncertain. When judges 'defer' to administrative expertise, which is often non-existent, they only compound the original problem.

These problems have less salience with the core prohibition against price-fixing. In contrast, the numerous activities of a dominant firm do not easily lend themselves to extensive pre-approval review by administrative agencies. To be sure, it is possible to set up institutions for review as part of consent decrees in individual cases. Just such a procedure was, for example, set up as part of the final settlement of the final US resolution in the Microsoft case, which adopted a neutral, expert, technical committee with broad powers to oversee the activities of the company. This procedure was sustained in the litigation challenging the decree.[8] But this decree itself is a rarity in US jurisprudence. Nor is it an unalloyed good. As Microsoft struggles to gain its balance in a highly competitive world, this decree, even though skilfully drafted, necessarily limits its competitive flexibility. Unfortunately, neither the USA nor the EC could devise a workable pre-approval process to govern the myriad activities of the modern large corporation so long as virtually any marketing strategy counts as a unilateral practice that can be examined, or invalidated, under the provisions of either Section 2 or Article 82. Couching the tests for legality in terms of 'reasonable' commercial practices gives only meagre guidance as to their legality. Inescapably, the broad-scale effort to regulate unilateral practices by dominant firms is in sharp tension with traditional rule-of-law concerns.

7 See, for example, *Babbitt* v. *Sweet Home Chapter of Communities for a Great Or.*, 515 U.S. 687 (1995); *Cohen* v. *Brown University*, 101 F.3d 155 (1st Cir. 1996): for my comments on Title IX, see Epstein (2003); for my comments on the Endangered Species Act, see Epstein (1997).

8 *Massachusetts* v. *Microsoft*, 373 F.3d 1199 (D.C. Cir. 2004).

Fairness – or efficiency?

There is a second, equally large difficulty with Article 82 in its approach to taming the world of unilateral practices. Any regulation of unilateral conduct must identify those practices that deviate from a competitive market in ways that generate systematic social losses. But the text of Article 82 does not march the reader off in that direction. Instead Article 82 is a drafting nightmare. The first reason is that the text is completely open-ended. It begins with the undefined terms 'abuse' and 'dominant position' which insist upon the existence of various practices and firms that the Article then fails to define or identify. One obvious first step is to develop an exhaustive list of abusive practices, but Article 82 does no such thing. Rather, its key transitional phrase is that 'such abuse *may, in particular,* consist in' (emphasis added). These words only make clear that the list that follows is not exhaustive, simply representative. In principle, without any kind of advance notice at all, additional practices could be described as abusive, letting loose a full range of civil sanctions in their wake. Broad uncertainty is embedded in Article 82, without any information as to the paradigmatic cases to which it applies.

In principle that information could be gleaned from the list that follows. But here again the language chosen is ill suited to undertaking any efficiency-based critique of unilateral practices. Just consider the first of the alleged abuses, namely 'directly or indirectly imposing unfair purchase or selling prices or other unfair trading conditions'. The proposition opens up at least as many problems as it resolves. Initially, it uses the term 'unfair' twice, first in connection with buying and selling, and second with respect to other trading conditions. What is certain from this brief account is that the abusive position can be held either by a buyer or a seller (or perhaps even both if they have dominant positions in their respective industries). We learn, second, that the pattern of abuse is not tied only to price terms, but also extends to any other term of the contract.

Note, however, the *only* clear features of Article 82 *expand* its scope.

There is no similar clarity about the rules that govern this extensive terrain after it is staked out. Thus we have no real definition of what the term 'unfair' means, which is a matter of immense concern because of the two diametrically opposed visions of the subject. Within the libertarian tradition, the notion of transaction fairness has multiple connotations. The first holds that a transaction is 'unfair' if it is tainted by force or fraud. In most cases of force and fraud, the question of competitive injury does not come to the fore. But it takes only a little ingenuity to forge the necessary connection. The party that fires guns at the customers of its business rivals is trying to create some kind of monopoly position, as is the firm that falsely disparages the quality of wares sold by a rival manufacturer.[9] In these cases, the desired results for competition policy are achieved by the straightforward application of a traditional tort norm that guards against interference with advantageous relationships by the use of illegal or improper means.

Most instructively, the English courts during the nineteenth century were wary of going beyond this boundary line, and thus explicitly refused to find tortious efforts (which ultimately failed) by a group of firms to gain market share by 'smashing' rates by offering rebates to shippers on the China to England run.[10] The stress here in good libertarian fashion was on 'intimidation, obstruction, and molestation'. Price competition was not covered. In addition, 'passing off' and product disparagement could both be actionable, as both involve the use of misrepresentation that hurts the plaintiff. With passing off the plaintiff claims that its inferior goods are those of a competitor. Similarly, with product disparagement, the plaintiff claims that the defendant made the plaintiff's product look worse than it truly was, thereby diverting sales to

9 On the first, see, e.g., *Tarleton* v. *McGawley*, 170 Eng. Rep. 153 (K.B. 1793) (firing shots to keep natives from trading with plaintiffs found actionable); on the second see, e.g., *Old Investors & Traders Corp.* v. *Jenkins*, 133 Misc. 213 (N.Y. Sup. Ct. 1928) (permitting a plaintiff to state a claim in suing to enjoin distribution of circulars with false and misleading information about plaintiff's products).

10 *Mogul Steamship Co.* v. *McGregor, Gow, & Co.*, 23 Q.B.D. 598 (1889), affirmed [1892] A.C. 25.

other parties, including the defendant. When there are more than two firms in the industry, this strategy will both hurt the plaintiff and give an unearned benefit to other firms that have committed no wrong. Neither rule required a comprehensive welfarist analysis to reach the right result in the individual case.

The second portion of the libertarian synthesis deals with the tort of 'inducement of breach of contract', which covers those cases where a defendant *with notice* that some third party is in a contractual relationship induces a breach of that contract. The term 'breach' is essential to the correct formulation of this tort. Thus the rule applies where the plaintiff has a term contract with a third party that the defendant wishes to break. Historically, the first case of this sort involved the famous operatic star Johanna Wagner, who was induced by one impresario to breach her contract for the season with a second.[11] But as before this tort also must be closely circumscribed, for otherwise it could shipwreck all competitive markets, by essentially denying one firm the opportunity to lure away the employees of the second at higher wages. The subsequent growth of that tort has never been read to block this kind of conduct, even though it will protect, for example, a firm whose key employees possess valuable trade secrets of use to a rival. Even here the remedy is carefully circumscribed with respect to both the new employments that are covered and the relief that is made available.

Second, the term 'fairness' refers to situations where persons in equal positions are entitled to equal treatment. This more abstract norm is harder to apply. It clearly works for certain corporate transactions, where, for example, the corporation must pay uniform dividends to all shareholders of the same class of stock. Making all shares equal in the eyes of the law (a) facilitates a thick market for their sale, and (b) reduces the discretion of the corporate board on disputes between shareholders. Yet these duties of uniform treatment may not apply to the board's treatment of outsiders to whom no fiduciary duty is owed (see, for example,

11 *Lumley* v. *Gye*, 118 Eng. Rep. 749 (K.B. 1853).

Fischel, 1983). Even with insiders, moreover, there are often subtle differences in the position of the various individuals within a class which make positions of parity difficult to identify.

Finally, we can identify a third use of the term 'unfairness' that is diametrically opposed to the first and in genuine tension with the second. The common-law framework uses the term 'unfair' to describe actions that advance competition rather than thwart it, as with the torts of passing off and disparagement. The inversion of this term started in rich profusion in the New Deal period when effective competition on price or terms was treated as unfair to competitors, even if it produced a net gain to consumers. Thus the codes of fair competition for the sale of meat and agricultural products were a staple of the period,[12] as were the 'unfair labor practices' under the National Labor Relations Act of 1935, which fostered the growth of monopoly unions. These and other elaborate statutory schemes moved the law in the exact opposite direction from the objectives of American antitrust law, by allowing political actors to decree whether competition or monopoly was the ideal goal for some market segment.

This point raises no passing fancy but exposes a deep structural fear. The now rejected European Constitution attempted to bridge the gap by announcing that it was for both 'free and fair trade',[13] without pausing to ask how much weight should be put on each of these two incompatible notions (for discussion, see Epstein, 2005b). Subsequently, the Treaty of Lisbon was signed on 13 December 2007. It will go into effect once, and only, if it is ratified by all member states. Most of its provisions have little to do with competition policy. But it does contain one short protocol that adopts as one objective of the EC a desire that the 'internal market' be regulated by 'a system ensuring that competition is not distorted',[14]

12 See, e.g., *A.L.A. Schecter Poultry Corp.* v. *United States*, 295 U.S. 495 (1935) (striking down the 'codes of fair competition' that imposed, among other things, minimum wage, maximum hours and collective bargaining for the poultry business). For discussion of the *Schecter* decision, see Epstein (2006a).

13 Treaty Establishing a Constitution for Europe, Art. 1–3(4).

14 Official Journal of the European Union, 2007/C 306/01, Treaty of Lisbon amending the Treaty on European Union and the Treaty Establishing the European Community, signed

without resolving the tension between fairness and freedom so evident in the earlier failed European Constitution. Unfortunately, the persistent tension between free and fair trade will filter down from constitutional principle to competition policy, for neither the American antitrust law nor the EC competition law has any rule that blocks the ability of disappointed firms to challenge successful innovations by their competitors. On this question two topics come to the fore. The first considers the various defences that have been put forward with respect to enforcement actions brought under Article 82, and the second examines some discrete cases that have tested its amorphous provisions.

The official ambivalence within the EC

In order to lend focus to this inquiry into the defences of Article 82, I shall start with the remarks of Neelie Kroes (2005) in a speech that she gave at the Fordham Corporate Law Institute in September 2005.[15] Kroes is a Dutch economist by training, and as the member of the European Commission in charge of competition policy she is now the top competition official within the EC. Her speech shows the extent to which she (and, by implication, the EC Commission) can speak in a way that offers olive branches to both sides in the debate over unilateral practices, without exposing the latent tensions within such ecumenical pronouncements. As will become evident later, this transition helps explain her elation after the European Court of First Instance largely sustained the Commission's findings against Microsoft,[16] which I shall discuss briefly in due course. Her initial remarks are somewhat soothing. She disdains

at Lisbon, 13 December 2007. Protocol on the internal market and competition, http://eur-lex.europa.eu/en/treaties/dat/12007L/htm/C2007306EN.01015601.htm.

15 For a more exhaustive treatment of dominant position, see DG Competition Discussion Paper on the Application of Article 82 of the Treaty to Exclusionary Abuses (Dec. 2005). To access this paper, go to http://ec/europa.eu/camm/competition/antitrust/art82, and then click on the link to the 'Staff Discussion Paper'.

16 *Microsoft Corp.* v. *Commission of the European Communities*, Judgment of the Court of First Instance (Grand Chamber), 17 September 2007 (Case T-201/04) (hereinafter *Microsoft CFI*).

any 'radical shift' in EC policy, and adopts the commendable American saying – commendable for regulators, not businesses – that 'if it ain't broke, then don't fix it'. She is also cognisant of the limited resources available to enforcement agencies. The initial tone seems in perfect conformity with the fundamental proposition of laissez-faire, which is to examine each proposal for an extension of government regulation into prices and terms under a presumption of error.

But this manifestation of good feelings does not last, for in her short address her mood rapidly darkens when she turns her attention to the two threshold concepts under Article 82. She recognises that the question of market dominance is associated with 'substantial market power', but she does not offer any workable test to decide whether a firm does or does not have that power. She is right to say that a simple examination of market share does not solve the problem, because every firm operates in fear that some major technological innovation, often from some unanticipated quarter, will quickly drive that market share down. Potential competition from unidentified new entrants places subtle but real pressures on firms, which know that others can enter under the price umbrella if prices are set too high. Accordingly, the shape of the market may depend on innovations that may come to light only after some enforcement action is begun but before it is concluded. So long as these possibilities are live, even precise information about current and past market shares offers little guidance as to how to proceed. Nonetheless, the current rules show little concern for these dynamic elements. Instead, a static model is used such that market shares of over 50 per cent have been regarded as presumptively dominant, even if lower shares from 25 to 50 per cent are not.[17] A fortiori, it is clear that EC law is virtually certain to treat market shares of over 75 per cent as dominant.[18]

A second difficulty with this test is that it does not pay attention to the structure of the remainder of the market. The point does receive

17 Case C-62/86, *AKZO Chemie BV* v. *Commission*, [1991] E.C.R. I-3359 (adopting broad definition of predation). See also DG Competition Discussion Paper, *supra* at note 15 at 4.2.1.

18 *Hoffman-La Roche*, *supra* at note 3.

some attention in the Director General's 2005 Discussion Paper on Article 82, issued shortly after that speech, where it is observed: 'It is very likely that very high market shares, which have been held for some time, indicate a dominant position. This would be the case where an undertaking holds 50% or more of the market, provided that rivals hold a much smaller share of the market.'[19]

The Discussion rightly draws attention in the last clause to the full state of the market, while abstracting away from the dynamic elements of market definition.[20] It matters whether the dominant firm has to contend with only one firm or with a number of firms in its niche. Clearly, the former configuration is more dangerous than the latter, for two firms will in general find it easier to collude. The point is evident from the familiar Herfindahl index, which measures concentration by taking the squares of the market shares of all the leading participants. With only two equal players, that index is equal to at least 0.50 (or $0.5^2 + 0.5^2$). But with three players, holding 50, 25 and 25 per cent shares respectively, the index drops to 37.5 (or $0.5^2 + 0.25^2 + 0.25^2$), a far lower number. But the DG Discussion Paper does not pursue these knotty issues, apart from the further observation that market dominance is 'more likely to be found in the market share range of 40% to 50% than below 40%'. Again, the tests are framed in terms of likelihood, not hard lines. Nor does the DG Discussion Paper try to tie the finding of dominance to the Herfindahl index, or even to provide a general rule that does not turn on the facts of each particular case. Its explanation for this shortfall is that market share is at most an imperfect measure of market power.[21] The point is true enough. From a structural point of view this will not do: it is imperative to have some stronger sense of who counts as a dominant firm given the onerous obligations that attach to that status. In principle, this sensible concession should be reason to slow down the Commission Express. But there is no sign that this has happened.

19 DG Competition Discussion Paper, at 4.2.1.

20 On which see, generally, Jones and Sufrin (2008: ch. 6, š 3, pp. 352–94).

21 DG Competition Discussion Paper, at 4.2.1.

After Ms Kroes speaks about dominant position, she moves on to the question of abuse, which she associates primarily with 'exclusionary abuses'. On this point, the potential list of practices is long indeed: tie-ins, predation, bundling and rebates are the usual suspects. I have already mentioned some of the reasons to tread warily in these areas given the real risk that excessive legal enforcement could have dramatic anti-competitive consequences. But nonetheless, Ms Kroes is not prepared to offer a clear demarcation between legal and illegal forms of firm behaviour. The rule-of-law anxieties are not eased, but heightened, for the points of firm vulnerability are enormous, because both price and non-price terms can be subject to Commission inquiry under Article 82. The Commission's powers start with the power of investigation, which allows it to seize papers and records of firms that it suspects of illegal practices, as recently happened in Munich when the EC raided two large retailers, Germany's huge Media Markt-Saturn and British electrical goods retailer DSG International Plc, in order to acquire information that it could use in hearings in Brussels that charge Intel with an abuse of its dominant position by reducing prices to drive Advanced Micro Devices out of business (Lawsky, 2008). Those raids could lead to heavy fines, injunctive relief or perhaps even a call to break up the competitor. For these kinds of remedies, especially in predation cases, the case for articulating a 'bright-line' rule on legality seems imperative. The more continuous the distribution of good and bad outcomes, the harder it is to make sense of the entire enterprise. Yet notwithstanding her initial cautionary remarks, Ms Kroes does not offer the dominant firm (however defined) a safe harbour against onerous liability.

On the price issue, which could easily prove decisive in the Intel/AMD dispute, the line between legality and illegality depends on whether a 'high' or 'low' price is charged for a given commodity, even though the distinction between these two states of the world is always blurry. Thus the use of high rebates to selective customers is regarded as improper but low rebates are not. The nub of the difficulty is that EC competition policy insists upon some Archimedean price point, which in key cases could prove unattainable. Let the price be too high, and the business is inefficient because of the adverse impact that it has on consumers, but let it fall too low and it is also inefficient because of its adverse impact on rival producers. There is thus a real risk that a firm that has proved successful in the marketplace cannot win before the EC Commission: this entire enterprise requires some external determination of the costs that the dominant firm has in production, without making it clear whether it is average or marginal cost which is involved. For agencies that are cost-constrained, it is a fair question whether it makes sense to invest resources in the full-scale investigation of pricing that takes into account 'the overall situation', which can be very complicated for large firms that compete in multiple markets simultaneously.

The ambivalence does not stop here. Once the dominant firm is identified, Ms Kroes notes that the firm is entitled to make an 'efficiency defence' under Article 82, but only under a stringent standard that requires the firm to prove that 'the unilateral conduct should be indispensable to realise these efficiencies'. The extensive litigation under this standard must necessarily sort out both the costs and benefits of various practices, not only for the dominant firm, but for all parties with whom it deals and competes. These calculations, moreover, must be made over the short and the long term. 'Indispensable' is one rigorous standard that does not sound remotely like 'if it ain't broke, don't fix it'. It is amazing how the cautious attitude towards Article 82 found on the first page of a speech gives way to a frontal assault against select dominant firms on the third!

The overall issue does not become any clearer in terms of general economic theory. Ms Kroes follows a familiar line when she insists that the ultimate test is said to ask whether the defendant's practices amount to 'competition on the merits', which in turn is said to occur 'when an efficient competitor that does not have the benefits of a dominant position, is able to compete against the pricing conduct of the dominant company'. The most obvious rejoinder to this test is to ask why we should bother with Article 82 at all. It is quite clear that there is no competition on the merits when a firm engages in intimidation or molestation, or passing off. But once those misdeeds are removed from the list, just what additional conduct should not count as competition on the merits? The best test of whether the non-dominant firm can compete against the dominant firm is whether the non-dominant firm has competed against the dominant firm, which it can do by making advantages in marketing or securing technical improvements that the established firm does not possess. There is a strong argument that a single firm can use various practices in network industries or common-carrier situations to take advantage of that monopoly power, which is in part why the initial claims against Microsoft, discussed below, have strong credibility on the liability side of the issue. Normally, common-carrier cases are subject to direct regulation because of the inability of courts to set rates in such industries as railways and electrical power. But with Microsoft that institutional disability does not matter if everyone agrees that interconnection should be made at a zero price. But once these important cases are put to one side, it is very hard to identify the particular terms or pricing strategies that do not count as competition on the merits in non-network industries where the new entrants do not have to depend on the cooperation and hence the good graces of a dominant firm.

The decision to use some independent test apart from survival to see whether competition is 'sound' or 'distorting' has this unfortunate effect on the analysis. The non-dominant firm, however defined, is not subject to the restraints in Article 82, so it is free from restraints on the choice of business practices that bind its larger rivals. In adopting its own business plan, that non-dominant firm will not routinely or willingly adopt strategies on pricing, bundling, tie-ins or rebates that make its operations inefficient. The pressure to survive is a far more accurate filter on good and bad practices than the oversight of any board or commission in either the USA or the EC. At this point, the use of practices by non-dominant firms offers a good market test of efficiency, albeit one that appears to hold no appeal to the European Commission.

Why, then, does it become improper for dominant firms to use these same practices? The usual explanation is that these practices also have restrictive or exclusionary effects given the size of the dominant firm. But even if these shadowy effects could be demonstrated (which is hard, to say the least), we know that any effort to rid the marketplace of restrictions also has the inescapable by-product of ridding it of efficient practices. This results in a kind of inverse unfair competition whereby the new entrant or smaller firm can use practices that are denied to its direct competitor, thereby removing basic parity from the marketplace. Yet under current EC law, the 'distortion' is said to come from the ability of all firms to use the same practices, *not* from the selective advantages conferred upon firms thought to be non-dominant. It becomes therefore something of a mystery as to why the techniques that a small firm uses in its rise to dominance must be abandoned once that exalted state has been reached. The overall efficiency gains that the ideal enforcement of Article 82 (or Section 2, to be fair) can achieve are therefore limited because we know that each and every application of sanctions knocks out *only* efficient practices with industry-wide appeal.

There is a second way in which dominant practices could influence the efficiency of economic markets. With patents the law is willing to give a person exclusive rights to a particular invention in order to spur innovation. The basic judgement here is that it is better to grant a monopoly – or more accurately an exclusive right – in some new device today than to have no device at all. The earlier innovation provides immediate gains that offset the increase in monopoly power. Nor need we worry about the long-term implications of the patent system. So long as the exclusive right is correctly limited, the risk of economic monopoly can be properly constrained. Patents are limited to devices, as opposed to entire fields – the telegraph, as opposed to the exclusive right to transmit signals at a distance over wire. It is for that reason that the US Supreme Court struck down Samuel Morse's 1840 patent claim covering exclusive use of 'electromagnetism, however developed for marking or printing intelligible characters, signs, or letters, at any distances',[22] while allowing the

22 *O'Reilly* v. *Morse*, 56 U.S. 62, 112–13 (1853).

narrower, but still enormously valuable, patent claims for his particular device. The patent forecloses imitative use of the device, not of the entire field of technology.

That same attitude should carry over to dominant practices. To take one example, in the USA it has proved possible for Apple to market its new iPhone through an exclusive arrangement with AT&T, with the product being extensively touted on the AT&T website, in part for its innovation in visual voicemail.[23] There can, and should, be all sorts of speculation as to whether this deal is good for either or both companies. But I see no reason to impose a duty on Apple to take its iPhone and license it on similar deals with all other carriers. The first objection here is generic. If Apple must deal with all comers, then some public body must oversee the compulsory licensing arrangements that govern not only price but also a whole range of technical issues, which may vary from carrier to carrier, and, of course, from state to state within the USA or nation to nation within the EC. In general, I think that there are good reasons to fear compulsory licences in many industries, especially pharmaceuticals, given the substantial risk of under-compensation (see Epstein, 2006b). In addition, the denial of the exclusive arrangement could easily upset useful technological sharing agreements, for AT&T would be uneasy about passing on information to Apple which it now knows could be used by its other licensees. And finally, the unwillingness to allow these exclusive arrangements should in expectation reduce the returns that Apple gains from its innovation, which, as in the patent context, should slow down the rate of its introduction.

These exclusives have provoked to my knowledge no legal antitrust response in the USA because Apple acquired iPhone through lawful actions and thus is entitled to market it in whatever form it sees fit. The reaction to these proposed exclusives has been mixed in Europe, where, as of December 2007, the German government was unable to prevent Apple from striking an exclusive arrangement with T-Mobile, even as,

23 www.wireless.att.com/cell-phone-service/specials/iPhoneCenter.jsp.

at last reckoning, the French government still imposes similar restrictions on dissemination within France.[24] At this point the economic losses, compounded by the threat of restrictive practices, are likely to have two effects. The first of these is to slow down innovation *worldwide* by reducing the return to any invention, wherever developed, no matter under what legal regime. The second is to work an implicit wealth transfer whereby (in this instance) the French gain the benefits of the implicit subsidy necessarily borne everywhere else. The application of EC (or US) rules therefore should not be thought of only as a matter of local concern in the light of their systemic global effects. The poor administrative judgement in France inflicts its own sort of regulatory injury on everyone else, which is no less real because it is immune from legal sanction. The extraterritorial effects of legal sanctions, either good or bad, are at least as important as the extraterritorial effects of the standard practice of dominant firms.

The analysis of the behaviour of dominant firms, both under Section 2 of the Sherman Act and Article 82, only becomes harder to organise once the inquiry turns to the causation questions that are necessarily embedded in competition policy. Quite simply, any claim that a particular practice 'distorts' the marketplace has a built-in causal component which is far more difficult to identify than that found in personal injury or property damage cases, where harm is usually limited to the use of force or the creation of traps or other dangerous conditions. Joint causation cases, always difficult, are usually infrequent in physical injury cases because it is not often that a person is hit by ten or more bullets at the same time. These physical limitations have no particular relevance in dealing with competition policy, so a more far-ranging inquiry becomes inescapable in virtually every case. More concretely, once a non-dominant firm fails, its behaviour has to be dissected to determine whether its demise or failure is attributable to its own faulty

24 Jacqui Cheng, 'T-Mobile wins back iPhone exclusivity in Germany', ars technica (2007), http://arstechnica.com/journals/apple.ars/2007/12/04/t-mobile-wins-back-iphone-exclusivity-in-germany.

business judgement or technical acumen, or alternatively to the use of certain contractual provisions by the dominant firm. If both elements have some role in the grand analysis, who sorts out their relative effects?

On this issue, my own examination of consent decrees under Section 2 of the Sherman Act concludes that in most instances particular contractual provisions that the dominant firm uses usually have small overall effects on the final results in a particular case (Epstein, 2007: 40–53). For example, the 60-year campaign against the exclusive-dealing provisions in the equipment leases of the United Shoe Company had little effect on its market share.[25] One objectionable leasehold provision after another was stripped away, but the market position of the firm remained in large measure because customers probably preferred to have 'end-to-end' protection from a single supplier to whom they could turn in the event that anything went wrong. The dominance of that firm ended only when the USA, frustrated by the slow rate of progress of rival firms, broke up the company, leading to its demise, just as its domestic position was coming under pressure from the foreign shoe manufacturers entering the American market.[26] Knocking down tariff barriers – a skill that is in short supply in the EC – turns out to be a far more effective remedy for major forms of abuse.

The lesson to be drawn from this litigation is that firms that think their protections are indispensable are themselves overstating the value of restrictive practices, so that it is hard to fault the regulators for making the same mistake. A prompt and unilateral surrender on all these points is clearly the preferred strategy because it makes it far more difficult for regulators or competitors to attribute the continued success of the dominant firm to illicit practices.

25 *United Shoe Machinery Corp.* v. *United States*, 258 U.S. 451, 456–57 (1922). A second set of terms were invalidated in *United States* v. *United Shoe Machinery Corp.*, 110 F. Supp. 295 (D. Mass. 1953), affirmed in *United Shoe Machinery Corp.* v. *United States*, 347 U.S. 521 (1954). The entire opinion reads: 'The case having been fully argued and the Court being satisfied that the findings are justified by the evidence and support the decree, the judgment is affirmed.'

26 *United States* v. *United Shoe Machinery Corp.*, 391 U.S. 244 (1968); Crandall and Winston (2003: 11–12).

A tale of two statutes

The overall theoretical concerns are the same for both the EC and the USA, despite differences in terminology. But it seems all too clear today that the EC enforcement under Article 82 proceeds at a much more vigorous clip than the analogous activity under Section 2 in the USA. It is useful to give a few examples of the overall difference.

Predation

One of the exclusive practices that attracted Ms Kroes's attention was predatory pricing, whereby the stated offence is to reduce prices below costs in an effort to drive out competitors in the hope of reaping monopoly profits when the competition vanishes. Within the American framework, there is no current rule of per se legality with respect to predation claims, although that position has powerful intellectual support (Easterbrook, 1981, critiquing the standard below-cost test of predatory pricing found in Areeda and Turner, 1975, which relies on some mixture of short-run marginal cost and average variable cost). I believe that it is for good reason that the US Supreme Court has taken a far more sceptical position than the EC Commission on this point in a line of cases that now stretches close to 25 years.[27]

The US decisions are correct and the EC worries far too much about predation. The initial intuition is that claims by disappointed competitors are always suspect, for it is intrinsically difficult to distinguish between lawful and unlawful competition solely by looking at price levels, which – secret rebates to one side – are observable, in their relationship to cost, which most definitely is not observable. That basic point is reinforced by noting the different challenges that face a monopolist or cartel

27 See, e.g., *Matsushita Electric Industrial Co., Ltd.* v. *Zenith Radio Corp.*, 475 U.S. 574 (1986) (conspiracy by foreign sellers of TV to lower prices not found to be predatory pricing); *Brooke Group Ltd.* v. *Brown & Williamson Tobacco Corp.*, 509 U.S. 209 (1993) (same, for allegations of below-cost pricing of cigarettes); *Weyerhaeuser* v. *Ross-Simmons HardWood Lumber Co.*, 127 S. Ct. 1069, 1073, 1077 (2007) (unanimously rejecting charge of buyer predation based on paying too much to preclude competitors for remaining in the market).

that seeks to reap extra profits not by raising prices, but by lowering them. Raising prices and cutting output gives an immediate gain which is worth having even if the cartel breaks down over time because of cheating. It is therefore rational for firms to enter into these arrangements if they are able to escape legal detection, which they are often able to do. It is for that reason that the USA has an amnesty programme that waives the trebling of damages against the party that provides the federal government with evidence against its co-conspirators.[28] Yet the situation is quite the opposite with predation. Now the firm has to take a loss on each item that it sells below costs in order to drive its rivals from the market. Worse still, the low prices have buyers flooding in, while rival sellers can often sit on the sidelines (or even become purchasers for later resale), pushing the predator's short-term loss still higher. The ability to knock out old competitors in the short run is dubious, as is the ability to capture monopoly gains in the long run. Once prices rise above competitive levels, the older sellers will come off the sidelines, or new sellers will enter the market. In the absence of any regulatory restraint against renewed competition, it is hard to see how the consumers who gain mightily in the short run will be hurt in the long run.

Nor, I might add, is it clear how to draw in practice the line between price cutting that is too aggressive and that which is just right. Even the Commission's present standards should not generate liability for firms that consciously calculate their price cuts in ways that are *sustainable* over the long run, wholly without regard to the response of the targeted competitors. It seems highly likely that the difference in pricing decisions under this standard and one that seeks to crush rivals in the short run is likely to prove rather small to matter in practice. The near-per se rule on legality thus allows firms to compete aggressively (of which Ms Kroes rightly approves) without being falsely tagged with groundless charges of predation. A virtual per se rule of legality looks even better. The US

28 See, e.g., *United States* v. *Stolt-Nielsen S.A.*, 524 F. Supp. 2d 609 (E.D. Pa. 2007), which shows the difficulties that can come from litigating a withdrawal from amnesty under the USA's Corporate Leniency Program, instituted in 1993.

cases have not formally gone that far, but there is no recent successful predation case under the US laws, and it is highly unlikely that any court will find predation today so long as they first ask whether the supposed predator has any successful recoupment strategy.[29] Why worry about the complex calculation of costs if recoupment is not possible no matter how they are calculated? The strong presumption operates close to a per se rule on the ground.

As noted, under Article 82 the Commission treats predation as a form of exclusionary conduct worthy of its special attention. Within the EC, the criticisms of Areeda/Turner tend to stress that the test allows too much freedom to the firm in making its decisions, not too little (Jones and Sufrin, 2008: 445–46). Accordingly, in terms of predation claims (as evidenced by the recent raids in connection with the Intel/AMD dispute) it tends to see real danger in pricing below average variable cost, which accordingly prompts aggressive Commission intervention.[30]

Ms Kroes does not detail the EC approach to predation cases in her short speech, but some sense of the inexorable expansion of Article 82 is found in the Economic Advisory Group for Competition Policy (EAGCP) (2005) report entitled 'An economic approach to Article 82'. The report mirrors the ambivalence in the Kroes speech, first by noting the presumption in favour of non-intervention, only to promptly invoke a 'rule of reason' that rejects the approach of virtual per se legality that largely characterises the modern US case law. From here it is only a short step to eroding the requirement of market dominance by holding that 'an anti-competitive effect is what really matters and is already proof of dominance' (EAGCP, 2005: 4), without drawing the line between legitimate and illegitimate pricing practices. At this point, the burden of proof is bifurcated such that 'Competition authorities have to show the presence of significant anti-competitive harm, while the dominant firm

29 See, e.g., *A. A. Poultry Farms, Inc.* v. *Rose Acre Farms, Inc.*, 881 F.2d 1396 (7th Cir. 1989).

30 *AKZO Chemie BV*, *supra* at note 17. For discussion, see Jones and Sufrin (2008: 447–59, making the simple but compelling point, for example, that low prices are sometimes used to remove excess stock; ibid. at 450).

should bear the burden of establishing credible efficiency arguments' (ibid.). How the two are distinguished is not clearly explained.

The upshot is that the basic theory of predation may be used to examine 'selective rebates', which could of course be meeting competition in certain geographical markets, or indeed simply charging 'more attractive prices or, more generally, offer[ing] better conditions to these customers' (ibid.: 5). In addition, the full range of loyalty and fidelity rebates becomes suspect as well. The initial presumption in favour of open markets becomes the opposite: an open season on aggressive forms of market competition. Official statements of principle are so pliable that it is impossible to tell before the axe falls whether a dominant-firm practice is protected by the general presumption in favour of free competition or upset by the equally robust willingness to ferret out all forms of predation.

Yet from a social point of view, it is hard to see what all the fuss is about. All the practices that are suspect under Article 82 have positive and negative effects for different firms over different time periods. To give but one example, it is uncertain whether the various rebates produce short-term benefits to consumers that exceed any possible long-term losses that they suffer.[31] The calculations are too tenuous to justify the enormous legal uncertainty that is created under any rule that looks to the totality of the circumstances in its examination of market definition or the practice in question. Even if administering this system were costless and unerring, it is at best an open question whether the marketplace works more smoothly with all these legal protections against ostensible distortions than without them. But no system is costless and error-free, especially in matters as unbounded as competition cases. Therefore, the right question to ask is whether the enforcement activities of the Commission produce gains in excess of the high administrative and error costs of their implementation. If the first question is (at best) in equipoise, then the answer to the second question is a no-brainer. No

31 See, e.g., Michelin, [1981] OJ L 353/33, [1982] 1 CMLR 643.

one has demonstrated and no one can demonstrate the clear social gains from chasing after unilateral practices under Article 82.

The Microsoft litigation

The danger of the aggressive position is apparent in the long-standing struggle that ended when Microsoft decided not to appeal the adverse judgment of the Court of First Instance ('CFI') entered in September 2007. The saga did not begin with that case but started far earlier in both the US and EC. It is interesting to contrast the litigation in both settings over the same issues.

Let me start with the US experience. The opening salvo was fired in 1993 when the Clinton Justice Department filed its initial complaint against Microsoft under section 2 of the Sherman Act. I think there is a strong argument that liability was proper in that case, on the ground that Microsoft should be treated as though it operated an essential facility in a network industry, which should therefore be subject to common carrier obligations of non-discriminatory treatment (Epstein, 2007: 74–111).

Microsoft, in my view, made a major mistake in the early stages of litigation by relying on its strong autonomy arguments, which claimed its exclusive ownership of its servers gave it an absolute right to determine how to configure its network and to whom to issue licences for its use. That claim gives it too much power in a network industry where competitive solutions are not attainable, given the need for extensive linkages and cooperation between supposed competitors. The situation is not made any easier because there are enormous efficiency advantages to having a single operating system, which sets a uniform standard for all players. Given the network status, the traditional rules of common carriers require it to allow hook-ups for all competitors, actual or potential, in those designated complementary markets. The upshot is that the antitrust laws could operate to require the firm to make interconnections with other firms whose applications could only run on the Microsoft platform.

The US litigation on this case veered from pillar to post and back again. In the early stages, Microsoft won an important victory when it prevailed in its claim that it was entitled to develop an 'integrated' product that incorporated its web browser into the basic design.[32] But as the litigation progressed, it seemed possible that Judge Thomas Penfield Jackson, the first district court judge, would break the firm up into two separate components, one that controlled the MS-DOS operating system and the other which controlled applications – which would have done nothing to address the interconnection question.[33] But the matter quickly passed out of Judge Jackson's hands. The appellate court for the District of Columbia first rejected the break up remedy,[34] and then it took the extraordinary step of removing Judge Jackson from the case.[35]

On remand, the case was assigned to a new district court judge, Colleen Kollar-Kotelly. Judge Kollar-Kotelly fashioned a sensible remedy that required the firm to allow interconnections on non-discriminatory terms, which was sustained on appeal against various legal attacks.[36] One subordinate piece of that decision required Microsoft to share its trade secrets with its competitors, but also required those firms to keep that information confidential and to use it solely for the purpose of implementing the connections.[37] The overall effect of the initial decree was

32 *United States v. Microsoft Corp.*, 1998 U.S. Dist. LEXIS 14231 (D.D.C. 1998) (Microsoft I).

33 *United States v. Microsoft Corp.* and *State of New York v. Microsoft Corp.*, 87 F.Supp.2d 30 (D.D.C. 2000) (finding liability); *United States v. Microsoft Corp.* and *State of New York v. Microsoft Corp.*, 97 F. Supp.2d 59 (D.D.C. 2000) (ordering break up).

34 *United States v. Microsoft Corp.*, 253 F.3d 34, 45–97 (D.C. Cir. 2001).

35 Ibid at 107–117. "Although we find no evidence of actual bias, we hold that the actions of the trial judge seriously tainted the proceedings before the District Court and called into question the integrity of the judicial process." Ibid. at 46.

36 *State of New York v. Microsoft Corp.*, 224 F.Supp. 2d 76 (D.D.C. 2002); *Commonwealth of Massachusetts v. Microsoft Corp.*, 373 F.3d 1199 (D.C. Cir. 2004).

37 'Microsoft shall disclose to [various equipment and service providers], for the sole purpose of interoperating with the Windows Operating System Product … the [various] APIs and related Documentation that are used by Microsoft Middleware to interoperate with a Windows Operating System Product.' *United States v. Microsoft Corp.*, 2002 U.S. Dist. LEXIS 22864,, at *9 (D.D.C. 2002) (2002 Consent Decree, at III(D)). 'Microsoft [must license] third parties … on reasonable and non-discrimi-

modest, at best, in large measure because the interconnection problem is not very difficult to overcome, given that rival and compatible web browsers can be downloaded from the Internet. There is some evidence that the overall market has not moved in areas that were subject to the earlier decree, which suggests that Microsoft's product has an efficiency advantage over its rivals, just as happened in the *United Shoe Machinery* case discussed above.

The initial five year period of 2002 consent decree expired in November 2007, and at this point, the case took a surprising twist as Judge Kollar-Kotelly extended the decree for an additional two years.[38] Her decision did not rest on any claim that Microsoft had not sought to comply with the decree. Instead, she held that her present decision was 'based upon the extreme and unforeseen delay in the availability of complete, accurate, and useable technical documentation relating to the Communications Protocols that Microsoft is required to make available to licensees under Section III.E of the Final Judgments.'[39] Section III.E requires Microsoft to 'make available' to its customers all communications protocols that allow Windows client operating systems to interoperate 'natively,' with Microsoft's own server operating system – that is, to operate together without the addition of any special software to forge the connection. The source of her conclusion about interoperability was that Microsoft had not been able to supply in detail all sorts of protocols about conceivable interconnection scenarios to both its customers and its users.[40]

As William Page and Seldon Childers have argued, however, the difficulties here had nothing to do with the day-to-day challenges of interconnection by actual end users.[41] Rather the complications arose

natory terms ... any communications protocol[s] ... [used by Microsoft] operating system[s] ... to interoperate, or communicate, [directly] ... with a Microsoft server operating system []'. Ibid. at *10 (2002 Consent Decree, at III.E).

38 New York v. Microsoft Corp., 531 F. Supp. 2d 141 (D.D.C. 2008).

39 Ibid. at 144.

40 Ibid. at 172.

41 William H. Page & Seldon J. Childers, 'Measuring Compliance with Compulsory Licensing Remedies in the American Microsoft Case', http://papers.ssrn.com/so13/papers.cfm?abstract_id=1149862 (Antitrust Law Journal, Forthcoming).

because of the large volume of requests to specify the protocols for all conceivable interconnections, whether or not these were needed in any particular case. Page and Childers note that these requests have required Microsoft to devote a large flotilla of technical experts – 630 as of January 2008 – to a problem that does not involve any actual harm to other firms in the industry.[42] It is hard therefore to resist their conclusion that this latest twist in the Microsoft saga has anticompetitive consequences by allowing Microsoft's rivals to use the consent decree process to impose costs on rivals.[43] Once again the key lesson to learn is that even a sensible interconnection proposal can go off the rails through its implementation.

The question of market dominance followed a different path in the EC, but also resulted in some anticompetitive outcomes. Here the Commission began its investigation of Microsoft in 1998 in response to a complaint of another American company, Sun Microsystems.[44] Competitor complaints are generally a sign of a weak case. The gist of Sun's complaint was that Microsoft had refused to disclose key protocols on the interfaces between the Microsoft operating system that would allow Sun and other competitors to create 'workgroup' systems that could interact with Microsoft's desktop and operating systems. With a 95 percent share in the server market, Microsoft could not well claim that it did not have a dominant market position. That claim was sustained in 2004 when the EC Commission imposed on Microsoft a fine in excess of 497 million Euros for the abuse of its dominant position, and ordered the company to make available the key information to its competitors.[45] The charges that sustained the complaint were that Microsoft had been guilty of 'stifling innovation in the impacted market and of diminishing consumers' choices by locking them into a

42 Ibid. at 18, 20–22.

43 Ibid. at 37–38.

44 For a concise account, see Jones and Sufrin (2008: 571–575).

45 *Microsoft*, Commission Decision, 24 March 2004, COMOP/C-3/37.792, [2005] CMLR 965.

homogenous Microsoft solution.'[46] The remedy ordered was interoperability. There was, however, virtually no discussion of what innovations had been thwarted, which seems like a serious omission in the light of the huge amount of new software that had been built by outside firms under Microsoft licences. Clearly, the company had some strong incentive to share its codes with other firms under various confidentiality agreements. The question that was never addressed was how further decrees on interoperability would improve the situation.

The gaps in the Commission's case were equally evident after Microsoft took its case to the CFI, where the liability finding was affirmed. On the remedial side two issues were critical. The first was the extent to which 'interoperability' standards that sufficed in the original US decree would suffice in the EU, so that further actions were required, particularly in connection with the sharing of trade secrets that related to the operation of the Microsoft systems. The second dealt with the question of the bundling of Microsoft's Windows Media Player.

On the first of these questions, the CFI judgment of 17 September 2007 is a model of obscurity that takes over 100 pages without giving any clear explanation as to what forms of disclosure should be required and why. In dealing with these issues all that is clear is that the definition of interoperability that commended itself to Judge Kollar-Kotelly in her initial consent decree was regarded as too narrow by the CFI. Yet exactly how and why it should be broadened was not clarified. It does not seem that other software and computer companies complained that their products could be downloaded to function on Microsoft's operating system, which is what interoperability should require. There is no question that the Kollar-Kotelly decree would allow for example rival suppliers of web browsers or word processing programs to challenge the question of whether they could interoperate on the Microsoft platform, and specific grievances of that sort could and should be worked out in a framework patterned on the original Kollar-Kotelly judgment.

46 Ibid. § 782.

The CFI did not adopt that line. And much of its verbal effort was to reassure its readership that its rulings would not allow Microsoft's competitors to 'clone'[47] or create a 'plug replacement.'[48] Nonetheless, it seems as if the CFI backed the Commission insofar as it held that

> in order to be able to be viably marketed, non-Windows work group server operating systems must be capable of participation in the Windows domain architecture – which consists of 'architecture' of both client/server and server/server interconnections and interactions, closely interlinked – on an equal footing with Windows work group server operating systems. That means, in particular, that a server running a non-Microsoft work group server operating system is able to act as domain controller within a Windows domain using Active Directory, and consequently, is capable of participating in the multimaster replication mechanism with the other domain controllers.[49]

In light of this pronouncement, it seems – where the precaution is not one of false modesty, but genuine confusion – therefore that interoperability does not mean just the ability to run one's programs on the Microsoft system. Rather it seems as though any competitor should be able to get enough information to substitute its own equipment for any portion of the basic Microsoft operating system so that it can market a composite operating system at its own discretion. Obviously, the only way that these substitutions can be made is to know the guts of the system well enough to facilitate the replacements in question, which goes a long way toward building a rival operating system on the back of Microsoft's hard labour.

The informational demands for this form of selective substitution is far greater than those for the interconnections contemplated under the original 2002 US consent decree, which helps explain why the CFI had to force Microsoft to disclose its trade secrets to remedy to an Article

47 *CFI Microsoft*, ¶ 212, 234.

48 Ibid at ¶ 212, 216.

49 Ibid at ¶ 390.

82 claim. It reached this conclusion on the ground that the protection that trade secrets receive under national law is less than that which is normally accorded to patents and to copyrights.[50] The point is correct in one sense, in that the law of trade secrets does not prevent the independent discovery of the same device or even, in most instances, the reverse engineering of a particular product to determine the content of any given trade secrets. But I am aware of no law that says that just because one party may acquire a trade secret in either of these two ways, it follows that the Commission can order a company to surrender its trade secrets to its competitors without compensation, which seems the clear purport of the CFI's position.

It is very hard to resist the conclusion that the CFI has forgotten the difference between competition and subsidy. In its zeal to strike at Microsoft for its dominant practices, it has not given any reason why the emergence of multiple modifications of the Microsoft server will result in any efficiency gain, let alone those on the scale of allowing interconnections US-style. Thus when Microsoft offered to open its system wider,[51] Neelie Kroes scoffed at its detailed proposal, only to impose a new fine of 899 million Euros for refusing to comply with its 2004 decision, without any further hearing.[52] The effect of her actions has been to create a real economic inefficiency by essentially ordering the cross-subsidy of new competitors who can share in Microsoft's technology without paying any compensation for what they have received. It is hard to conceive of any action that is more anticompetitive than the subsidies that the CFI has ordered.

The second portion of the 17 September judgement is in my view

50 Ibid at 280.

51 See Microsoft, Virtual Pressroom: 'Microsoft Makes Strategic Changes in Technology and Business Practices to Expand Interoperability', http://www.microsoft.com/presspass/presskits/interoperability/default.mspx, 21 February 2008).

52 Neelie Kroes, "Decision to impose EUR 899 million penalty on Microsoft for non-compliance" (27 February 2008), http://europa.eu/rapid/pressReleasesAction.do?reference=SPEECH/08/105&format=HTML&aged=0&language=EN&guiLanguage=en

more bizarre than the first. In it the CFI upheld the position of the Commission that Microsoft had engaged in an abuse of its dominant position insofar as it refused to market a version of its operating system without its Windows Media Player. The apparent abuse in this situation was the failure to offer less for more. The argument for this novel position was so long as WMP was on the basic system neither original equipment manufacturers (OEMs) nor consumers could choose to have just some other system. The effective demand for this product has been, according Microsoft, less than one sale in 10,000,[53] which suggests that the Commission had made much ado about nothing. Nonetheless, the CFI insists that its broad definition of coercion covers the case, even if Microsoft does not charge any more for the inclusion of WMP.[54] There is then this irony. The first portion of the CFI judgment is massively coercive, but its later portion reads more like an irritant than a constructive engagement with any of the issues of market power.

In conclusion, it is hard to resist the judgment that the jurisprudence that has developed under Article 82 is both more intrusive and more mischievous than the US case law under Section 2 of the Sherman Act, which has its own fair share of unfortunate surprises. The question is why then do the Commission and the CFI show such a determination to engage in decisions that are far more likely to hurt the cause of innovation and competition than to abandon it? That answer is hard to come by. One possible explanation is that there is an implicit willingness to aggressively apply Article 82 against US firms, since these are far more likely to have a dominant position than firms that are located in the EC. Perhaps it is not an accident that Microsoft and Intel have been the most conspicuous targets of EC actions, but it is clear that other of the Commission's misguided decisions have not involved US firms at all, so that it may well be that a large part of the truth lies in the observation

53 "Backgrounder: Microsoft's Competition Case in Europe", http://www.microsoft.com/presspass/legal/european/EU_Competition_Overview.mspx, which notes that approximately .005% of consumers have chosen this option.

54 *CFI Microsoft*, ¶¶962–965.

that the EC is led by a more corporatist and less individualist mindset than US courts. Ideas, both good and bad, do matter in the way in which they shape the intellectual orientation to particular debates. All this speculation, however, has to wait for another day. The simple and stark conclusion here is that the aggressive condemnation of unilateral practices by dominant firms has, especially in the EC, created far more harm than good. Score one more intellectual victory – and practical defeat – for the defenders of limited government in the classical liberal tradition.

References

Areeda, P. & D. F. Turner (1975), 'Predatory Pricing and Related Practices Under Section 2 of the Sherman Act,' *Harvard Law Review*, Vol. 88, pp. 697–733.

Easterbrook, F. H. (1981), 'Predatory Strategies and Counterstrategies,' *University of Chicago Law Review*, Vol. 48, pp. 263–337.

Economic Advisory Group for Competition Policy (2005), 'An Economic Approach to Article 82,' http://ec.europa.eu/comm/competition/publications/studies/eagcp_july_21_05.pdf (accessed June 22, 2006).

Epstein, R.A. (2004), 'The Coordination of Public and Private Antitrust Actions', (on file with editor).

Epstein, R.A. (2005a), 'Monopoly Dominance or Level Playing Field: The New Antitrust Paradox,' *University of Chicago Law Review*, Vol. 72, pp. 49 – 72.

R. A. Epstein (2005b), 'American Lessons for European Federalism,' *New Frontiers Foundation*.

Epstein, R.A. (2006), *Overdose: How Excessive Government Regulation Stifles Pharmaceutical Innovation*, Yale, New Haven.

Epstein, R.A. (2007), *Antitrust consent decrees in theory and practice: Why less is more*, American Enterprise Institute, Washington, D.C.

Evans, D. & J. Padilla (2005), 'Designing Antitrust Rules for Assessing Unilateral Practices: A Neo-Chicago Approach,' *University of Chicago Law Review*, Vol. 72, pp. 73–98.

Fischel, D. R. (1983), 'The Appraisal Remedy In Corporate Law', *Am. Bar Found. Res. J.* pp. 875 – 902.

Hovenkamp, H. (2005), *The Antitrust Enterprise: Principle and Execution*, Harvard University Press, Cambridge, Mass. & London, UK

Jones, A. & B. Sufrin (2008), *EC Competition Law: Text, Cases, and Materials*, Oxford, Oxford University Press.

Kroes, N. (2005), 'Preliminary Thoughts on Policy Review of Article 82,' http://europa.eu.int/rapid/pressReleasesAction.do?reference=SPEECH/05/537 (accessed February 11, 2008).

Lawsky, D. (2008), 'EU conducts antitrust raid on Intel, retailers', Tuesday, 12 February 2008 07:12:32 RTRS [nL12166662].

Locke, J. (1690), *Second treatise of government*, Hackett Publishing Company, Indianapolis, IN (1980) Ch. IX.

Page W.H. & S. J. Childers, Measuring Compliance with Compulsory Licensing Remedies in the American Microsoft Case, http://papers.ssrn.com/s013/papers.cfm?abstract_id=1149862 Antitrust Law Journal, Forthcoming).

Rubinfield, D.L. (2005), '3M's Bundled Rebates: An Economic Perspective,' *University of Chicago Law Review*, Vol. 72, pp. 243 – 264.

Appendix

The Sherman Act, 15 U.S.C. §§ 1–2 (2006)

Section 1. Trusts, etc., in restraint of trade illegal; penalty

Every contract, combination in the form of trust or otherwise, or conspiracy, in restraint of trade or commerce among the several States, or with foreign nations, is declared to be illegal. Every person who shall make any contract or engage in any combination or conspiracy hereby declared to be illegal shall be deemed guilty of a felony, and, on conviction thereof, shall be punished by fine not exceeding $10,000,000 if a corporation, or, if any other person, $350,000, or by imprisonment not exceeding three years, or by both said punishments, in the discretion of the court.

Section 2. Monopolization; penalty
Every person who shall monopolize, or attempt to monopolize, or combine or conspire with any other person or persons, to monopolize any part of the trade or commerce among the several States, or with foreign nations, shall be deemed guilty of a felony, and, on conviction thereof, shall be punished by fine not exceeding $10,000,000 if a corporation, or, if any other person, $350,000, or by imprisonment not exceeding three years, or by both said punishments, in the discretion of the court.

7 Clayton Act, 15 U.S.C. § 18

Acquisition by one corporation of stock of another
No person engaged in commerce or in any activity affecting commerce shall acquire, directly or indirectly, the whole or any part of the stock or other share capital and no person subject to the jurisdiction of the Federal Trade Commission shall acquire the whole or any part of the assets of another person engaged also in commerce or in any activity affecting commerce, where in any line of commerce or in any activity affecting commerce in any section of the country, the effect of such acquisition may be substantially to lessen competition, or to tend to create a monopoly.

No person shall acquire, directly or indirectly, the whole or any part of the stock or other share capital and no person subject to the jurisdiction of the Federal Trade Commission shall acquire the whole or any part of the assets of one or more persons engaged in commerce or in any activity affecting commerce, where in any line of commerce or in any activity affecting commerce in any section of the country, the effect of such acquisition, of such stocks or assets, or of the use of such stock by the voting or granting of proxies or otherwise, may be substantially to lessen competition, or to tend to create a monopoly.

Article 81 of the Treaty Establishing the European Community (Nice consolidated version) (ex Article 85)

1. The following shall be prohibited as incompatible with the common market: all agreements between undertakings, decisions by associations of undertakings and concerted practices which may affect trade between Member States and which have as their object or effect the prevention, restriction or distortion of competition within the common market, and in particular those which:
   (a) directly or indirectly fix purchase or selling prices or any other trading conditions;
   (b) limit or control production, markets, technical development, or investment;
   (c) share markets or sources of supply;
   (d) apply dissimilar conditions to equivalent transactions with other trading parties, thereby placing them at a competitive disadvantage;
   (e) make the conclusion of contracts subject to acceptance by the other parties of supplementary obligations which, by their nature or according to commercial usage, have no connection with the subject of such contracts.
2. Any agreements or decisions prohibited pursuant to this Article shall be automatically void.
3. The provisions of paragraph 1 may, however, be declared inapplicable in the case of:
   - any agreement or category of agreements between undertakings,
   - any decision or category of decisions by associations of undertakings,

- any concerted practice or category of concerted practices, which contributes to improving the production or distribution of goods or to promoting technical or economic progress, while allowing consumers a fair share of the resulting benefit, and which does not:
  (a) impose on the undertakings concerned restrictions which are not indispensable to the attainment of these objectives;
  (b) afford such undertakings the possibility of eliminating competition in respect of a substantial part of the products in question.

Article 82 of the Treaty Establishing the European Community (Nice consolidated version) (ex Article 86)

Any abuse by one or more undertakings of a dominant position within the common market or in a substantial part of it shall be prohibited as incompatible with the common market in so far as it may affect trade between Member States.

Such abuse may, in particular, consist in:

(a) directly or indirectly imposing unfair purchase or selling prices or other unfair trading conditions;
(b) limiting production, markets or technical development to the prejudice of consumers;
(c) applying dissimilar conditions to equivalent transactions with other trading parties, thereby placing them at a competitive disadvantage;
(d) making the conclusion of contracts subject to acceptance by the other parties of supplementary obligations which, by their nature or according to commercial usage, have no connection with the subject of such contracts.

10 PRIVATE VERSUS PUBLIC REGULATION OF THE ENVIRONMENT

Julian Morris

Introduction

When environmental issues are discussed in the media or the classroom, the standard presumption is that a problem has been caused by private business and must be solved by government stepping in to regulate. The reader may therefore be surprised to learn that many environmental problems have in fact been caused by governments, sometimes in spite of attempts by private individuals or businesses to stop them. Meanwhile, private regulation of the environment has a long history. The purpose of this chapter is to compare and contrast private with public regulation of the environment. The focus is primarily on controlling pollution, but the results are readily extended to conservation.

The chapter begins with a discussion of the standard theory of environmental policy, which is now widely used as a justification for government regulation. This is followed by criticisms of that theory and its practical application. Private alternatives to public regulation are explained and discussed. The chapter concludes with an assessment of how to improve the mix of public and private environmental regulation.

The theory of environmental policy

The theory of environmental policy (e.g. Baumol and Oates, 1988) posits that in the absence of regulatory intervention, economically rational individuals and firms will generate negative 'externalities'; that is to say, they will impose an uncompensated cost on third parties. It is further posited that various policies might be followed that would enable the 'internalisation' of these externalities. It is important to note that this is not necessarily the same as saying that adversely affected third parties will be fully compensated for the harm imposed upon them, or that the harm will be eliminated. Rather, what it usually means is that the externality will be reduced to the 'socially optimal' or 'social-welfare-maximising' level.

So, for example, if the externality in question results from smoke released as a result of burning bituminous coal, then one policy that might reduce the extent of this externality is the imposition of a regulation restricting the burning of such coal. The question then arises as to what type and degree of regulation are desirable. To the environmental economist the answer is that the optimal regulation sets the level of smoke emissions (or, perhaps more likely, ambient concentrations of smoke) at a level that maximises net social welfare.

Now, you may well be wondering how one identifies the social-welfare-maximising level of smoke. To the theoretical environmental economist this question is simply answered: by identifying the point at which the marginal social benefit and marginal social cost curves intersect. To the practically minded environmental economist, the question is a little more difficult, since it will be necessary to identify what the social cost and social benefit functions look like. But we will come back to that later (this section is about theory, after all).

Once one has established the optimum level of emissions (within some range of error), the question becomes one of what policy is most effective at achieving the necessary reduction in emissions. At this stage, three options are usually put on the table: command-and-control regulation, tradable emissions permits (TEPs) and emission charges.

Command-and-control regulations take various forms, including technological standards (such as BAT: best available technology), flow limits (e.g. maximum and/or average end-of-pipe emission limits) and stock limits (i.e. restrictions on the degree to which emissions into a flow of water may consume oxygen in the water). Often, such regulations are not fixed in statute but are set by regulators, who must obtain detailed information about the functioning of any specific plant being regulated. The implementation and enforcement of such regulations set an implicit price on emissions, though this will usually not be transparent (i.e. observable to other operators of similar plant in similar circumstances).

TEPs, first suggested by Dales (1968), in principle offer a means of achieving similar controls on emissions to those that would be obtained by command-and-control, but at lower cost. Under a TEP system, the government sets the total permissible ambient levels of a particular substance (sometimes these are a combination of maximum and average levels), then allocates permits to emit the substance to various sources. Allocation may be by 'grandfathering' to existing emitters, or by auction, or by some combination of the two.

Once emission permits have been allocated, trades may take place.[1] Allowing permit holders to trade enables emitters with relatively low abatement costs to sell some or all of their permits to emitters with higher abatement costs. This is both economically and environmentally more efficient than most command-and-control-type regulations, for the following reasons:

- First, it enables continued use of older plant with higher abatement costs, when a BAT requirement might have led to the decommissioning of the plant. So it reduces the level of investment required to achieve any particular environmental goal and it reduces the waste of resources inherent to any capital item.
- Second, if permit trades occur in a reasonably open market environment, this generates explicit prices. These prices enable more effective use of decentralised information about which technologies to use. They also incentivise the development and use of lower-cost low-emission and emission-abatement technologies.

1 Usually these trades are subject to rules that are intended to ensure that ambient concentrations of specific pollutants do not exceed the desired level. Often this means that trades are complex, since they must follow a formula that accounts for the differential impact on concentrations of emissions from plants located in different places.

Another method for reducing emissions is the emission charge. Whereas a TEP works by imposing restrictions on the amount of emissions allowed, enabling permit holders to establish a market price for each unit of emissions, a charge works by imposing a price on emissions and allowing emitters to decide how much to pay in fees and how much to invest in abatement.

As with TEPs, emission charges incentivise the use and development of low-cost emission-abatement technologies, but do not specify which technologies to use. They also allow plant that has high abatement costs to continue to be operated – if it is still profitable to do so once the charge has been paid.

Environmental policy in practice

When we look at the real world, it is clear that governments have primarily used command-and-control-type measures to control pollution. The history of such measures can be traced at least to 1306, when Edward I passed an Act banning the burning of 'sea coal' (smoky, bituminous coal of the kind typically brought by sea from Newcastle) in London's kilns when Parliament was in session. Parliament became more active in passing air pollution legislation in the nineteenth century, beginning with the Smoke Abatement Act of 1854 and the Alkali Acts of 1863 and 1874. The twentieth century saw an explosion of environmental legislation, not only in the UK but around the world, nearly all of which has been of the command-and-control type.

Seeking to explain why command-and-control has been the preferred option for governments, Buchanan and Tullock (1975) analysed the incentive effects of the different systems. They showed that incumbent firms would prefer 'direct' (command-and-control) regulations because they could act as a means of limiting entry of new firms, reducing competition and increasing the profitability of the incumbents.

While the real world is inevitably more complicated than Buchanan and Tullock's model, researchers have found that such regulations often do benefit a set of incumbent interests. For example, Ackerman and Hassler (1981) argue that the seemingly perverse Section 111 of the US Clean Air Act Amendments of 1977 can be explained by the fact that it substantially benefited coal producers in the eastern USA. To understand why, we will briefly recount the history of the Clean Air Act (CAA).

Under the 1970 CAA, the Environmental Protection Agency (EPA) was required to set emission standards for coal-fired boilers. The original standard it set was 1.2 pounds of coal per million BTU of energy. The operators of boilers (mainly power companies) were allowed to meet this standard in whatever way they deemed to be most cost-effective. Since coal from the west of the USA is cleaner than that in the east, many companies chose to use the cleaner western coal, instead of installing expensive scrubbers.

Rather than mandating new emissions standards, the 1977 Amendments required the EPA to ensure that the 'best available technology' for reducing sulphur dioxide pollution was installed on new coal-fired boilers. By forcing power companies to install scrubbers on new boilers, the Amendments removed the incentive to use the cleaner western coal. Ackerman and Hassler (ibid.) argue that the Amendments were effectively a massive subsidy to eastern coal producers, which had lobbied for their inclusion.

The requirement also had a perverse environmental effect. Since scrubbers were required only on new plants, companies had incentives to continue to use older, less efficient coal-fired boilers for longer, thereby delaying environmental improvements that otherwise would have occurred and in some cases even increasing ambient levels of sulphur dioxide.[2]

2 See also Pashigan (1985), who found evidence that the 'prevention of significant deterioration' requirement in the 1977 Clean Air Act Amendments benefited vested interests in northern urban areas over those in western and southern rural areas – and that the pattern of congressional voting was more consistent with this benefit than any putative party bias.

Another clear instance occurred in the phase-out of chlorofluorocarbons (CFCs). In the early 1980s, there was a push to phase out the use of CFCs globally, on the grounds that they were causing stratospheric ozone to break down, weakening the shield that protects the earth's inhabitants from harmful ultraviolet radiation. Initially, producers of CFCs lobbied hard against such a phase-out. Nevertheless, an international agreement to that effect, the Vienna Convention on Substances that Deplete the Ozone Layer, was signed in 1985. Then things got interesting.

Following the signing of the Convention, the CFC industry began to lobby for a more rapid phase-out of CFCs than had originally been envisioned. Why did it do this? Two reasons: first, the companies had patented various molecules they believed would be substitutes for the CFCs, which were by that time no longer protected by patent. By forcing the rapid phase-out of CFCs, they would create a larger market for these alternatives, increasing their profitability. Second, the large producers of CFCs reasoned – correctly – that they would obtain allowances to produce under the supply restrictions, enabling them to reap windfall profits. Environmentalist organisations and some politicians also supported a shorter timescale. In the context of this perfect storm, in 1987 a Protocol to the Convention was signed at Montreal, which supported this more rapid phase-out. Subsequent meetings of the parties likewise speeded up the process and the CFC producers made a killing (Morrisette, 1989).

A similar scenario played out with the waste management industry in the UK, which lobbied the government to implement environmental regulations that would eliminate 'cowboy' operators by setting minimum standards for the construction and operation of waste management facilities. The ploy worked – to an extent: following the passage of legislation in 1990, the apparent restrictions on supply drove up the price of landfill sites and some of the incumbent operators cashed in by selling to larger firms. In the implementation phase, however, smaller operators obtained concessions enabling them to continue to operate, leading to a temporary reduction in landfill site prices (Morris, 1995).

More recently, we have also seen the gaming of the TEP system established in Europe to reduce emissions of greenhouse gases (GHGs). Permits were grandfathered to existing GHG emitters, many of whom had low abatement costs. The result was that large incumbents were able to make a tidy profit by selling permits to smaller incumbents and new entrants with higher abatement costs (Open Europe, 2006).

This finding suggests that there may be benefits in using charges over either command-and-control or TEPs, since the latter will have additional social deadweight losses in the form of resources diverted to lobbying and in the form of reduced competition, lower levels of innovation and higher prices. It also suggests, however, that politically it may be more difficult to implement charges, since incumbents will lobby for command-and-control regulations or grandfathered TEPs.

Given the concentration of interests in regulated industries, it is not surprising that there have been very few cases in which TEPs or charges have been used to *replace* existing environmental regulations. Rather, what has typically happened is that charges or permits have been applied on top of existing regulatory regimes.

The experience with permits has been mixed. As noted above, permit trading schemes have often been gamed by vested interests. Nevertheless, there have been some relatively successful schemes. Schmalensee et al. (1998) argue that the Southern California Air Quality Management District scheme saved billions of dollars on emissions abatement costs relative to the previous command-and-control-based system. Generally speaking, permit trading schemes have been most successful when the permits have been clearly defined, readily transferable and not subject to arbitrary expropriation – in other words, they work when they are closest to being *de jure* property rights.

Unfortunately, very few if any schemes actually meet these criteria – unless one broadens the category of tradable permits to include other resource management issues. In particular, Iceland and New Zealand's systems of tradable permits for fisheries are worth noting. Like TEPs, individual transferable quotas (ITQs) offer a way of more efficiently managing a scarce resource: in the case of TEPs the scarce resource is clean air or clean water; in the case of ITQs, the scarce resource is ocean species such as fish and lobster. Unlike most TEP schemes, however, the ITQ systems put in place in New Zealand and Iceland do closely resemble property rights. The establishment of these schemes has dramatically altered the incentives faced by fishermen and the agencies setting the total allowable catch, and has improved the sustainability of the system.

Prior to the introduction of ITQs in New Zealand and Iceland, the fisheries in both countries had been going the way of government-regulated fisheries the world over, which follows roughly the following pattern: (1) the fishing industry grows and becomes more technologically sophisticated; (2) legitimate concerns are raised about the sustainability of the harvest in the absence of intervention; (3) limits are imposed on the amount of fish each boat may catch and on the number of days they may put to sea; (4) fishers over-invest in boats and other equipment, and fisheries producer organisations lobby for increased catch levels; (5) regulations are imposed on the types of equipment that can be used; (6) fishers identify ways of getting around the restrictions, either legally or illegally; (7) repeat (3) to (6) until fish stocks fall to levels at which fishing is no longer economically viable; (8) fishers receive subsidies that help eliminate the stocks altogether, or are given welfare and told never to fish again.

Following the introduction of ITQs, the owners of quotas called for lower total allowable catch levels. They did this because their quota represented a clearly defined and readily transferable share of the total allowable catch and they could see that the future value of their quota would rise if stock levels rose, which is the logical consequence of lower catch levels. Furthermore, in New Zealand boat owners voluntarily accepted a system of monitoring that enables the quota management authorities to see where their boats are and to identify potential instances of illegal fishing. In addition, the more efficient fishers bought out the quotas of less efficient fishers. Overall, the ITQ system in both countries has raised levels of efficiency, reduced conflict over the use of the scarce resource, and increased the sustainability of the fisheries system (see, for example, Arnason, 2006; Newell et al., 2002).

While the experience with TEPs has been mixed, the experience with charges has mostly been abysmal, with governments frequently using the premise of environmental damage as a justification for imposing revenue-raising taxes. Successive UK governments have been particularly guilty, with the Fuel Duty Escalator, Landfill Levy and other taxes that have little or no environmental merit being introduced on a 'green' ticket. The main problem with these taxes is that they are applied to inputs rather than outputs: a tax on fuel gives some incentive to reduce fuel consumption, which may lead to increased efficiency of burn and reduced emissions, but it is a poor proxy for an emissions charge. A tax on the disposal of waste by landfill will likely reduce the amount of waste going to landfill (but only if alternatives are available at a price differential less than the tax); in many cases, however, landfilling may be the environmentally superior disposal option, so the tax will have the perverse effect of incentivising environmentally damaging recycling or incineration (Eshet et al., 2006).

Problems with the theory of environmental policy

If one accepts the proposition that in principle it is desirable to set environmental policy goals on the basis of what is considered socially optimal, we then have the challenge of actually identifying that optimum. In a world of fixed technologies, it is possible within some margin of error to identify the private costs of restricting emissions (but see above the implications of information asymmetries between producers and regulators and the potential this creates for gaming the system). The larger problems come when trying to identify the social benefits of restricting emissions.

To put it bluntly, there are no truly reliable means of estimating external benefits. Economists have devised all manner of sophisticated proxies, from measuring the difference in prices of properties (houses, apartments) apparently associated with differing environmental conditions (so-called 'hedonic pricing') to estimating the amount individuals appear to be willing to pay to visit a place of natural beauty on the basis of how much it costs them to get to the place (the so-called 'travel cost method') to asking people questions about what they would be willing to pay for a less polluted environment (so-called 'contingent valuation method' or CVM). All these methods, however, rely on assumptions that are for the most part invalid.

Hedonic pricing relies on the assumption that it is possible to specify all the criteria upon which people make decisions and, by performing a regression analysis, deduce the implied value of one or more environmental characteristic(s). The problem is that we cannot actually know what individual characteristics people value unless we ask them, and even when we ask them, the reliability of their answers is questionable (see below under CVM). Meanwhile, the value people place on specific characteristics varies; even if one could identify all the characteristics, a regression analysis will provide only an average of what value a certain group of individuals puts on each characteristic – and that average might well not be representative of the group for whom the social cost–benefit analysis is being carried out.

CVM is highly problematic. Among other concerns is the 'embedding problem': if subjects are asked questions in an order that does not conform to their own hierarchy of priorities and/or does not include all relevant items in that hierarchy, then they may well respond inconsistently (Kopp et al., 1997). So, for example, if a person is asked how much they are willing to pay to preserve the snow leopard, they might answer £5,000; when the same person is asked first how much they are willing to pay to preserve all the world's non-human species (£10,000), then how much all non-human mammals (£5,000), then all leopards (£500), then the snow leopard, they might say £250, or £50, or £5 – but almost certainly not £5,000. In spite of attempts to overcome this by embedding questions (on the basis of prior surveys), or by giving respondents 'time to think', the problem cannot be eliminated (e.g. Whittington et al., 1997). At best, CVM is a sophisticated means of ranking society's preferences (Mitchell and Carson, 1989; Coursey, 1998).

Another, related, problem is that people being asked such questions rarely have regard to real budget constraints, which can make their answers unreal. To control for this, researchers have attempted to identify ways of giving theoretical budget constraints, for example by making it clear that any investment/regulation would come as a result of a rise in taxes that would impact on them. But at the end of the day, unless the budget constraint is believed to be real it will not have the same impact.

A further problem with many attempts to identify the socially optimal level of pollution is that the putative harm is often expected to materialise only in the future, yet a decision must be made today. When given the option, people typically choose to have money now rather than in the future – which is part of the reason why they demand interest on money lent to others: they are being compensated for being deprived of that money for the duration of the loan.[3] Given this preference, it follows that future benefits and costs will be worth less today than current benefits and costs, so decisions regarding limits on emissions should discount benefits and costs at an appropriate rate. But people discount the future at different rates, so it is difficult to identify a single 'social' discount rate.

There is also a more fundamental problem with making decisions on behalf of future people: they are not yet born, so are not capable of having preferences (e.g. Beckerman, 2007). We can thus rely only on the preferences of people alive today when making long-term decisions – and these may well not be the same as those of people who are born in the future.

Perhaps the most egregious problem with the theory of environmental policy is that even at the 'optimum' level of emissions, there will often remain some people who are harmed by the externality. As noted

3 The other reason for interest is that the money might not be repaid, so lenders demand a 'risk premium'.

earlier, the theory says nothing about compensating those third parties on whom costs are imposed. I have always found this difficult to swallow; it somehow offends my sense of equity: how can it be 'optimal' that some people should be harmed? On whose say-so?

A related problem was identified by Coase (1960), who argued that externalities are reciprocal, not unilateral. Take, for example, a coal-burning factory operating next to a laundry such that the white sheets placed outside to dry by the laundry are tainted black by soot. Conventionally, the factory would be said to be causing a negative externality. Coase argues, however, that the externality has been caused by both the factory and the laundry – it is reciprocal – since the damage done to the white sheets occurs only because the laundry places them outside.

Coase analysed various situations in which such reciprocal externalities existed and showed how the common law resolved them. His analysis inspired a considerable degree of further work looking at possible common-law solutions to environmental problems. Among other things, such solutions have the potential to overcome the potential iniquities that result when the state intervenes through the imposition of regulations, permits or charges. The following section draws on this literature.

Private regulation of the environment

Unpleasant sights, smells and noise have surely troubled man since his earliest days. Attempts to resolve these problems can be traced back at least to Greek and Roman law, which had provisions protecting property owners against damage caused by neighbours. Meanwhile, the laws of Solon – the constitution of ancient Athens – included land-use planning rules, such as 'minimum distances between homes, and the permissible interposition of walls, ditches, wells, beehives, and certain trees' (Madden, 2005).

In the common law of England and Wales, injunctions and damages have been available to those subjected to vile smells and unbearable noise for hundreds of years. In 1608 William Aldred brought an action at the Norfolk assizes against his neighbour, Thomas Benton, who had built a pigsty adjacent to Aldred's house. The judge decided that the resultant stink interfered with Aldred's rights and ordered Benton to move the pigsty.[4]

But not any interference was deemed a nuisance. In his famous treatise on the Laws of England, Sir Edward Coke (1628) used *Aldred's Case* to clarify the rule: property holders have a right to use and enjoy their property free from interference, but the extent of this right is only that of ordinary comfort and necessity, not delicate taste: 'In a house four things are desired [habitation of man, pleasure of the inhabitant, necessity of light, and cleanliness of air], and for nuisance done to three of them an action lies.'[5]

The underlying principle was derived from the Roman maxim '*sic utere tuo ut in alienum non laedas*': so use your own property as not to injure your neighbours.[6] This rule was employed in numerous seventeenth-century cases and seems to have been applied quite generally (see Morris, 2003, and references therein). It was affirmed by the great jurist William Blackstone, who wrote in his Commentaries:

> [I]f one erects a smelting house for lead so near the land of another that the vapor and smoke kills his corn and grass, and damages his cattle therein, this is held to be a nuisance … [I]f one does any other act, in itself lawful, which yet being done in that place necessarily tends to the damage of another's property, it is a nuisance: for it is incumbent on him to find some other place to do that act where it will be less offensive. (Blackstone, 1765–69, Bk 3, ch. 13, pp. 217–18)

By clearly delineating the boundaries of acceptable action, the *sic utere* rule provided a framework within which economic activity could take place in such a way as to limit the environmental damage inflicted on

4 *Aldred's Case*, 77 Eng. Rep. 816 (K.B. 1611).
5 Ibid.
6 Ibid.

others. The rule discouraged activities that led to environmental damage and ensured, at least in principle, that if such damage occurred the perpetrator would be compelled to stop it and to compensate those affected.

Liability is strict; public benefit is no defence

Under the *sic utere* rule, liability is strict; that is to say, if an activity on A's property has caused a nuisance to B's property, A is liable notwithstanding the fact that A did not intend to cause the nuisance, notwithstanding the fact that A may have taken all reasonable precautions to prevent the nuisance from occurring, and notwithstanding any putative benefit to the public that might have resulted from the nuisance-causing action. Fundamentally, once it is established that activities occurring on A's property caused a nuisance to B's property, then under the *sic utere* rule A is liable – full stop.

Thus, in *Aldred's Case*, Benton argued in his defence that 'the building of the house for hogs was necessary for the sustenance of man, and one ought not to have so delicate a nose, that he cannot bear the smell of hogs'. This attempt to use a 'public benefit' argument failed, however.[7]

Acquiring the right to pollute by prior appropriation

While the *sic utere* rule was strict, it was not absolute: there were exceptions. In 1791, the Crown brought a case in public nuisance[8] against one Neville, a 'maker of kitchen stuff and other grease', for fouling the air.[9] But Neville had been carrying on his trade for some time without objection from his neighbours and Lord Kenyon advised the jury that 'where

7 Ibid.

8 Public nuisance is a separate action to private nuisance. It relates to harms to the general public and is primarily enforced by the Crown, although individuals may also argue a case in public nuisance if the extent of harm they suffer is greater than that suffered by other members of the public.

9 *R* v. *Neville*, 170 Eng. Rep. 102 (1791).

manufacturers have been borne within a neighbourhood for many years, it will operate as a consent of the inhabitants to their being carried on, though the law might have considered them as nuisances, had they been objected to in time'.[10] The jury acquitted the defendant. Following this reasoning, a person may acquire a prescriptive right to pollute if nobody brings an action in nuisance within a reasonable time.

Subsequent cases clarified the rule. In *Bliss* v. *Hale*,[11] the court ruled that since the defendant had been causing a nuisance only for three years, he had not acquired a prescriptive easement to continue, for which at least twenty years' continuous operation would have been necessary. In *Sturges* v. *Bridgeman*,[12] the court made clear that the harm itself, not merely the action causing the harm, must have continued for a period of 20 years in order for a right to have been acquired by prescription.

The zoning function of nuisance law

In *R* v. *Neville*, Lord Kenyon offered the observation (*obiter dicta*) that the consent to pollute would not apply to a newcomer who made the air 'very disagreeable and uncomfortable'.[13] This was taken to imply that a newcomer whose actions made only a marginal difference to air quality would not be liable for their portion of the harm caused to neighbouring properties.[14] In *Sturges* v. *Bridgeman*,[15] the court granted an injunction to the plaintiff whose ability to carry on his trade as a doctor in Wimpole Street was adversely affected by the very noisy activities of a neighbouring confectioner, the judge remarking: 'Whether anything is to be considered a nuisance or not is a question to be determined not merely by an abstract consideration of the thing itself, but in reference to its

10 Ibid.
11 7 Eng. Rep. 122 (1838).
12 11 Eng. Rep. 852, at 865 (Ch. D. 1879).
13 170 Eng. Rep. 102 (1791).
14 Ibid.
15 11 Eng. Rep. 852 (Ch. D. 1879).

circumstances. What would be a nuisance in Belgrave Square would not necessarily be so in Bermondsey.'[16]

In other words, nuisance law could provide a land-use planning, or 'zoning', function,[17] describing the boundaries where certain activities may or may not take place.[18]

In *St Helen's Smelting Co.* v. *Tipping*[19] a distinction was made between physical damage to property, which was deemed to be actionable regardless of the location of the property, and interference with the beneficial use of that property, which would be actionable only in areas that were not 'zoned' as industrial. It is important to understand what was going on here: the common law seeks where possible to use objective standards; in 'industrial' areas the objective standard against which a person's or company's behaviour may be compared will be different from the objective standard in non-industrial areas. At the time of the case in point (1865), it would not have been possible to prove that the noxious vapours emitted by the St Helen's Smelting Company were injurious to human health. In addition, given that there were several other industrial concerns in the neighbourhood, it was reasonable to suppose that the contribution of the smelter to the general unpleasantness of the air was both difficult to identify and perhaps marginal.[20]

16 Ibid.

17 See *Colls* v. *Home and Colonial Stores*, 1904 A.C. 179 ('a dweller in towns cannot be expected to have as pure air, as free from smoke, smell, and noise as if he lived in the country, and distant from other dwellings, and yet an excess of smoke, smell and noise may give a cause of action, but in each case it becomes a matter of degree').

18 Coase (1960) points out that the two parties would have been free to bargain around this judgement – the doctor selling his right to peaceful enjoyment of his property to the sweet manufacturer – if they so wished. This point is important but, nevertheless, if such a bargain were struck it would not have affected the general right, as a resident of the West End of London, to be free from the noise of pestles and mortars, so the planning function of the law would remain. (Although, presumably, a point would come where so many defendants had bargained around their respective injunctions that the character of the area would have changed.)

19 11 Eng. Rep. 1483 (H.L. 1865).

20 The judge in the lower court instructed the jury that the law was not concerned with 'trifling inconveniences' and that where noxious vapours were concerned 'the injury to be actionable must be such as visibly to diminish the value of the property and the comfort

So, the only 'objective' harm that could be identified was the direct physical damage to Mr Tipping's property.

By establishing clear and readily enforceable property rights in this way, nuisance law enabled parties to strike a balance between environmental amenities and cost. People buying a property in the West End of London knew that they had a right to be free from air pollution, noise and other interferences. People buying property in Bermondsey or St Helens knew that they would not be able to take an action against a marginal polluter unless the pollution caused physical damage to their property. The differences in property prices in these districts no doubt reflected the differences in amenities.

Nuisance law also contains an efficiency aspect. In areas where interference with peaceful enjoyment is rare, as in Berkeley Square and Wimpole Street, it is more efficient to grant injunctions against those who cause a nuisance, since the transaction costs of bargaining will be relatively low. By contrast, in areas such as Bermondsey, where historically there would have been many parties causing such interferences, the imposition of an injunction against one party seems iniquitous, yet the imposition of an injunction against all would cause great problems. The transaction costs of bargaining would be very high and if, as a result, many firms were to close, the costs to the local people could be great.[21] Moreover, as a neighbourhood becomes less industrial, judges may look more favourably on claims that an individual source of noise or noxious emission constitutes a nuisance, thus helping those seeking to improve the environmental amenities in an area that was formerly industrial.[22]

and enjoyment of it' (ibid.).

21 If many firms were faced with injunctions, they would have to bargain with each of the affected parties, which may be time-consuming and expensive – and most likely some parties would simply refuse any compensation. In the absence of low-cost abatement technologies, the only alternative for many firms might be to move the plant elsewhere.

22 Another option for improving the environment in an area 'zoned' for industrial use would be for those affected by the pollution to bargain with the companies. The coordination costs of such an activity might, however, be high. Moreover, the bargaining power of those so affected would probably be weak since the very nature of places that are 'zoned' for industrial use implies that the residents are poor.

Finally, the establishment of property rights through decentralised private nuisance actions is arguably both more equitable and more efficient than the creation of rights through a system of administrative planning. In the latter system, state administrators decide a priori where industry can locate and bargaining cannot take place, because rights created by administrative planning are inalienable.

Nuisance law as a means of preventing industrial pollution

It is often claimed that civil liability is not an appropriate remedy in cases where there are multiple sources of pollution or multiple affected parties. In other words for most instances of what nowadays would be called 'environmental pollution'. The nineteenth-century cases show, however, that this is not so.

St Helen's was the site not only of a copper smelter (the St Helen's Smelting Company) but also an alkali manufacturer. The fact that the Lords saw fit to hold the smelting company liable for the damage done to Tipping's property even though the alkali works was also causing pollution is prima facie evidence that nuisance law can work in multiple-source situations. Moreover, following Mr Tipping's victory, the farmers living around St Helen's were able to obtain compensation from the smelting company; indeed, they did so en masse, through William Rothwell, a land agent and valuer in St Helen's, who acted as arbitrator between the St Helen's Smelting Company and numerous farmers who were adversely affected (House of Lords, 1862). In 1865, Mr Tipping won an injunction against the smelting company, which led to the closure of the plant and no doubt put him and his neighbours on a surer footing to bargain with the alkali works.[23]

The implication is that if it could be shown that the emissions from a specific plant were causing objectively verifiable damage to a person's property – which today would reasonably be taken to include harm to

23 *Tipping* v. *St. Helen's*, 11 Eng. Rep. 1483 (H.L. 1865).

the health of the occupants – then the appropriate remedy is an injunction against the owner of that plant. Armed with an injunction, the injured property owner(s) would then be able to choose whether to be free from the nuisance or to negotiate with the polluter – and perhaps accept some compensation in return for permitting some or all of the harmful emissions to continue. In situations where there are multiple sources, an injunction against one plant sends a strong signal to owners of other polluting plants that they must at least enter into negotiations with affected property owners. Meanwhile, where there are many affected parties, there would be incentives for agents like Mr Rothwell to act on behalf of all affected parties and thereby protect the community and the environment. The standard of protection would be that desired by the property owner who was least willing to accept harmful emissions – which might be different from the standard that would be established by government.

Multiple sources: the combined-effect rule and collective action

Another argument often made in support of statutory regulation over the use of the common law is that the latter is unable to address situations where individual sources of emissions are harmful only when combined with other sources. This is simply false, as can be seen with regard to pollution of streams and rivers.

In *Young and Co.* v. *Bankier Distillery Co.*,[24] Lord McNaghten specified the rights of riparian owners as follows:

> A riparian proprietor is entitled to have the water of the stream, on the banks of which his property lies, flow down as it has been accustomed to flow down to his property, subject to the ordinary use of the flowing water by upper proprietors, and to such further use, if any, on their part in connection with their property as may be reasonable under the circumstances. *Every riparian owner is thus entitled to the water of his stream, in its natural flow, without sensible*

24 [1893] 69 L.T. 838.

diminution or increase and without sensible alteration in its character or quality.[25]

This robust riparian doctrine has remained more or less unchanged.[26] Moreover, multiple sources have been held jointly liable for harms. In *Blair & Sumner* v. *Deakin*,[27] each contributor to a nuisance was held liable for his contribution to the pollution, even though individually their actions would not have constituted a nuisance – this is known as the combined-effect rule. In the *Pride of Derby Angling Club* v. *British Celanese*,[28] this was extended to cases where a co-defendant has already admitted liability. Thus, a defendant D will be held liable as long as he has contributed to a nuisance, even though another defendant C has admitted liability and even though D would not have committed a nuisance but for the actions of C.[29]

The clarity of riparian rights was utilised in an innovative way by John Eastwood, KC, who in 1952 established the Anglers Co-operative Association (ACA).[30] The ACA acts on behalf of anglers and other riparian users – taking actions against polluters. This typically involves indemnifying the riparian owner(s) against the costs of taking action.[31] As Roger Bate has shown, the ACA has successfully prosecuted thousands of actions, using money obtained in damages and through bargaining around injunctions to fight subsequent cases (Bate, 2002).

The ACA offers an example of the role that environmental organisations might play if private law took a more prominent role in protecting the environment. Instead of lobbying for environmental regulations – and engaging in all manner of publicity stunts to raise public awareness

25 Ibid. at 839.

26 *Pride of Derby & Derbyshire Angling Club* v. *British Celanese Ltd*, 2 W.L.R. 58 (C.A. 1953).

27 [1887] 57 L.T.R. 522.

28 2 W.L.R. 58 (C.A. 1953).

29 Ibid.

30 The ACA has since changed its name to the Anglers' Conservation Association.

31 The right to support such an action through indemnity was challenged unsuccessfully (with an allegation of 'maintenance') in *Martell and Others* v. *Consett Iron Co. Ltd*, [1955] 1 All E.R. 481.

of problems (real and alleged) – they would simply get on with the business of suing polluters by stepping into the shoes of affected parties.

Using contracts to improve environmental amenities

While nuisance law offers a potentially powerful means of protecting the environment, it is, as has been observed, suitable only where 'objective' harm has been done. Thus, where harm is subjective, alternative mechanisms are needed.

One option is to use contracts: i.e. for the party who wishes to achieve a higher level of environmental protection to pay the counterparty not to cause the unwanted environmental harm. For example, if A has a spectacular view that she wishes to protect and her neighbour, B, owns the land immediately in front of her property, then it might be in A's interest to contract with B not to develop B's land.

A good example is the use of contracts to impose constraints on the development of garden squares in towns. In *Tulk* v. *Moxhay*,[32] a covenant was included in the title deed of a parcel of land in Leicester Square sold in 1808, which required the purchaser to keep the square 'uncovered with buildings', in order that it remain a pleasure ground. The defendant purchased the parcel in full knowledge of the covenant but claimed he was not privy to the contract and so was not bound by it. The court ruled that the defendant was bound by the covenant because he had been given notice of it. Thus was Leicester Square preserved from the developers: in essence the court had created a way of converting a contract from a right *in personam* to a right *in rem* (a property right).

Many garden squares in England and Wales are protected by such covenants, as are other natural and architectural features. A famous example is the frontage at Llandudno, which since the mid-nineteenth century has been protected by deed covenants.[33]

32 [1848] 41 E.R. 1143.

33 The covenants were introduced by the Mostyn family. See: www.mostyn-estates.co.uk/you_and.htm.

Contracts also enable protection from fumes that otherwise might not be subject to restraint by the courts. In the nineteenth and early twentieth centuries, homeowners in the private places of St Louis, Missouri, agreed not to burn more noxious bituminous coal and thereby achieved lower pollution levels than was the case in the places controlled by the municipal government (Beito, 1990).

Private versus public regulation of the environment

Given the apparent advantages of private regulation – through tort law and contracts – over public regulation, the question arises as to why the latter has become so dominant. One reason is that in practice many people were not able to avail themselves of actions in private nuisance; in part this was because of the high cost of taking legal action, in part because of rulings such as *St Helen's* v. *Tipping,* which made it difficult to obtain redress when the 'only' harm was to human health and where it was difficult to show cause and effect. As a result, there was a genuine deterioration of the environment in towns and industrial settings in most common-law jurisdictions. In response, various organisations were established which sought to persuade Parliament to introduce stricter anti-pollution legislation (Ashby and Anderson, 1981). The result was the elaboration of the various pieces of environmental legislation mentioned earlier.

At the same time, the law of nuisance has been gradually diluted over the past 150 years. One reason is the introduction of the defence of 'statutory authority'. This is essentially an instance of the 'public benefit' defence that was disallowed under the *sic utere* rule: if a plant operates under statute, it is presumed that the state has deemed the operation of the plant to be beneficial to the public, and so long as it is operated according to all relevant statutes, it cannot be held liable for any nuisance thereby created. Statutory authority effectively abrogates the rights of neighbouring property owners to peaceful enjoyment of their property.

Thus, in the case of *Allen* v. *Gulf Oil Refining*,[34] the plaintiff complained that the peaceful enjoyment of his property had been adversely affected by dust and noise created by the operation of a nearby oil refinery. The plaintiff was, however, denied redress. Lord Wilberforce explained:

> To the extent that the environment has been changed from that of a peaceful unpolluted countryside to an industrial complex (as to which different standards apply) Parliament must be taken to have authorised it. So far, I venture to think, the matter is not open to doubt. But in my opinion the statutory authority extends beyond merely authorising a change in the environment and an alteration of standard. It confers immunity against proceedings for any nuisance which can be shown ... to be the inevitable result of erecting a refinery on the site, not, I repeat, the existing refinery, but any refinery, however carefully and with however great a regard for the interest of adjoining occupiers it is sited, constructed and operated. To this extent and only to the extent that the actual nuisance (if any) caused by the actual refinery and its operation exceeds that for which immunity is conferred, the plaintiff has a remedy.[35]

More recently, the law of nuisance has essentially been replaced by the law of negligence (see Morris, 2003), which requires that the plaintiff or claimant (alleged victim) demonstrate fault on the part of the defendant (alleged polluter). Moreover, the interaction between these three factors (the expansion of public regulation, the dilution of nuisance law and its replacement by the law of negligence) has further undermined the utility of private actions, since compliance with all environmental regulations would likely be considered sufficient to satisfy the requirement that the defendant has not been negligent.

While some degree of public regulation of the environment is perhaps inevitable, there is nevertheless a strong case for enhancing the role of private regulation – on both equity and efficiency grounds.

34 [1981] 1 All E.R. 353.

35 Ibid. at 857–858, per Lord Wilberforce.

Possible reforms

Several reforms might be taken which would enable more effective private regulation without immediately interfering with the system of statutory controls, some of which are outlined below:

- Generally, return to the late-nineteenth-century doctrine of strict liability (the *sic utere* rule).[36]
- Create separate rules for cases of injury to persons or property that occur in places controlled directly by the state (e.g. public highways, public waterways, and so on).[37]

36 For an actionable private nuisance this would entail establishing:
a) Interference with another's right
(i) For physical damage to property or harm to the persons occupying that property, this would merely require showing that harm has occurred or is likely to occur in the future (this latter applying especially to harms that take time to develop and have multiple causes, such as cancers). Combined with better scientific understanding of the causes of these problems and with better monitoring techniques – enabling readier and cheaper identification of the sources of pollution – this should offer an effective and objective means of dealing with modern air pollution problems.
(ii) For interference with beneficial use of property, this would require showing that the interference was 'unreasonable' in the circumstances. Reasonableness in this context would be dependent principally on the extent of the interference, the location of the claimant, the time the interference occurred, and its duration. This distinction accords with the common law's general predilection for objectivity. Physical interference – including impacts on the health of occupants – can be objectively determined. By contrast, interference with beneficial use is inherently subjective.
(b) Causation: it would be necessary to demonstrate that the interference with the claimant's right emanated from the defendant's property. It should not be necessary, however, to show that the harm resulted uniquely from the defendant's actions, or indeed that the defendant's actions would have resulted in harm but for the actions of another. It should only be necessary to show that the defendant's actions contributed, in the circumstances, to the interference.
(c) Foreseeability and fault: liability should be strict; it is enough that something has emanated from the defendant's property that *might* interfere with another's property. It does not matter that the specific interference itself is unforeseeable. The test is whether a 'reasonable man' should have foreseen some potential interference. It does not matter that the defendant took every care to ensure that his operation was conducted in compliance with industry standards.

37 The reason is simply that the activities in such places are not subject to the same sphere

- Constrain or eliminate the defence of statutory authority – for example, by construing statutes such that they are assumed *not* to override the common-law rights of property owners except where expressly stated.[38]
- Remove the more general defence of public benefit, which compels judges to make impossible calculations (weighing up the interests of many different parties).[39]
- In case there is any confusion, the primary remedy for continuing nuisances should be the injunction.[40]

By enhancing the ability of private individuals to achieve their own environmental objectives, these amendments would likely reduce the

of control that pertains in private spaces. It is, for example, not usually possible to enter into a contract with the state to prevent persons from walking past one's building on the public footpath. Perhaps the solution in such cases is for the state to be liable under the same rules as apply in private nuisance.

38 This was essentially the approach adumbrated by Lord Denning in the Court of Appeal decision in *Allen* v. *Gulf Oil*: 'But I venture to suggest that modern statutes should be construed on a new principle. Wherever private undertakers seek statutory authority to construct and operate an installation which may cause damage to people living in the neighbourhood, it should not be assumed that Parliament intended that damage should be done to innocent people without redress. Just as in principle property should not be taken compulsorily except on proper compensation being paid for it, so also in principle property should not be damaged compulsorily except on proper compensation being made for the damage done. No matter whether the undertakers use due diligence or not, they ought not to be allowed, for their own profit, to damage innocent people or property without paying compensation. They ought to provide for it as part of the legitimate expenses of their operation, either as initial capital cost or out of the subsequent revenue.' *Allen* v. *Gulf Oil Refining Ltd*, [1979] 3 All E.R. 1008, [1979] 3 W.L.R. 523 [1980] R.V.R. 126 per Lord Denning.

39 To the extent that 'public benefit' is of relevance, it is incorporated into the locality criterion. Moreover, if the benefit of continuing a nuisance is sufficiently great, then in some cases the defendant may be able to buy out the plaintiff(s).

40 Whereas in some cases courts may be able accurately to assess damages for past nuisances, it seems extremely unlikely that they will be able to assess damages for future nuisances, making the injunction a more appropriate remedy from the perspective of protecting the rights of those who are adversely affected. Moreover, in cases where many people are adversely affected, an injunction brought by one party would effectively protect the rights of many and thereby protect the environment as a whole. Such a reformation of nuisance law seems to offer at least a partial solution.

pressure for further public environmental regulation, thus ensuring a greater balance between the two systems moving forward.

References

Ackerman, B. and W. Hassler (1981), *Clean Coal, Dirty Air*, Newhaven, CT: Yale University Press.

Arnason, R. (2006), 'Property rights in fisheries: Iceland's experience with ITQs', *Reviews in Fish Biology and Fisheries*, 15(3): 243–64.

Ashby, E. and M. Anderson (1981), *The Politics of Clean Air*, Oxford: Clarendon Press.

Bate, R. (2002), *Saving Our Streams*, London: Institute of Economic Affairs.

Baumol, W. J. and W. Oates (1988), *The Theory of Environmental Policy*, 2nd edn, Cambridge: Cambridge University Press.

Beckerman, W. (2007), 'The chimera of sustainable development', *Electronic Journal of Sustainable Development*, vol. 1, available at: www.ejsd.org/public/journal_article/3.

Beito, D. T. (1990), 'The formation of urban infrastructure through non-governmental planning: the private places of St Louis, 1869–1920', *Journal of Urban History*, 16: 263–301.

Blackstone, W. (1765–69), *Commentaries*. See also: www.lonang.com/exlibris/blackstone/bla-313.htm.

Buchanan, J. M. and G. Tullock (1975), 'Polluters profits and political response', *American Economic Review*, 65: 139–47.

Coase, R. H. (1960), 'The problem of social cost', *Journal of Law and Economics*, 4: 1–44.

Coke, E. (1628–), *The Institutes of the Laws of England* (in several parts), London: Brooke.

Coursey, D. (1998), 'The revealed demand for a public good: evidence from endangered and threatened species', *New York Electronic Law Journal*, 6, www.law.nyu.edu/journals/envtllaw/issues/vo16/2/6nyuelj411.html.

Dales, J. H. (1968), *Pollution, Property and Prices*, Toronto: University of Toronto Press.

Eshet, T., E. Ayalon and M. Shechter (2006), 'Valuation of externalities of selected waste management alternatives: a comparative review and analysis', *Resources, Conservation and Recycling*, 46: 335–64.

House of Lords (1862), *Select Committee on Noxious Vapours*, Parliamentary Papers, 14, Minutes of Evidence 21 QQ 220–2.

Kopp, R. J., W. W. Pommerehne and N. Schwartz (1997), *Determining the Value of Non-Marketed Goods*, Berlin: Springer.

Madden, M. S. (2005), 'The Graeco-Roman antecedents of modern tort law', Berkeley Electronic Press Working Paper, October, http://law.bepress.com/expresso/eps/823/, p. 31.

Mitchell, R. C. and R. T. Carson (1989), *Using Surveys to Value Public Goods: The Contingent Valuation Method*, Washington, DC: Resources for the Future.

Morris, J. (1995), 'The impact of Part II of the Environmental Protection Act 1990 on the waste management industry', MPhil dissertation thesis, Department of Land Economy, University of Cambridge.

Morris, J. (2003), 'Climbing out of the hole: sunsets, subjective value, the environment and English common law', *Fordham Environmental Law Journal*, 14(2): 343–74.

Morrisette, P. M. (1989), 'The evolution of policy responses to stratospheric ozone depletion', *Natural Resources Journal*, 29: 793–820.

Newell, R. G., J. N. Sanchirico and S. Kerr (2002), *An Empirical Analysis of New Zealand's ITQ Markets*, available at: www.motu.org.nz/pdf/Newell_Sanchirico_Kerr_IIFET.pdf.

Open Europe (2006), *The High Price of Hot Air: Why the European Emissions Trading Scheme is an Environmental and Economic Disaster*, London: Open Europe.

Pashigan, B. P. (1985), 'Environmental regulation: whose self-interests are being protected?', *Economic Inquiry*, 23: 551–84.

Schmalensee, R., P. L. Joskow, A. D. Ellerman, J. P. Montero and E. M. Bailey (1998), 'An interim evaluation of sulfur dioxide emissions trading', *Journal of Economic Perspectives*, 12(3): 53–68.

Whittington, D., C. KyeongAe and D. Lauria (1997), 'The effect of giving respondents "time to think" on tests of scope', in Kopp et al. (1997).

ABOUT THE IEA

The Institute is a research and educational charity (No. CC 235 351), limited by guarantee. Its mission is to improve understanding of the fundamental institutions of a free society by analysing and expounding the role of markets in solving economic and social problems.

The IEA achieves its mission by:

- a high-quality publishing programme
- conferences, seminars, lectures and other events
- outreach to school and college students
- brokering media introductions and appearances

The IEA, which was established in 1955 by the late Sir Antony Fisher, is an educational charity, not a political organisation. It is independent of any political party or group and does not carry on activities intended to affect support for any political party or candidate in any election or referendum, or at any other time. It is financed by sales of publications, conference fees and voluntary donations.

In addition to its main series of publications the IEA also publishes a quarterly journal, *Economic Affairs*.

The IEA is aided in its work by a distinguished international Academic Advisory Council and an eminent panel of Honorary Fellows. Together with other academics, they review prospective IEA publications, their comments being passed on anonymously to authors. All IEA papers are therefore subject to the same rigorous independent refereeing process as used by leading academic journals.

IEA publications enjoy widespread classroom use and course adoptions in schools and universities. They are also sold throughout the world and often translated/reprinted.

Since 1974 the IEA has helped to create a worldwide network of 100 similar institutions in over 70 countries. They are all independent but share the IEA's mission.

Views expressed in the IEA's publications are those of the authors, not those of the Institute (which has no corporate view), its Managing Trustees, Academic Advisory Council members or senior staff.

Members of the Institute's Academic Advisory Council, Honorary Fellows, Trustees and Staff are listed on the following page.

The Institute gratefully acknowledges financial support for its publications programme and other work from a generous benefaction by the late Alec and Beryl Warren.

The Institute of Economic Affairs
2 Lord North Street, Westminster, London SW1P 3LB
Tel: 020 7799 8900
Fax: 020 7799 2137
Email: iea@iea.org.uk
Internet: iea.org.uk

Other papers recently published by the IEA include:

WHO, What and Why?
Transnational Government, Legitimacy and the World Health Organization
Roger Scruton
Occasional Paper 113; ISBN 0 255 36487 3; £8.00

The World Turned Rightside Up
A New Trading Agenda for the Age of Globalisation
John C. Hulsman
Occasional Paper 114; ISBN 0 255 36495 4; £8.00

The Representation of Business in English Literature
Introduced and edited by Arthur Pollard
Readings 53; ISBN 0 255 36491 1; £12.00

Anti-Liberalism 2000
The Rise of New Millennium Collectivism
David Henderson
Occasional Paper 115; ISBN 0 255 36497 0; £7.50

Capitalism, Morality and Markets
Brian Griffiths, Robert A. Sirico, Norman Barry & Frank Field
Readings 54; ISBN 0 255 36496 2; £7.50

A Conversation with Harris and Seldon
Ralph Harris & Arthur Seldon
Occasional Paper 116; ISBN 0 255 36498 9; £7.50

Malaria and the DDT Story
Richard Tren & Roger Bate
Occasional Paper 117; ISBN 0 255 36499 7; £10.00

A Plea to Economists Who Favour Liberty: Assist the Everyman
Daniel B. Klein
Occasional Paper 118; ISBN 0 255 36501 2; £10.00

The Changing Fortunes of Economic Liberalism
Yesterday, Today and Tomorrow
David Henderson
Occasional Paper 105 (new edition); ISBN 0 255 36520 9; £12.50

The Global Education Industry
Lessons from Private Education in Developing Countries
James Tooley
Hobart Paper 141 (new edition); ISBN 0 255 36503 9; £12.50

Saving Our Streams
The Role of the Anglers' Conservation Association in Protecting English and Welsh Rivers
Roger Bate
Research Monograph 53; ISBN 0 255 36494 6; £10.00

Better Off Out?
The Benefits or Costs of EU Membership
Brian Hindley & Martin Howe
Occasional Paper 99 (new edition); ISBN 0 255 36502 0; £10.00

Buckingham at 25
Freeing the Universities from State Control
Edited by James Tooley
Readings 55; ISBN 0 255 36512 8; £15.00

Lectures on Regulatory and Competition Policy
Irwin M. Stelzer
Occasional Paper 120; ISBN 0 255 36511 X; £12.50

Misguided Virtue
False Notions of Corporate Social Responsibility
David Henderson
Hobart Paper 142; ISBN 0 255 36510 1; £12.50

HIV and Aids in Schools
The Political Economy of Pressure Groups and Miseducation
Barrie Craven, Pauline Dixon, Gordon Stewart & James Tooley
Occasional Paper 121; ISBN 0 255 36522 5; £10.00

The Road to Serfdom
The Reader's Digest *condensed version*
Friedrich A. Hayek
Occasional Paper 122; ISBN 0 255 36530 6; £7.50

Bastiat's *The Law*
Introduction by Norman Barry
Occasional Paper 123; ISBN 0 255 36509 8; £7.50

A Globalist Manifesto for Public Policy
Charles Calomiris
Occasional Paper 124; ISBN 0 255 36525 X; £7.50

Euthanasia for Death Duties
Putting Inheritance Tax Out of Its Misery
Barry Bracewell-Milnes
Research Monograph 54; ISBN 0 255 36513 6; £10.00

Liberating the Land
The Case for Private Land-use Planning
Mark Pennington
Hobart Paper 143; ISBN 0 255 36508 x; £10.00

IEA Yearbook of Government Performance 2002/2003
Edited by Peter Warburton
Yearbook 1; ISBN 0 255 36532 2; £15.00

Britain's Relative Economic Performance, 1870–1999
Nicholas Crafts
Research Monograph 55; ISBN 0 255 36524 1; £10.00

Should We Have Faith in Central Banks?
Otmar Issing
Occasional Paper 125; ISBN 0 255 36528 4; £7.50

The Dilemma of Democracy
Arthur Seldon
Hobart Paper 136 (reissue); ISBN 0 255 36536 5; £10.00

Capital Controls: a 'Cure' Worse Than the Problem?
Forrest Capie
Research Monograph 56; ISBN 0 255 36506 3; £10.00

The Poverty of 'Development Economics'
Deepak Lal
Hobart Paper 144 (reissue); ISBN 0 255 36519 5; £15.00

Should Britain Join the Euro?
The Chancellor's Five Tests Examined
Patrick Minford
Occasional Paper 126; ISBN 0 255 36527 6; £7.50

Post-Communist Transition: Some Lessons
Leszek Balcerowicz
Occasional Paper 127; ISBN 0 255 36533 0; £7.50

A Tribute to Peter Bauer
John Blundell et al.
Occasional Paper 128; ISBN 0 255 36531 4; £10.00

Employment Tribunals
Their Growth and the Case for Radical Reform
J. R. Shackleton
Hobart Paper 145; ISBN 0 255 36515 2; £10.00

Fifty Economic Fallacies Exposed
Geoffrey E. Wood
Occasional Paper 129; ISBN 0 255 36518 7; £12.50

A Market in Airport Slots
Keith Boyfield (editor), David Starkie, Tom Bass & Barry Humphreys
Readings 56; ISBN 0 255 36505 5; £10.00

Money, Inflation and the Constitutional Position of the Central Bank
Milton Friedman & Charles A. E. Goodhart
Readings 57; ISBN 0 255 36538 1; £10.00

railway.com
Parallels between the Early British Railways and the ICT Revolution
Robert C. B. Miller
Research Monograph 57; ISBN 0 255 36534 9; £12.50

The Regulation of Financial Markets
Edited by Philip Booth & David Currie
Readings 58; ISBN 0 255 36551 9; £12.50

Climate Alarmism Reconsidered
Robert L. Bradley Jr
Hobart Paper 146; ISBN 0 255 36541 1; £12.50

Government Failure: E. G. West on Education
Edited by James Tooley & James Stanfield
Occasional Paper 130; ISBN 0 255 36552 7; £12.50

Corporate Governance: Accountability in the Marketplace
Elaine Sternberg
Second edition
Hobart Paper 147; ISBN 0 255 36542 X; £12.50

The Land Use Planning System
Evaluating Options for Reform
John Corkindale
Hobart Paper 148; ISBN 0 255 36550 0; £10.00

Economy and Virtue
Essays on the Theme of Markets and Morality
Edited by Dennis O'Keeffe
Readings 59; ISBN 0 255 36504 7; £12.50

Free Markets Under Siege
Cartels, Politics and Social Welfare
Richard A. Epstein
Occasional Paper 132; ISBN 0 255 36553 5; £10.00

Unshackling Accountants
D. R. Myddelton
Hobart Paper 149; ISBN 0 255 36559 4; £12.50

The Euro as Politics
Pedro Schwartz
Research Monograph 58; ISBN 0 255 36535 7; £12.50

Pricing Our Roads
Vision and Reality
Stephen Glaister & Daniel J. Graham
Research Monograph 59; ISBN 0 255 36562 4; £10.00

The Role of Business in the Modern World
Progress, Pressures, and Prospects for the Market Economy
David Henderson
Hobart Paper 150; ISBN 0 255 36548 9; £12.50

Public Service Broadcasting Without the BBC?
Alan Peacock
Occasional Paper 133; ISBN 0 255 36565 9; £10.00

The ECB and the Euro: the First Five Years
Otmar Issing
Occasional Paper 134; ISBN 0 255 36555 1; £10.00

Towards a Liberal Utopia?
Edited by Philip Booth
Hobart Paperback 32; ISBN 0 255 36563 2; £15.00

The Way Out of the Pensions Quagmire
Philip Booth & Deborah Cooper
Research Monograph 60; ISBN 0 255 36517 9; £12.50

Black Wednesday
A Re-examination of Britain's Experience in the Exchange Rate Mechanism
Alan Budd
Occasional Paper 135; ISBN 0 255 36566 7; £7.50

Crime: Economic Incentives and Social Networks
Paul Ormerod
Hobart Paper 151; ISBN 0 255 36554 3; £10.00

The Road to Serfdom *with* The Intellectuals and Socialism
Friedrich A. Hayek
Occasional Paper 136; ISBN 0 255 36576 4; £10.00

Money and Asset Prices in Boom and Bust
Tim Congdon
Hobart Paper 152; ISBN 0 255 36570 5; £10.00

The Dangers of Bus Re-regulation
and Other Perspectives on Markets in Transport
John Hibbs et al.
Occasional Paper 137; ISBN 0 255 36572 1; £10.00

The New Rural Economy
Change, Dynamism and Government Policy
Berkeley Hill et al.
Occasional Paper 138; ISBN 0 255 36546 2; £15.00

The Benefits of Tax Competition
Richard Teather
Hobart Paper 153; ISBN 0 255 36569 1; £12.50

Wheels of Fortune
Self-funding Infrastructure and the Free Market Case for a Land Tax
Fred Harrison
Hobart Paper 154; ISBN 0 255 36589 6; £12.50

Were 364 Economists All Wrong?
Edited by Philip Booth
Readings 60; ISBN 978 0 255 36588 8; £10.00

Europe After the 'No' Votes
Mapping a New Economic Path
Patrick A. Messerlin
Occasional Paper 139; ISBN 978 0 255 36580 2; £10.00

The Railways, the Market and the Government
John Hibbs et al.
Readings 61; ISBN 978 0 255 36567 3; £12.50

Corruption: The World's Big C
Cases, Causes, Consequences, Cures
Ian Senior
Research Monograph 61; ISBN 978 0 255 36571 0; £12.50

Choice and the End of Social Housing
Peter King
Hobart Paper 155; ISBN 978 0 255 36568 0; £10.00

Sir Humphrey's Legacy
Facing Up to the Cost of Public Sector Pensions
Neil Record
Hobart Paper 156; ISBN 978 0 255 36578 9; £10.00

The Economics of Law
Cento Veljanovski
Second edition
Hobart Paper 157; ISBN 978 0 255 36561 1; £12.50

Living with Leviathan
Public Spending, Taxes and Economic Performance
David B. Smith
Hobart Paper 158; ISBN 978 0 255 36579 6; £12.50

The Vote Motive
Gordon Tullock
New edition
Hobart Paperback 33; ISBN 978 0 255 36577 2; £10.00

Waging the War of Ideas
John Blundell
Third edition
Occasional Paper 131; ISBN 978 0 255 36606 9; £12.50

The War Between the State and the Family
How Government Divides and Impoverishes
Patricia Morgan
Hobart Paper 159; ISBN 978 0 255 36596 3; £10.00

Capitalism – A Condensed Version
Arthur Seldon
Occasional Paper 140; ISBN 978 0 255 36598 7; £7.50

Catholic Social Teaching and the Market Economy
Edited by Philip Booth
Hobart Paperback 34; ISBN 978 0 255 36581 9; £15.00

Adam Smith – A Primer
Eamonn Butler
Occasional Paper 141; ISBN 978 0 255 36608 3; £7.50

Happiness, Economics and Public Policy
Helen Johns & Paul Ormerod
Research Monograph 62; ISBN 978 0 255 36600 7; £10.00

They Meant Well
Government Project Disasters
D. R. Myddelton
Hobart Paper 160; ISBN 978 0 255 36601 4; £12.50

Rescuing Social Capital from Social Democracy
John Meadowcroft & Mark Pennington
Hobart Paper 161; ISBN 978 0 255 36592 5; £10.00

Paths to Property
Approaches to Institutional Change in International Development
Karol Boudreaux & Paul Dragos Aligica
Hobart Paper 162; ISBN 978 0 255 36582 6; £10.00

Prohibitions
Edited by John Meadowcroft
Hobart Paperback 35; ISBN 978 0 255 36585 7; £15.00

Trade Policy, New Century
The WTO, FTAs and Asia Rising
Razeen Sally
Hobart Paper 163; ISBN 978 0 255 36544 4; £12.50

Sixty Years On – Who Cares for the NHS?
Helen Evans
Research Monograph 63; ISBN 978 0 255 36611 3; £10.00

Taming Leviathan
Waging the War of Ideas Around the World
Edited by Colleen Dyble
Occasional Paper 142; ISBN 978 0 255 36607 6; £12.50

Other IEA publications

Comprehensive information on other publications and the wider work of the IEA can be found at www.iea.org.uk. To order any publication please see below.

Personal customers

Orders from personal customers should be directed to the IEA:

Bob Layson
IEA
2 Lord North Street
FREEPOST LON10168
London SW1P 3YZ
Tel: 020 7799 8909. Fax: 020 7799 2137
Email: blayson@iea.org.uk

Trade customers

All orders from the book trade should be directed to the IEA's distributor:

Gazelle Book Services Ltd (IEA Orders)
FREEPOST RLYS-EAHU-YSCZ
White Cross Mills
Hightown
Lancaster LA1 4XS
Tel: 01524 68765, Fax: 01524 53232
Email: sales@gazellebooks.co.uk

IEA subscriptions

The IEA also offers a subscription service to its publications. For a single annual payment (currently £42.00 in the UK), subscribers receive every monograph the IEA publishes. For more information please contact:

Adam Myers
Subscriptions
IEA
2 Lord North Street
FREEPOST LON10168
London SW1P 3YZ
Tel: 020 7799 8920, Fax: 020 7799 2137
Email: amyers@iea.org.uk

Pirate Attack

Felice Arena and Phil Kettle

illustrated by

Susy B

RISING STARS

First published in Great Britain by
RISING STARS UK LTD 2005
76 Farnaby Road, Bromley, BR1 4BH

For information visit our website at:
www.risingstars-uk.com

British Library Cataloguing in Publication Data

A CIP record for this book is available from the British Library.

ISBN: 1-904591-96-5

First published in 2004 by
MACMILLAN EDUCATION AUSTRALIA PTY LTD
627 Chapel Street, South Yarra, Australia 3141

Visit our website at www.macmillan.com.au

Associated companies and representatives throughout the world.

Project Management by Limelight Press Pty Ltd
Cover and text design by Lore Foye
Illustrations by Susy Boyer

Printed and bound in Great Britain by
Mackays of Chatham plc, Chatham, Kent

Contents

Tom *Joey*

CHAPTER 1

High Sea Dreaming

Best friends Tom and Joey have been told by Joey's mother that they should go outside and play.

Tom "Whoa! Look at that! It takes up the whole garden."

Joey "Yes, it's Dad's new boat. He got it last week. Cool huh?"

Tom "Yes. It's huge!"

Joey "I know, we're lucky. Dad's dreamed of owning a boat all his life. And now he does."

Tom "Hey, I reckon it'd make a great pirate ship."

Joey "Yes, I s'pose so."

Tom "Hey, imagine if we were pirates. We could capture all the treasure in the world and sell it."

Joey "Yes, that'd be cool. But why do you think pirates' treasure always turns out to be jewellery?"

Tom "Maybe they have lots of girlfriends?"

Joey "Gross."

Tom "Yes, if I was a pirate I'd want to get bikes and PlayStations and stuff like that—things I could use."

Joey "So, want to go on board my dad's boat, I mean, our pirate ship?"

CHAPTER 2

Captain 'n' Crew

The boys go out into the backyard and climb onto the boat.

Tom "This is so cool!"

Joey "Raise the anchor and make ready to sail."

Tom "Who made you captain?"

Joey "Okay, well maybe we could both be captains?"

Tom "Good idea. I want to be 'Captain Blood'. The most feared pirate in the world!"

Joey "Cool. Then I'll be 'Captain Splash'."

Tom "That's a weird name for a pirate."

Joey "Well, if anybody tries to board the boat, they'll see how scary I look."

Tom "And ... ?"

Joey "Then they'll jump overboard, of course ... and then *splash*! Get it? Captain Splash."

Tom "Good one. Right, are we ready to sail, Captain Splash?"

Joey "We've got to get supplies before we can sail."

Tom "Like what?"

Joey "We need to get weapons to fight other pirates with, and we've got to get some food, too. We might be at sea for a really long time."

Tom and Joey go ashore. A lady pirate, who looks a lot like Joey's mother, is working in the galley, which looks a lot like a kitchen. The lady pirate helps pack plenty of food for Captain Blood and Captain Splash.

CHAPTER 3

Blood and Guts

In the meantime, Captain Blood and Captain Splash collect a load of water bombs. Soon the pirates are back on board ready to set sail.

Tom "We should have a really good name for our ship."

Joey "Well, Dad's given it a name already—'Lady Breeze'."

Tom "That doesn't sound like the name of a pirate ship. I know! We should call it 'Blood and Guts'."

Joey "Yes, much better—the 'Blood and Guts'. Captained by the most feared pirates in the world: Captain Blood and Captain Splash."

Tom "Captain Splash, we should stack our bombs at the pointy end of the ship."

Joey "That's a good idea, Captain Blood, but I think the pointy end is called the sharp end."

The ship sets sail for the open sea. The sea looks a lot like Joey's garden.

Tom "We've been sailing for a long time, Captain."

Joey "That's what I was thinking, Captain. Maybe we should anchor and take a lunch break? What have we got?"

Tom opens the lunch box and looks inside.

Tom “We’ve got peanut butter sandwiches and more peanut butter sandwiches.”

Joey “Well, it’s a good thing that pirates love peanut butter.”

Tom and Joey sit down and eat their lunch. All of a sudden a water bomb splatters on top of Joey’s head.

Tom "We're under attack!"

Joey "Yes, and I've been soaked."

Tom "No time to lose. Time to fight back."

Tom and Joey stand up and look out to sea. In the distance is a huge wave that looks a lot like a fence.

Tom "Whoever ambushed us must be hiding behind that big wave."

Joey "I bet it's those girl pirates from next door."

Tom "Well, it's time to show them why boys rule—it's time to defend ourselves!"

Joey "Yes, it's time for Captain Blood and Captain Splash to rule the seas!"

The boys race to the front of the boat and collect all the bombs that they brought on board.

Tom "This could be the greatest pirate war ever."

Joey "Look out, here comes another bomb. Dive for cover."

CHAPTER 4

Full-on Battle

Splash! Another water bomb explodes on the deck of the "Blood and Guts".

Tom "Phew! That was close. When we defeat them we'll take all their treasure."

Joey "They're only girl pirates. They haven't got any treasure that we'd want."

Tom "Maybe they've got some food. Because to be honest with you Captain Splash, there's only so much peanut butter most feared pirates like us can eat."

Suddenly, *splat*! A scream is heard coming from behind the fence.

Joey “Yes, got them! Sounds like a direct hit.”

Joey throws two more bombs. Tom throws three. There are more screams from the other side of the fence.

Tom "I think we're going to win this pirate war."

Joey "Yes, *arrrrr, me hearty*. I think you're right."

Captain Blood and Captain Splash keep throwing their bombs, one after the other.

Joey "I haven't heard any more screams. Maybe they've drowned or sailed away? It's quiet—too quiet."

Tom "Well, we'll just keep bombing them—to make sure that we really win this pirate war. Pass me another bomb."

Joey "We haven't got any more bombs left—we've run out!"

Suddenly, from behind the fence the sounds of "Attack! Attack! Attack!" echo across the water.

Captain Blood and Captain Splash look worriedly at each other.

Tom "Oh no! I think we're in big trouble."

CHAPTER 5

The White Flag

The boys crouch down and discuss their next course of action.

Joey "Don't worry, Captain Blood, because the best form of defence is attack."

Tom “Yes, if only we had something to attack with. Look out! Here comes another one! We’re going to be hit!”

Joey “*Captain Splash, the greatest pirate ever to sail the seas, to the rescue!*”

Joey flies through the air, as if he is saving a goal in football and, remarkably, catches the water-filled balloon without breaking it.

Tom "Great catch, Captain Splash!"

Joey throws the balloon back. A scream from the girl pirates can be heard across the sea. Suddenly, a stream of water-filled balloons is tossed at the boys. The boys duck for cover.

Joey "Look out, Captain Blood!"

Splash! Tom is hit and is drenched.

Joey "Are you wounded?"

Tom "Just a graze. It's okay, I'm Captain Blood, I'll just fight on."

Joey "Look! They're waving a white flag."

Tom "That means they want to surrender. That's weird. They were winning. Maybe they've run out of bombs."

Joey "Or they're more wounded than we are. Should we ask them what they want?"

Tom "We don't have to. Look, they're holding up a sign."

A cardboard sign appears from behind the fence. It reads, “Do you want something to eat?”.

Captain Blood and Captain Splash look at each other.

Joey “I wonder what they’ve got to eat.”

Tom "Maybe we should invite them aboard. I bet it's good, whatever they've got."

Joey "Yes. Okay. But once we've eaten their food we'll make them walk the plank and let the sharks eat them."

Tom "Brilliant idea, Captain Splash. But let's find out what they've got first."

Joey "Okay. Hold on, I'll swim to shore and make a sign."

Joey runs into the house and then returns to the boat with a sign that reads, "What sort of food do you have?". He holds it up for the girl pirates to see.

Tom "I hope it's crisps or chocolate. Real treasure!"

A few minutes later the girls hold up another sign. It reads, "We have peanut butter sandwiches!". And with that, the boys instantly lose their appetite.

BOYS RULE!

Pirate Lingo

Tom

Joey

bow The front of a sailing ship, or the pointy end.

"man overboard!" A cry for help! Somebody has fallen overboard.

poop deck The highest deck on the ship—usually above the captain's quarters.

sea legs When you get used to the rocking of a ship in the water.

stern The back of a sailing ship, or the blunt end.

walk the plank When you're forced by pirates to walk out on a plank over the side of the ship and drop into the ocean to be eaten by sharks.

Pirate Must-dos

☞ Lift the anchor before you try to sail.

☞ Wear a patch over one eye.

☞ Have a big earring in at least one ear.

☞ Learn to say "aye aye, Captain".

☞ Carry a sword.

☞ Know how to read a compass. This is very important if you don't want to get lost in your own garden.

☞ Carry water bombs. You never know when girl pirates might attack.

☞ Make sure that you always take plenty of food. You never know how long you might have to stay at sea.

☞ Fly a flag from your ship with the words "Boys Rule!" written on it.

☞ Make sure you have a plank on your ship (just in case you might have to make some girl pirate walk it)—and no, not your mum's ironing board.

☞ Put together a treasure chest and then bury it in a secret spot.

☞ Draw a map to show where your treasure is buried—mark the spot with an "X".

Pirate Instant Info

- Pirates always fly a special flag when they are about to attack another ship.
- A pirate's flag has a skull and crossbones on it.
- One of the most famous pirates of all time was Blackbeard. His real name was Edward and he was from England.
- "Pirates of the Caribbean" is a Disneyland theme park ride and also a blockbuster movie starring Johnny Depp and Geoffrey Rush.

- In the classic story "Peter Pan", Peter's arch rival is an evil pirate called Captain Hook.

- A favourite treasure for pirates from hundreds of years ago were doubloons, which were Spanish coins made from pure gold.

- Pirate ships usually had lots of men in their crew.

Think Tank

1 Should you wear a life jacket when you are on a pirate ship?

2 Who's the famous pirate in the classic story "Peter Pan"?

3 What's usually on a pirate flag?

4 What do the words "man overboard!" mean?

5 What does it mean to "walk the plank"?

6 What do pirates hunt for?

7 Name some things that would belong to a pirate.

8 What does "aye aye, Captain!" mean?

Answers

1 Yes, you should always wear a life jacket when you are on a pirate ship.

2 The famous pirate is called Captain Hook.

3 A skull and crossbones are usually on a pirate flag.

4 A cry for help! Someone has fallen overboard.

5 You are forced by pirates to walk out on a plank and jump into the water.

6 Pirates hunt for treasure.

7 Pirates would have things like a ship, a patch, a rope, treasure and a sword.

8 It means "yes, Captain".

How did you score?

- If you got all 8 answers correct then *shiver me timbers*, you're born to be a pirate in your own garden.
- If you got 6 answers correct you love to hunt for treasure, but aren't keen on wearing a fluffy pirate shirt and patch.
- If you got fewer than 4 answers correct, pirate life may not be for you, but you don't mind watching pirate movies.

Hi Guys!

We have heaps of fun reading and want you to, too. We both believe that being a good reader is really important and so cool.

Try out our suggestions to help you have fun as you read.

At school, why don't you use "Pirate Attack" as a play and you and your friends can be the actors. Set the scene for your play. Make a pirate flag and map and bring them to school to use as props, but whatever you do, don't throw any water bombs in the classroom. Pretend you and your crew are boarding an enemy ship.

So ... have you decided who is going to be Tom and who is going to be Joey? Now, with your friends, read and act out our story in front of the class.

We have a lot of fun when we go to schools and read our stories. After we finish the kids all clap really loudly. When you've finished your play your classmates will do the same. Just remember to look out the window—there might be a talent scout from a television station watching you!

Reading at home is really important and a lot of fun as well.

Take our books home and get someone in your family to read them with you. Maybe they can take on a part in the story.

Remember, reading is a whole lot of fun.

So, as the frog in the local pond would say, Read-it!

And remember, Boys Rule!

BOYS RULE!

When We Were Kids

Felice

Phil

Phil "Have you ever played pirates?"

Felice "Plenty of times. Have you?"

Phil "Yeah, and I was in a boat that sank."

Felice "That's terrible! What happened?"

Phil "I was playing pirates in my father's boat and it tipped over!"

Felice "Gee, what did you do?"

Phil "Well, I just let the boat sink to the bottom then I swam to safety!"

Felice "Gee, that must have been scary."

Phil "Yeah, it could have been if I hadn't been in the swimming pool."

What a Laugh!

Q How does a boat show its affection?

A It hugs the shore.